Project AIR FORCE

Measuring Interdiction Capabilities in the Presence of Anti-Access Strategies

Exploratory Analysis to Inform Adaptive Strategy for the Persian Gulf

Paul K. Davis
Jimmie McEver
Barry Wilson

Prepared for the
UNITED STATES AIR FORCE

RAND

The research reported here was sponsored by the United States Air Force under Contract F49642-96-C-0001. Further information may be obtained from the Strategic Planning Division, Directorate of Plans, Hq USAF.

Library of Congress Cataloging-in-Publication Data

Davis, Paul K., 1943-
Measuring interdiction capabilities in the presence of anti-access strategies : exploratory analysis to inform adaptive strategy for the Persian Gulf / Paul K. Davis, Jimmie McEver, Barry Wilson.
p. cm.
"MR-1471."
Includes bibliographical references.
ISBN 0-8330-3107-4
1. United States—Armed Forces—Combat sustainability. 2. National security—Persian Gulf Region. 3. Strategy. I. McEver, Jimmie. II. Wilson, Barry, 1959- III. Title.

UA23 .D288 2002
355'.033273—dc21

2001057888

RAND is a nonprofit institution that helps improve policy and decisionmaking through research and analysis. RAND® is a registered trademark. RAND's publications do not necessarily reflect the opinions or policies of its research sponsors.

Published 2002 by RAND
1700 Main Street, P.O. Box 2138, Santa Monica, CA 90407-2138
1200 South Hayes Street, Arlington, VA 22202-5050
201 North Craig Street, Suite 102, Pittsburgh, PA 15213-1516
RAND URL: http://www.rand.org/
To order RAND documents or to obtain additional information, contact Distribution Services: Telephone: (310) 451-7002; Fax: (310) 451-6915; Email: order@rand.org

PREFACE

This monograph stems from a project on long-term force planning for the Persian Gulf. The project was commissioned by Lt General M. Esmond, who was then the Deputy Chief of Staff of the United States Air Force (USAF) for Air and Space Operations (AF/XO), and Lt General Charles Wald, commander of the 9th Air Force. The monograph presents analytical methods for capabilities-based planning of interdiction missions and models to implement the methods. It considers both the halt campaign and other counter-maneuver-force operations.

Our purpose in this monograph is to help inform development of military strategies that are *adaptive* over time. U.S. operational capabilities for fighting a war today in the Persian Gulf region are adequate and well understood, but changes are on the horizon and uncertainties—such as anti-access strategies—loom. Planners are therefore interested in anticipating needed adaptations and in developing related hedge capabilities. No study is needed to know that bigger threats are more troublesome, that warning is important, that more stealth is desirable, or that advanced munitions are valuable. It is useful, however, to have quantitative methods for measuring the potential value of enhanced capabilities. Analysis can illuminate tradeoffs when it comes time to allocate resources and action priorities. The most valuable analysis sheds light on how flexible, adaptive, and robust a given capability would be across circumstances and assumptions, and on how much of that capability would be enough. It follows that higher-level planning can benefit from exploratory analysis across the dimensions of uncertainty—so long as the analysis is fast, broad, flexible, and understandable. In what follows we develop a state-of-the-art model and methodology for such analysis. We also summarize insights from analysis to date.

Our work was largely conducted in the Strategy and Doctrine Program within RAND's Project AIR FORCE. The scope was extended to be useful also to a project sponsored by the Air Force Research Laboratory that seeks to advance the theory and technology of multiresolution modeling, an important enabler of advanced analysis. The work should be useful to military and civilian analysis organizations, to students in war colleges, and to segments of the academic community.

Research for this report was completed in March 2001.

PROJECT AIR FORCE

Project AIR FORCE, a division of RAND, is the Air Force's federally funded research and development center (FFRDC) for studies and analysis. It provides the USAF with independent analysis of policy alternatives affecting the deployment, employment, combat readiness, and support of current and future air and space forces. Research is performed in four programs: Aerospace Force Development; Manpower, Personnel, and Training; Resource Management; and Strategy and Doctrine.

CONTENTS

FIGURES

TABLES

SUMMARY

STUDY OBJECTIVE: HELPING TO DEFINE AN ADAPTIVE STRATEGY

U.S. military capabilities for the Persian Gulf are currently adequate to defend Kuwait because of the weakness and posture of Iraq's military forces, the forward stationing of U.S. forces, the substantial infrastructure of regional bases and prepositioning, and the high readiness of U.S. forces for a Persian Gulf contingency. This monograph is not about today's capabilities, but rather about what the Air Force (and the United States more generally) can do to ensure that such capabilities remain adequate as circumstances change. We provide methods and a model for broad, high-level, *exploratory* analysis of such issues. We also summarize insights from analysis to date, which suggest key elements of an adaptive capabilities-based strategy over the years ahead.

We believe that the methodology is applicable not just to a halt campaign in a new invasion of Kuwait, but—with adjustments—to many large and small counter-maneuver missions, such as providing timely help to an enclave of friendly forces about to be attacked or tying down enemy maneuver units during an early insertion of U.S. ground forces.

BACKGROUND: TRENDS AND ANTI-ACCESS CHALLENGES

As mentioned above, U.S. capability in the Persian Gulf is currently good. Further, U.S. capabilities are improving as advanced weapons are procured and as platforms, logistics, concepts of operation, and command and control for the region mature. The U.S. regional posture appears to be sustainable. In contrast, Iraq's military capabilities are modest. If anything is certain, however, it is that change will occur. Some of those changes might be for the better, but our interest here is with potential problems.

Many troublesome possibilities exist. Sanctions may end and Iraq may rebuild its forces—not as a mirror image of its 1990 forces, but as something better tailored to deal with U.S. strengths and weaknesses. Iraq might emphasize netted, mobile, long-range air defenses; short-warning attack capability; dispersed formations; and missiles with weapons of mass destruction (WMD) that could coerce regional states and threaten forward operating bases. More generally, Iraq could combine a number of such tactics and shape a coherent anti-access strategy—a strategy that would impede American use of regional bases and otherwise hinder efficient operations in the region.

Political-military context may also change in troublesome ways. For example, if sanctions were lifted, Saddam Hussein might behave well for a time and regional states might then be inclined to ask the United States to adopt an over-the-horizon posture with less forward basing. That would increase vulnerability to quick moves by Iraq.

The point is that changes will occur. How, then, can the United States—and the Air Force in particular—anticipate possible changes, hedge accordingly, and adapt as smoothly as possible? Understanding such matters is the key to adaptive capabilities-based planning. It is also important when diplomatic issues come under debate, because decisionmakers will need to know what changes in military posture would be most and least desirable from a security perspective—i.e., to know the positions most worth fighting for in negotiations.

THE "MISSION-SYSTEM PERSPECTIVE" IN MEASURING CAPABILITIES

To understand such matters it is helpful to have a systematic approach to capabilities-based planning. The intended output of planning should be that future U.S. commanders have all the material and other resources necessary to conduct successful operations in wartime—in a wide variety of circumstances and under diverse assumptions. Because this view of output goes beyond normal systems analysis, we use the terms *mission-system capabilities* (MSC) and *mission-system analysis* (MSA) to highlight our emphasis on realistically assessed future operational ability to accomplish missions despite uncertainty. Our perspective gives meaning to attributes such as flexibility, adaptiveness, and robustness. To put it differently, it addresses a variety of operational risks.

Figure S.1 summarizes the mission-system approach. It begins (left side) by defining the military mission and measures of success at the operational level of war. It then evaluates alternative sets of capabilities (top center). A particular capabilities set addresses not only forces but also weapon systems, command and control systems, logistical systems, doctrine, force employment concepts, and even the skills and readiness levels intended for the future forces. As when developing a weapon system, the evaluation is accomplished not just for some standard case but for the plausible range of operating conditions (bottom center). That is, the evaluation is accomplished across a *scenario space* representing uncertainties in (1) political-military context, (2) strategies and tactics, (3) forces, (4) force capabilities, (5) environmental factors, and (6) other assumptions of modeling and analysis. The result is an assessment—including discussion of risks and ways to reduce them—of mission-system capability (right side).

DEFINING THE MISSION OF INTEREST

The Early-Halt Mission

The Air Force has numerous core missions; in this monograph about capabilities for the Persian Gulf we focus on the mission of interdicting and defeating a mechanized invasion quickly—i.e., in bringing about an *early* halt.

The Joint Context

Almost always, the Air Force will conduct its operations as part of a larger joint and combined campaign. Interdiction might or might not be the principal component of a future campaign and, depending on circumstances, interdiction's success might depend on integrated jointness—not merely for deconfliction but also to obtain the benefits of synergy—with naval aviation and missiles, and with U.S. and defended-ally ground forces. We discuss some of these synergies in the monograph and have discussed elsewhere the potentially critical role of ground forces (Gritton, Davis, Steeb, and Matsumura, 2000). See also Defense Science Board (1998).

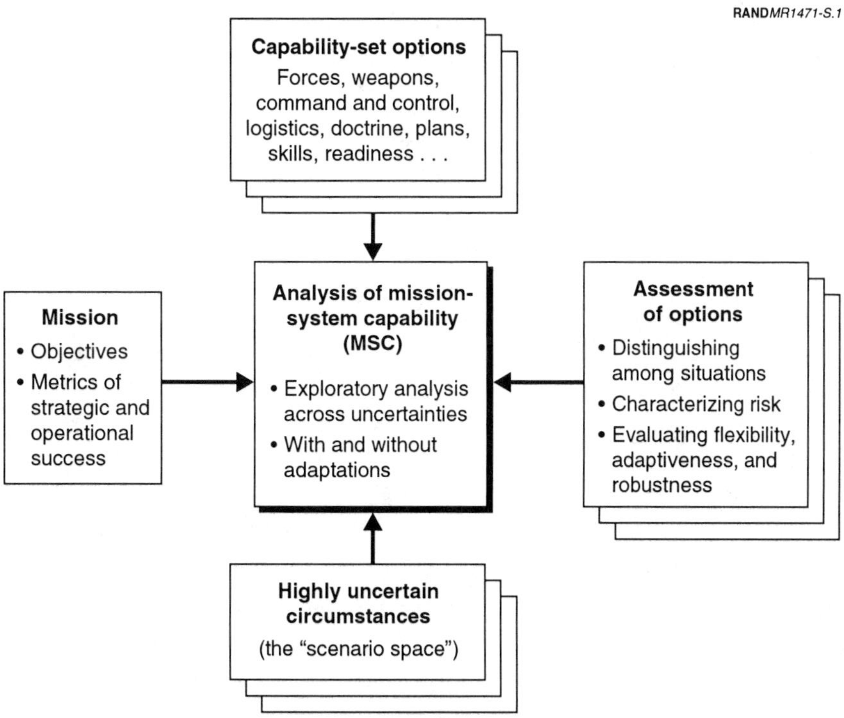

Figure S.1—Assessing Mission-System Capabilities

This said, the Air Force is responsible for providing certain core component capabilities to the future joint commander. Interdiction capability is one of those core capabilities and our discussion here is focused on what the Air Force can do to maintain it in the years ahead—both by acting unilaterally with its eye on the joint context and by advocating certain diplomatic measures and actions by or with other services.

Early-Halt Capability as a Surrogate for Broader Counter-Maneuver-Force Capability

A convenient measure of interdiction capability for the Persian Gulf is the ability to halt an invading army early—within Kuwait. Even if the capability is never used to halt another Iraqi invasion, its existence strongly affects deterrence. It affects both the reality and perceptions about the regional balance of power involving Iraq, Iran, Kuwait, Saudi Arabia, and the other Gulf states. *Significantly, early-halt capability is also a surrogate for more general counter-maneuver-force capabilities.* At issue might be operations such as protecting Kurdish or Shia groups from regular Iraqi ground forces, suppressing Iraqi maneuver during a period of U.S. ground-force maneuvers, or supporting the actions of a revolutionary group. Any of these would benefit from the same types of capability needed for the classic halt mission under diverse and stressful conditions.

A MODEL FOR EXPLORATORY ANALYSIS

The halt problem has been studied in war games and computer simulations, many of them dependent on official detailed databases and scenarios. Mission-system analysis, however, requires comprehensive exploratory analysis emphasizing breadth rather than depth, and confronting massive uncertainty rather than accepting standard assumptions.

Exploratory analysis is facilitated by relatively simple, fast-running models that resemble decision aids. It can be accomplished with a variety of models. However, for the purposes of this study, we developed a closed-form analytical model (i.e., a "formula model") that deals with this study's particular issues while permitting extremely efficient *simultaneous* exploration of roughly a dozen parameters—even in interactive group settings in which participants ask both "what if?" questions and more sophisticated questions of the form "Under what circumstances would we succeed?" or "When would we fail?" The development followed design principles of multiresolution, multiperspective modeling (MRMPM) (Davis, 2000). As a result, the user has significant latitude regarding the level of detail and choice of variables to be inputted. For example, he may input various warning times, the time that base access is granted, and various related deployment rates. Or he may simply input the number of D-Day shooters. This ability to abstract mitigates the curse of dimensionality while maintaining comprehensiveness and awareness about underlying variables.

The model developed here is called EXHALT-CF (the "CF" for closed-form) because it is closely related to and supported by the more detailed simulation model EXHALT (see McEver, Davis, and Bigelow, 2000a, and Appendix C). EXHALT provides day-by-day simulation of the interdiction operation and distinguishes among the many aircraft types, munitions, loads, and so on, whereas EXHALT-CF uses "equivalent shooters." The data for the full EXHALT model also cover many other "shooters" such as the Army Tactical Missile System (ATACMS) missiles with the Brilliant Antiarmor Munition (BAT) and Army attack helicopters. For some aspects of our work with the EXHALT models, including data, we have drawn on past RAND work for the Air Force (Ochmanek, Harshberger, Thaler, and Kent, 1998) and work led by Ochmanek for the Joint Staff and Office of the Secretary of Defense.

The value of such exploratory-analysis models depends fundamentally on whether they are rooted in a deeper understanding of issues. Indeed, the history of highly aggregated models is mixed: There are probably as many instances of naive and deceptive aggregate representations as of brilliantly insightful ones. We therefore urge using the family-of-models-and-games philosophy (Davis, Bigelow, and McEver, 1999). That philosophy values not only high-level exploratory analysis but also high-resolution simulation to illuminate phenomenological details; human war gaming to illuminate issues in the domains of political-military constraints, command and control, and force employment; theater-level modeling to provide integration and explore higher-level issues of joint and combined strategy; and experimentation, which can lead to discovery and, of course, empirical data. In this monograph, however, our emphasis is on broad, agile, exploratory analysis of the halt mission—with special emphasis on higher-level issues related to scenario-dependent risks, anti-access strategies, and potential U.S. adaptations.

The model documented in this monograph generates capability measures in the form of interdiction-limited halt time, interdiction-limited penetration distance, and the ability to delay and reduce attacking forces before they reach specified defense lines where ground forces would await. Table S.1 indicates the kinds of variables that can be inputted. Although EXHALT-CF is an attrition model, it can be used to study many issues that go well beyond attrition per se. For example, it has been used to illustrate how effects-based operations that take

Table S.1

VARIABLES REPRESENTED IN CLOSED-FORM ANALYTICAL MODELS (PARTIAL LIST)

Category of Variable	Variable
Attacking force and strategy	Size of threat (number of divisions, armored fighting vehicles per division)
	Maneuver scheme (number of axes, number of columns per axis, dispersion along each column)
	Unimpeded movement speed; delays if subject to very early strikes
	Quality of air defense (as proxied by defense-suppression time and attrition rate prior to suppression)
	Cohesion and morale as proxied by overall and local break points
Interdiction force	Size of D-Day interdiction force (as a function of forward presence, warning times, times at which access to bases is granted, and deployment rates). Measured in equivalent shooters with the F-16 as the standard shooter.
	Deployment rates after strategic warning, after decision to mount full-scale deployment, and after full access to bases is granted
	Fraction of shooters devoted to anti-armor missions (reflecting issues of suppression of enemy air defenses [SEAD], command and control [C^2], and command, control, communications, computing, intelligence, surveillance, and reconnaissance [C^4ISR]), by phase of operation
	Kills per shooter day (determined by kills per sortie or shot and by sorties or shots per day)
	Early strikes causing movement delays
	Limited stocks of high-effectiveness anti-armor munitions
Defending ground forces	Capability of ground forces as proxied by size of the residual enemy force they could halt at a specified defense line and the time at which the defense line could be active
Weapons of Mass Destruction (WMD)	Effects of WMD, as proxied by reduced sortie rates, deployment rates, and theater capacities
C^4ISR capabilities	Reduced early effectiveness as command-control efficiency spins up and as reconnaissance, surveillance, and target acquisition (RSTA) systems are more fully exploited (via assumptions about the length of operational phases, forces employed in phases, and their effectiveness)
	Impact on effectiveness of terrain, maneuver schemes, en route retargeting, command-control delays, weapons mix, and other factors (reflected crudely by adjusting parameters based on other studies)[a]
Blue strategy	Relative effectiveness of in-depth and leading-edge interdiction
	Commander's tradeoff between halt distance and losses
	Effect of being able to use a red line for warning and early employment

[a]More detailed representation of these issues is particularly important in mixed terrain. See Davis, Bigelow, and McEver (2000a).

into account situation-dependent shortcomings in the attacker's morale and cohesion can dramatically affect the assessment of alternative strategies (Davis, 2001a).

OBSERVATIONS FROM EXPLORATORY ANALYSIS OF THE HALT PROBLEM

We observe the following from exploratory analysis. The qualitative statements can be given quantitative expression by using the model described in the monograph with realistic numbers.

Critical Enablers of the Early-Halt Mission

Figure S.2 is one depiction of the mission-system perspective for the halt problem. It is not just a decomposition into components, but rather a success tree (a positively stated version of a fault tree) highlighting the various *critical* components—each of which must separately be successful for mission success. These are, starting from the left: avoiding a sudden surprise takeover, building up adequate numbers of shooters, establishing high-effectiveness command and control, suppressing or evading air defenses, and conducting the interdiction operations themselves effectively.

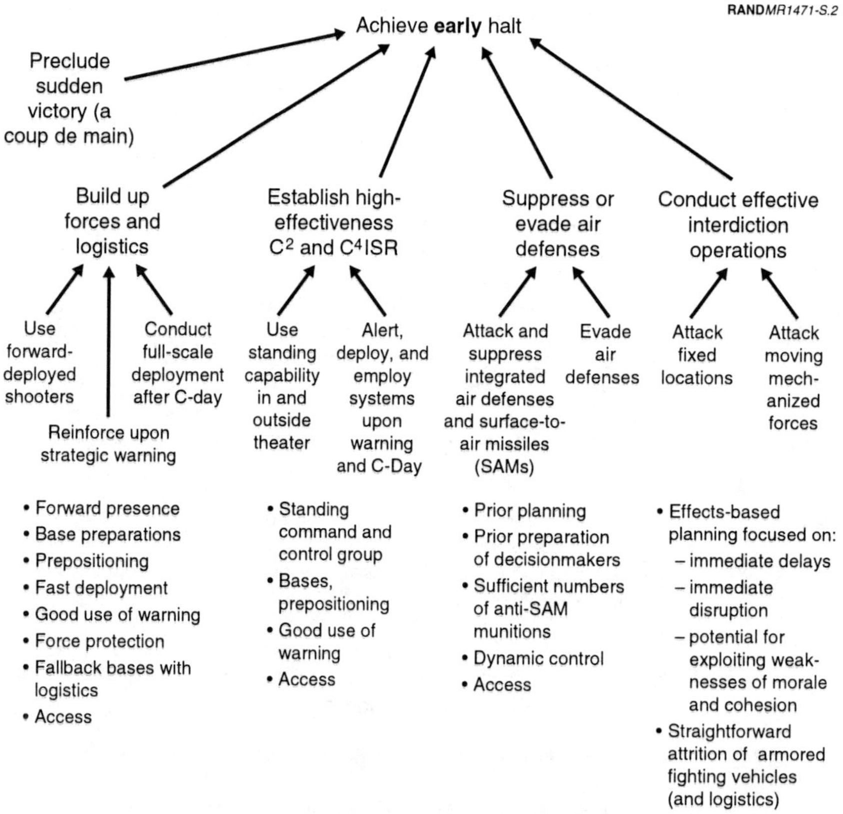

NOTE: Depicts interdiction-only case; preference is for integrated operations, including use of ground forces. Precluding a coup de main is not treated further here. All top-layer components are critical; not all subcomponents are necessary.

Figure S.2—Critical Interacting Components of an Early Halt

Preventing a surprise takeover (i.e., a coup de main) is outside the scope of this study, but it deserves a prominent place in the system depiction. For the context of Iraq threatening Kuwait, the concerns here include a fast attack into Kuwait City itself by small, elite units. As in 1990, such an attack would likely involve air-mobile units and various special forces, accompanied by a relatively small force of regular ground units.[1]

The other critical components of Figure S.2 are at the heart of this study. Analysis demonstrates quantitatively their criticality for the early halt:

- Having substantial anti-armor shooters *in place by D-Day*. These shooters can include Air Force fighter aircraft, long-range bombers, naval aircraft and missiles, and ground-force systems such as attack helicopters and long-range missiles (e.g., ATACMS/BAT). The result is a premium on forward presence, long-range bombers, aggressive use of strategic warning, and at least moderate base access.
- Ability to employ the shooters from D-Day onward, rather than only after a SEAD campaign, the length of which could be difficult or impossible to control.
- Having highly effective command-control and C^4ISR from D-Day onward, rather than only after a potentially lengthy SEAD campaign and a potentially lengthy buildup of command-group cohesiveness and efficiency.
- Having effective shooters, which—given good C^4ISR as highlighted in the third branch—is largely associated with having adequate stocks of high-quality munitions (e.g., Joint Direct Action Munition [JDAM] or more advanced weapons such as the Low Cost Autonomous Attack System [LOCAAS]) and the avionics to exploit them.
- Focusing force employment on immediate slowing of enemy movement and exploiting potential shortcomings of morale and cohesion that could bring about a halt much more quickly than would be estimated by conservatively calculated massive attrition. That is, effects-based operations, to use the current vernacular, are essential for an early halt. Such operations could include prompt strikes on assembly areas and choke points, a leading-edge strategy of force employment, and possible cyber attacks on the enemy's command and control. Other methods of slowing an attack could in principle include actions by allied forces in peacetime or during crisis and include erection of barriers defended by fires or plans for a mobile delaying defense, perhaps with augmentation during a period of ambiguous warning.

Individually, these observations should not be surprising. What is significant, arguably, is the system perspective that emphasizes that success in *all* of them is necessary.[2] Although a commander at the time would be well aware of the many critical components, it is difficult in peacetime defense planning to avoid the tendency to work only parts of such a problem.

---

[1]On August 2, 1990, the Iraqi attack began at 1 am. Victory was claimed by Baghdad radio by 11 am and forces secured Kuwait City by 7 pm. The emir had fled in the morning. Iraq's invasion was led by three Republican Guard divisions and a special operations force that made heliborne and amphibious assaults (DoD, 1992, p. 3; Hiro, 1992, Ch. 2). Other relatively quick and painless takeovers have included the Soviet-British invasion of neutral Iran in 1941 (Stewart, 1988) and the Soviet invasion of Afghanistan in 1979.

[2]We did not address logistical issues in this study, but they also can be limiting factors as shown in work for the U.S. Air Force led by colleague Don Stevens. One chronic problem has been failure to preposition adequate stocks of high-lethality anti-armor munitions.

Other Factors Are Less Important

Although important, some factors are less important for the *early* halt than might have been expected before analysis. These include:

- The sheer size of the enemy attack force
- Sustained deployment rates of fighter aircraft (as distinct from initial deployment rates, which can have a big impact on D-Day shooters)
- A large in-theater bed-down capability for fighter aircraft (i.e., unrestricted access to bases)
- The size of the eventual force that could be brought to bear by the United States (i.e., the size of a nominal major-theater-war building block in force structure).

A smaller enemy force can be halted sooner than a large one, but early-halt capability requires having substantial D-Day effectiveness, in which case a large enemy force is not a great deal more difficult to deal with than a smaller one—especially if it can be slowed by the interdiction itself or by concerns about having to engage ground forces. Similarly, higher deployment rates are always better than smaller ones, but achieving an early halt depends primarily on shooters present at D-Day, which means that later deployments have less leverage. In the same way, the difference between unlimited theater capacity and something more limited is more relevant to a long large-scale low-efficiency attrition campaign than to the early-halt problem on which we have focused.

The correct way to interpret these points is not to imagine that these other factors are not important—indeed, they might be pivotal for other missions if the war continued, if a counteroffensive into enemy territory were made, or if the enemy achieved an initial fait accompli and had to be evicted from urban areas. Rather, the point here is that

> **The early-halt mission depends critically on up-front system capabilities rather than on overall force structure or mass.**

Other Observations

A variety of other observations can be made, some representing different expressions of insight already drawn. In particular:

- *Forward presence.* Because D-Day capability is so critical, and because having and using warning time well cannot prudently be assumed, forward presence will continue to be critical. Forward presence affects not only the number of D-Day shooters but also the likely real-world status of command- control and C^4ISR, and the plausibility of efficient coordination with regional forces and support personnel.
- *Red lines.* Should reduced sanctions be contemplated, maintaining a red line has high potential value in reducing the ambiguity of warning and thereby enhancing the likelihood of timely regional-state cooperation. Immediate strikes could devastate the attacker or seriously delay its advance. In the context of negotiations, then, preserving red-line constraints has high value. Unfortunately, effective use of red lines cannot be assured. Thus, they should be regarded as potentially quite valuable, but not as something to be counted upon. See Chapter 2.

- *Immediate anti-armor operations.* Because the time required to destroy air defenses will likely be increasingly uncertain in the future, the Air Force should plan to attack armor almost immediately—before SEAD is complete—depending instead on a combination of continuing SEAD operations, standoff weapons, stealth, electronic countermeasures, and geographically focused attacks that would permit better protection of shooters.
- *Missiles, UCAVs, and attack helicopters.* Because the air defense problem is inherently difficult, the United States may need to depend—for its immediate anti-armor missions—on long-range missiles and, as they develop, unmanned combat aerial vehicles (UCAVs). If present, attack helicopters might also be usable immediately for attacks—perhaps with less vulnerability in the halt mission to long-range SAMs than fighter aircraft and bombers. The Army could be encouraged to build mobile "brigades" with ATACMS missiles and attack helicopters and to consider related cooperative programs with Kuwait, which could facilitate augmentation during periods of ambiguous warning.[3]
- *Early C^4ISR.* Because of the projected problem of long-range SAMs, which would threaten traditional platforms such as the Joint Surveillance [and] Target Attack Radar System (JSTARS) aircraft, there will predictably be a premium on high-altitude long-endurance stealthy platforms such as unmanned aerial vehicles (UAVs) and satellites. There may also be a greater-than-appreciated role for elite ground forces that could target invasion forces.
- *Joint strike force (or joint response force).* If permanent U.S. presence were reduced, then having a joint strike force (or joint response force) with sufficient ground forces able to operate from and even in front of a forward defense line could be valuable—although the feasibility of inserting such a forward ground force would depend heavily on the assured effectiveness of long-range fires and local forces. Such a joint strike force is a candidate for joint transformation, since it could be initiated in the near term and evolve with technology and doctrine. It would have many benefits outside of the Persian Gulf.[4]

POTENTIAL ADAPTATIONS IN REVIEW

Actions and Reactions

Against this background, Table S.2 summarizes in its first column a number of potential actions by Iraq that would decrease U.S. counter-maneuver capability, including halt capability. The second column shows potential U.S. counters, both Air Force and joint. Finally, the third column suggests steps that could be made by regional states to support U.S. efforts.

---

[3]Each of these systems has substantial vulnerabilities and shortcomings, as do fighter aircraft. Such issues (e.g., vulnerability of attack helicopters) often must be addressed with high-resolution simulation and field tests. Results are sensitive to terrain and mission.

[4]The joint strike force concept has been studied in several versions by the Defense Science Board (DSB, 1998), RAND (Gritton, Davis, Steeb, and Matsumura, 2000), and the Institute for Defense Analyses (in work led by Colonel Rick Lynch). It is closely related to the Rapid Decisive Operation (RDO) being studied in depth by the U.S. Joint Forces Command (USJFCOM) as its first integrating concept. The recent transformation panel reporting to Secretary of Defense Rumsfeld recommended an early-entry joint response force consistent with the past work (McCarthy, 2001).

Table S.2

POTENTIAL ACTIONS AND COUNTER ACTIONS

Potential Iraqi Actions	U.S. Counters	Counters by Gulf States
Short-warning attacks: Create ambiguity during attack preparations. Plan to capture Kuwait City and oil facilities; hold population and facilities hostage.	Increase permanent presence. Routinely use strategic warning; punish Red politically and militarily for causing buildups. Insist on agreed red line. Hedge with increased long-loiter, large-capacity bombers.	Support U.S. presence, use of strategic warning, and red line. Participate in routinized punishing of Red for provocative actions and costly Blue responses.
Anti-access strategies: Pose WMD threat to forward bases, prepositioning, forces, and Gulf-state cities.	Deter with announced plans for reprisal attacks. Enhance capacity and stocking of secure but more distant regional bases. Enhance naval air's capabilities. Enhance bomber capability: more stealth and standoff weapons, larger weapon payloads, and prepositioning.	Support U.S. reprisal plan to enhance deterrence. Provide gas masks for population; suits for critical workers at bases. Enhance capability and stocking of more distant regional bases.
Advanced mobile, netted air defenses, plus metered use to extend SEAD time.	Use very large number of Joint Air-to-Surface Standoff Missiles (JASSMs) to suppress air defenses well enough to permit early anti-armor operations. Ready semi-stealthy UAVs and space systems for early C4ISR. Protect early shooters with stealth, electronic countermeasures (ECM), and attacks focused on front. Reassess risk; accept some losses.	Assist U.S. targeting efforts with elite troops on ground, reinforced by U.S. early-entry forces.
Increase size of army.	Increase buys of best-effectiveness weapons per platform (e.g., small smart bombs).	
Attack on multiple axes and columns, and perhaps off-road, reducing effectiveness of leading-edge attacks.	Plan to deal with axes sequentially. Focus more on road-bound logistics. Develop weapons with larger, cross-column footprints.	Develop maneuver capabilities sufficient, in principle, to force concentration.
Increase movement rate of dash to first objective.	Maintain vigilance to preclude surprise attack. Exploit red line; preempt attack and delay initial movement by days. Hedge by planning attacks on logistics to isolate forces in cities.	Maintain ready forces to prevent a sudden and easy coup de main. Embrace red line concept; incorporate in exercises. Have rapid-action ground forces for delay and disruption, rather than stand-and-die operations. Create temporary barriers to road-bound logistics; cover with fires.
Devise "hides" (e.g., using camouflage) to permit episodic dashes to frustrate continuous interdiction efforts (less plausible for the long-distance invasion through the desert; more plausible within Iraq).	Support CAP stations[a] with long-endurance, high-lethality platforms (e.g., stealthy bombers, UCAVs, or even fighter aircraft with small smart bombs). Employ strip-alert forces able to augment CAP stations on short notice.	Provide elite ground forces (perhaps augmented by U.S. forces) able to penetrate deep into enemy territory to provide improved warning of when maneuvers will begin. Commit ground-force ambush teams that could prolong the duration of marches.

[a]A Combat Air Patrol station might consist of one or a few orbiting aircraft able to loiter for hours rather than minutes. Supporting CAP stations requires many aircraft, but ensures coverage during enemy maneuvers.

Hedging Actions

It is one thing to recognize that many adaptations would be possible in principle. It is another to take measures now to ensure that the adaptations are possible in practice when needed. Some of the long-lead-time hedge actions that seem particularly useful—including some already ongoing—are as follows:

- Maintain standing teams for C^2 and C^4ISR teams able to operate with minimal spinup time even in relatively complex early joint operations (ongoing at 9th Air Force).
- Pursue development and initial deployment of the "small smart bombs" that will, if successful, substantially improve the kill potential of individual aircraft. This would leverage the capabilities of the relatively small numbers of aircraft present on D-Day in cases with little warning. Such development is well under way.
- Pursue development and deployment of survivable reconnaissance, surveillance, and tracking systems (e.g., stealthy UAVs or satellites) with the requirement that they be usable from the outset of war.
- Pursue development and deployment of stealthy platforms with long loiter times and large numbers of anti-armor munitions.
- Develop appropriate concepts of operations, including logistics, for anti-armor operations from CAP stations.
- Develop and maintain high-readiness competence in joint operations with Navy forces during the first days of war when Navy aviation and missiles might be especially critical for air defense and SEAD operations conducted simultaneously with early anti-armor attacks.

Our remaining suggestions relate to activities that the Air Force could support in the interagency domain or in joint operations:

- Continue to make the diplomatic case for permanent forward presence, even if sanctions are lifted and Iraq's behavior appears temporarily benign.
- Lay the diplomatic groundwork for permanent red lines—even in a post-sanctions regime.
- Urge reorientation of regional ground-force efforts to emphasize slowing of invasion forces; defeating special-forces attacks on bases, ports, and other critical sites; and perhaps providing early targeting information. This would be a long-lead-time effort because it would require different skills.
- As mentioned earlier, develop a joint strike force (or joint response force) that could be employed within days of deployment decision and that would have significant mechanized capabilities within a week (Gritton, Davis, Steeb, and Matsumura, 2000). Such a force would have numerous benefits, but would also increase the likelihood of slowing and concentrating invasion forces—thereby making them more vulnerable to interdiction. As part of this, plan early augmentation of regional forces with U.S. allied-support forces that could leverage regional forces with C^4ISR, air coverage, and other long-range fires. These could be followed by mobile light infantry and then medium-weight mechanized units. Such planning could include augmenting Kuwaiti personnel with U.S. personnel in attack-helicopter units.

Consistent with all of the above, we recommend that the Air Force (and Department of Defense) adopt planning scenarios that stress assured mission-system capability for the early halt under conditions with modest or ambiguous warning and differing degrees of regional cooperation. We also recommend that, even if some of the problems discussed in this monograph materialize, the easy course of reducing objectives to defending somewhere deep in Saudi Arabia *not* be taken—especially because real-world Iraqi capabilities are not now and are not likely soon to be as formidable as is often assumed in studies. The difficulty of bringing about a halt might be far less than is often assumed, given plausible U.S. adaptations.

ACKNOWLEDGMENTS

The final version of this monograph benefited from two very useful reviews by colleagues Tom Hamilton and Russ Shaver. The work also benefited from past work by and conversations with colleagues Glenn Kent, Edward Harshberger, and David Ochmanek.

ACRONYMS

AFV	Armored fighting vehicle
ATACMS	Army Tactical Missile System
BAT	Brilliant Antiarmor Munition
CAOC	combined air-operations center
CAP	combat air patrol
CF	closed form
CVBG	aircraft carrier battle group
C^2	command and control
C^4ISR	command, control, communications, computing, intelligence, surveillance, and reconnaissance
ECM	electronic countermeasures
EDR	equivalent deployment rate
ISR	Intelligence, Surveillance, and Reconnaissance
JASSM	Joint Air-to-Surface Standoff Missile
JICM	Joint Integrated Contingency Model
JSF	Joint Strike Fighter
JSTARS	Joint Surveillance [and] Target Attack Radar System
KPSD	kills per shooter day
LOCAAS	Low Cost Autonomous Attack System
MLRS	Multiple Launch Rocket System
MRM	multiresolution modeling
MRMPM	multiresolution, multiperspective modeling
MSC	mission-system capability
PGM	precision-guided munition
RSAS	RAND Strategy Assessment System
SAM	surface-to-air missile
SEAD	suppression of enemy air defenses
SEAS	System Effectiveness Analysis Simulation
UAV	unmanned aerial vehicle
UCAV	unmanned combat aerial vehicle
WMD	weapons of mass destruction

1. INTRODUCTION

1.1 BACKGROUND AND OBJECTIVES

The Early-Halt Problem

The "early-halt problem" in defense planning (Cohen, 1999, p. 16) is identifying and obtaining the military capability to halt an invading mechanized army quickly.[1] *Under ideal circumstances*, and with advanced weapon systems that are being procured now in limited quantities, the United States should be able to interdict, halt, and heavily degrade such an invading army with tactical and long-range air forces alone. This would set the stage for gaining control of the ground and for later counteroffensives. But ideal circumstances are hard to come by.[2] Complicating factors that would undercut any interdiction capability include the enemy's scheme of maneuver, the threatened use of mass-destruction weapons, or political delays in U.S. access to regional bases. These elements of an anti-access strategy are under the control of a determined invader, while others are more intrinsically related to the particular theater's terrain or to chance.[3] It is therefore of great interest to know what the United States and its regional allies could do even if confronted with an attempted anti-access strategy.

The Halt Problem as a Measure of More General Counter-Maneuver Capability

The halt problem not only measures capabilities to stop a stereotyped re-invasion of Kuwait, it also measures capabilities for countering maneuver forces more generally. Suppose, for example, that the United States wanted to prevent Saddam Hussein from moving a significant army into an area of rebellion or from engaging a rebel army. To the extent that it would be necessary for Saddam's army to expose itself

---

[1]General Ronald Fogleman, then Chief of Staff of the Air Force, highlighted this problem in 1996–1997. In commenting on the Air Force's contribution to the 1997 Quadrennial Defense Review, he said (Fogleman, 1997): "Perhaps our most important contribution was assisting the Secretary of Defense as he crafted a new national military strategy. In it, we see a reflection of increased appreciation for the advantages and possibilities responsive and capable forces provide to the nation. The strategy included a new special emphasis on the critical importance of an early, decisive halt to armed aggression—an area in which air and space forces have disproportionate value. I firmly believe more examination of the phases of this strategy—halt, buildup, and counter-offensive—is warranted."

[2]For extensive discussion of when ground forces are necessary early in conflict, see Gritton, Davis, Steeb, and Matsumura (2000).

[3]The halt problem has been studied in some depth. See particularly Ochmanek, Harshberger, Thaler, and Kent (1998); Davis, Bigelow, and McEver (1999); and Defense Science Board (1998, Vol. 1, pp. 279 ff). The earliest treatment of which we are aware was Bowie, Frostic, et al. (1993). Effects of base-access problems were discussed at some length by Davis and others in a limited-circulation 1997 study for the Office of the Assistant Secretary of Defense for Strategy and Threat Reduction. Riggins and Snodgrass (1999) discuss the halt problem from a joint perspective and note controversies and points of potential agreement, as in observing that the halt-problem challenge is closely related to what the Army calls "strategic preclusion."

during a fairly lengthy march, the same forces useful in a classic halt campaign could be used to deter such a march—or to interdict it if it occurred. Just as in the stereotyped halt problem, U.S. capabilities would depend sensitively on in-place forces, immediately effective command and control (C^2) and command, control, communications, computing, intelligence, surveillance, and reconnaissance (C^4ISR), per-sortie effectiveness, and so on. However, the size of the threat to be defeated might be much smaller than in traditional planning scenarios involving a large and rejuvenated Iraqi army. It follows that using the halt problem to measure capability—and its sensitivity to a host of situational details—is a surrogate—albeit imperfect—for measuring capability for diverse lesser uses of force. It is a particularly good measure for some aspects of air force capability.[4] Obviously, it is not especially relevant for assessing capability for fighting in urban sprawl or forests, nor for dealing with many of the situations that demand ground forces.

Monograph's Objectives

The objective of this monograph is twofold: to motivate, derive, and document a series of increasingly rich closed-form analytical models; and to summarize insights from use of such models. The most sophisticated of these models is called EXHALT-CF ("CF" for "closed form"). It is closely related to a more detailed simulation model named EXHALT (now in version 1.5 as described in Appendix C). We refer to EXHALT-CF in shorthand as an "analytical model," to distinguish it from a simulation.

Although we focus entirely on EXHALT-CF in this monograph, we strongly embrace the approach of using a *family* of models and human war games to study subjects such as the halt problem. This is not a matter of paying lip service to other methods, but rather recognizing that different models and games lead to different insights, make use of different classes of information, and are useful in different contexts (Davis, Bigelow, and McEver, 1999; Defense Science Board, 1998). Table 1.1 emphasizes this by summarizing the methods we and colleagues have used on the halt problem alone. A corollary here is that readers who find themselves uncomfortable with some of EXHALT-CF's simplifications should understand that this monograph is merely part of a larger tapestry. It is very good for some issues and inappropriate for others. As indicated, it is extremely fast and appropriate for interactive simultaneous exploratory analysis of roughly 10 parameters.

1.2 APPROACH: USE OF CLOSED-FORM ANALYTICAL MODELS

The classic argument for analytical solutions is that insights can be obtained by doing the derivations, which can clarify phenomenology, and by viewing the resulting mathematical forms to observe the nature of dependencies (e.g., linear, inverse, or exponential). Ideally, the insights reveal forests rather than trees. That argument applies to the halt problem as described in early chapters of this monograph.

---

[4]Higher-resolution treatment of the halt problem is needed, however, to address issues such as the ability to maintain continuous combat-air-patrol (CAP) stations sufficient to deal with small maneuvers over short periods of time.

Table 1.1

MEMBERS OF MODEL AND GAMES FAMILY USED FOR HALT-PHASE WORK

Model Name	Type	Comments
EXHALT-CF	Complex closed-form analytical model.	For high-level extremely fast and interactive exploration. Example: 10,000 cases varying 10 parameters simultaneously can be run in about 5–10 seconds on a personal computer. Displays then react instantaneously to interactive changes of one or another parameter. Written in Analytica®.
EXHALT[a]	Moderately simple simulation.	For high-level exploration with more detailed characterization of platform-weapon combinations. Fast (but not nearly as fast as the CF version). Written in Analytica.
Simple spreadsheet models (unnamed)	Simple spreadsheet simulations.	For traditional high-level sensitivity studies[b] and limited exploratory analysis.[c] Extremely fast. Written in Microsoft Excel.®.
PEM[d]	Simple analytical model focused on certain high-resolution aspects of halt problem.	For connecting entity-level simulation of long-range fires in mixed terrain to parameters of EXHALT and EXHALT-CF. Written in Analytica.
JICM[e]	Complex theater-level simulation of joint and combined operations.	For analytical war gaming and exploratory analysis of multi-theater conflicts. Moderate data preparation. Very flexible and fast running for a theater model (minutes per case on a workstation). Written in C with friendly interfaces.
START[f]	A complex spreadsheet simulation derived from JICM and enriched for Air Force issues.	For high-level exploration. Moderate data preparation. Written in Excel. Very flexible. Minutes per case.
RAND suite of high-resolution simulations with Janus game board[g]	Entity-level tactical models following individual vehicles in digitized terrain.	Explicit treatment of terrain, weapons, and joint maneuver operations for regiment-sized battles. Written in multiple languages and runs on UNIX workstations. Run times may be many minutes. Many weeks of database preparation, although many changes can be readily made within a basic scripted scenario.
SEAS (System Effectiveness Analysis Simulation)[h]	Entity-level personal-computer model for studying effects of particular C^4ISR systems on local ground-force battles. Agent-based modeling can represent some behaviors and decisions.	Explicit treatment of orbits and coverage of platforms, some communications, and effects on tactical battle. Runs in many minutes on personal computer. May require many weeks of data-base preparation. Very flexible.
No name[i]	Tactical force-employment human game for studying competitive tactics in presence of alternative C^4ISR systems.[g] Moderate database preparation. In development.	For study of issues such as the value of alternative types of information in resolving tactical problems created by terrain masking, deceptive tactics, and the limited number of aircraft available for immediate attack of emerging targets. Being written in Microsoft's Visual Basic®. Will probably require 1–3 hours per game.

[a]McEver, Davis, and Bigelow (2000a) and Appendix C.

[b]Bowie, Frostic, et al. (1993) and Ochmanek, Harshberger, Thaler, and Kent (1998).

[c]Davis and Carrillo (1997).

[d]Davis, Bigelow, and McEver (2000a).

[e]The Joint Integrated Contingency Model was used in early exploratory analysis of the halt problem in 1995–1996 by Paul Davis, Carl Jones, and Arthur Bullock. For JICM information, contact Daniel Fox in RAND's Arlington, VA office.

[f]For recent work using START, contact Don Stevens in RAND's Santa Monica, CA office.

[g]Matsumura, Steeb, Gordon, Glenn, Herbert, and Steinberg (2000).

[h]See Gonzales, Moore, Pernin, Matonick, and Dreyer (2001).

[i]For information on this developmental effort, contact Russ Shaver in RAND's Arlington office.

Later chapters add further levels of sophistication, resolution, and complexity. Although the models remain small, the resulting formulas proliferate to cover many distinct cases; they are not transparent and at that point only an inveterate lover of mathematics would claim that the approach is simple. We make no such claims and we and our colleagues do most of our related work with computer simulations such as EXHALT, which are in some respects *easier* to understand despite their greater detail. Nonetheless, the analytical approach still has several major advantages that are not widely appreciated:

- It can motivate and evaluate good abstractions, performance and capability metrics, and approximations that are often useful in the more complex simulations and for explaining results (Davis and Bigelow, 1998).
- It allows extremely fast calculations, which can be invaluable for interactive exploratory analysis driven by a portable personal computer (Davis, 2000; Davis and Hillestad [forthcoming]).
- The analytic models provide a reasonably independent check on the simulation models (and vice versa), since the errors in algebraic work tend to be different from those in simulation. They can be checked or obtained with Mathematica®.[5]
- They can be quickly implemented in any platform or language convenient to users (e.g., C, Excel, Visual Basic, or Analytica).

Using the closed-form solutions is somewhat akin to solving certain physics or chemistry problems under assumptions of equilibrium or steady state: Such solutions are frequently quite useful and very much to the point, even though they do not describe the system's dynamics, as simulations do.

1.3 STRUCTURE OF MONOGRAPH

We have organized this monograph to document EXHALT-CF and discuss substantive insights from analysis. Readers interested primarily in issues of policy, strategy, and broad analytical approach should focus on the summary. The main text of the monograph, in contrast, is organized in a bottom-up manner that may be of more interest to modelers and analysts needing to understand details. As shown in Table 1.2, the rest of this monograph starts with a simple discussion and then adds more effects in successive chapters.

Chapter 2 provides an overview of the full problem. Readers will see that the approach is highly abstract in some respects, but that it addresses key issues often not dealt with even in much more detailed analysis. Chapter 3 then begins the analytical discussion by presenting solutions for simple cases. This chapter addresses factors such as the time when deployment begins, deployment rates, sortie rates, effectiveness per sortie, enemy movement rate, and so on. It also includes important variables such as strategic and tactical warning, the potential for U.S. forces to begin interdiction early when the enemy may be particularly subject to disruption, and potential effects of the enemy using or credibly threatening to use mass-destruction weapons (WMD).

---

[5]We experimented with Mathematica in the current study, but found it less useful than in other domains because our problem had so many discontinuities, which created a multitude of separate cases.

Table 1.2

PROGRESSION OF COMPLETENESS WITHIN MONOGRAPH

Subject Treated	Ch. 3	Ch. 4	Ch. 5	Ch. 6	Ch. 7	Ch. 8
Simple race	•	•	•	•	•	
Access delays	•	•	•	•	•	•
WMD	•	•	•	•	•	•
Delays due to early strikes	•	•	•	•	•	•
Capacities	•	•	•	•	•	•
SEAD phase		•	•	•	•	•
Losses		•	•	•	•	•
Ground forces			•	•	•	•
Best-weapon shortages, C^2 and C^4ISR				•	•	•
Analysis of uncertainty and risk					•	•
Illustrative analysis						•

Chapter 4 generalizes the problem by accounting for attrition to the defender and, more important, by representing a phased interdiction operation in which portions of the shooters are withheld temporarily because of their high vulnerability to air defenses. Later, after a time sufficient to suppress air defenses, all shooters can operate without attrition, but that time may be excessive—the attacker may already have reached his objective. Thus, there are tradeoffs between waiting to use some aircraft for fear of losses and achieving the goal of an early halt. The choice of wait time can be optimized if the tradeoff relationship is specified (McEver, Davis, and Bigelow, 2000b).

Chapter 5 extends the analysis by allowing for the synergy of defending ground forces, which attempt to halt the invader at a defense line. The defending force is characterized by the size of the enemy force it could defeat while holding ground at the operational level, and by the time at which it would be available at the defense line.[6]

Chapter 6 draws on recent studies to add a number of important factors that are often ignored, even in complex war games. In particular, it treats exhaustion of best weapons in considerable detail. It also sketches how other factors, such as command and control, maneuver tactics, terrain, and weapon mix, can be reflected indirectly.

Chapter 7 describes how the models can be implemented to account for both deterministic and stochastic uncertainties. This is easy in either Analytica® or the combination of Microsoft Excel® with an appropriate add-in such as Crystal Ball®. We

[6]Richer depictions of the ground-force issues need to be addressed with war gaming and simulation. We need insights as to how quickly a relatively small but modern ground force could take up positions at a key defense line, and how large an enemy force it could deal with.

show examples of exploratory analysis using both Analytica and a system under development by Evolving Logic Inc. called CARs™.

Finally, Chapter 8 presents some illustrative analysis (see also Defense Science Board, 1998).

Appendix A generalizes the models to account explicitly for many shooter types: different types of fixed-wing aircraft, attack helicopters, multiple rocket launchers with brilliant munitions (Multiple Launch Rocket System [MLRS] or High Mobility Artillery Rocket System [HIMARS]/Army Tactical Missile System [ATACMS]), and naval missiles. This material uses array notation, which allows us to show how simple the generalization is from the viewpoint of formal mathematics. However, when explicit representation of systems is needed, we usually recommend moving to simulation models in a suitable modeling and gaming environment. We and colleagues have used the Analytica-based EXHALT model for relatively simple and transparent work and either JICM or START for more sophisticated joint and combined work (see Table 1.1).

Appendix B is a compact summary of all the variables used in the text, along with brief descriptions. Appendix C describes EXHALT 1.5, which is an extended version of EXHALT to which the EXHALT-CF of this monograph is a simpler companion. Appendices D and E provide mathematical details of some of the derivations. Appendix F describes implementation and testing in Analytica.

2. OVERVIEW OF THE HALT PROBLEM

2.1 GENERIC GEOGRAPHY

The generic problem is illustrated in Figure 2.1. The models developed in the monograph do not represent the details of Figure 2.1, but rather deal with mathematical abstractions such as average movement rate and average penetration distance. Nonetheless, having an overview picture is useful in formulating the model.

The invader (Red) lives to the north, above the international boundary. He[1] invades on a generally southeastern course, before swinging southward. His primary objective is shown as a large shaded rectangle. His invasion may be on more than one axis (two in the figure) and may have more than one column of advance on each main axis (not shown).

2.2 THE FORCES

The invader is using classic mechanized forces that are mostly road-bound. They consist of numerous divisions, each with a certain number of armored fighting vehicles (AFVs), which are an appropriate focus of attention in capabilities analysis.[2] Because the invader moves without substantial opposition on the ground, he is assumed to move at a constant average speed—except possibly for special delays at the invasion outset or shortly after it commences. Later, we consider effects-based approaches to interdiction that could cause more slowing.

The defender (Blue) is the defended country assisted by the United States. The United States interdicts the invader with long-range precision fires that could in principle come from Air Force bombers and tactical aircraft, naval aircraft, Army attack helicopters, and both naval and Army missiles. In this monograph, our examples focus on Air Force and Navy aircraft. Interdiction forces include those that were present from the outset and those deployed subsequently. Their numbers may be affected by losses to air defenses and constraints on theater air-base capacity. Their effectiveness may be affected by the threat or actual use of mass-destruction weapons, air defenses, shortages in high-quality munitions, command and control, and the force-employment strategy itself.

The defended country is assumed to have modestly capable ground forces. Small elite units might mount harassment and disruption operations (see X's in Figure 2.1) and regular forces might participate in defense at one or another identified defense

[1]Perhaps the guardians of gender-correct language will grant us license here, especially since nearly all historical invasions have been led by men.

[2]In real wars, actually killing AFVs is frequently much less important than forcing changes in the invader's strategy or tactics, precluding certain operations, and reducing the effectiveness of enemy forces generally (Keaney and Cohen, 1993). That said, such effects can be regarded as deriving ultimately from the defender's *capability* to cause attrition promptly and flexibly. Force planning, then, can reasonably focus on such capabilities as measured by the mathematics of an idealized war.

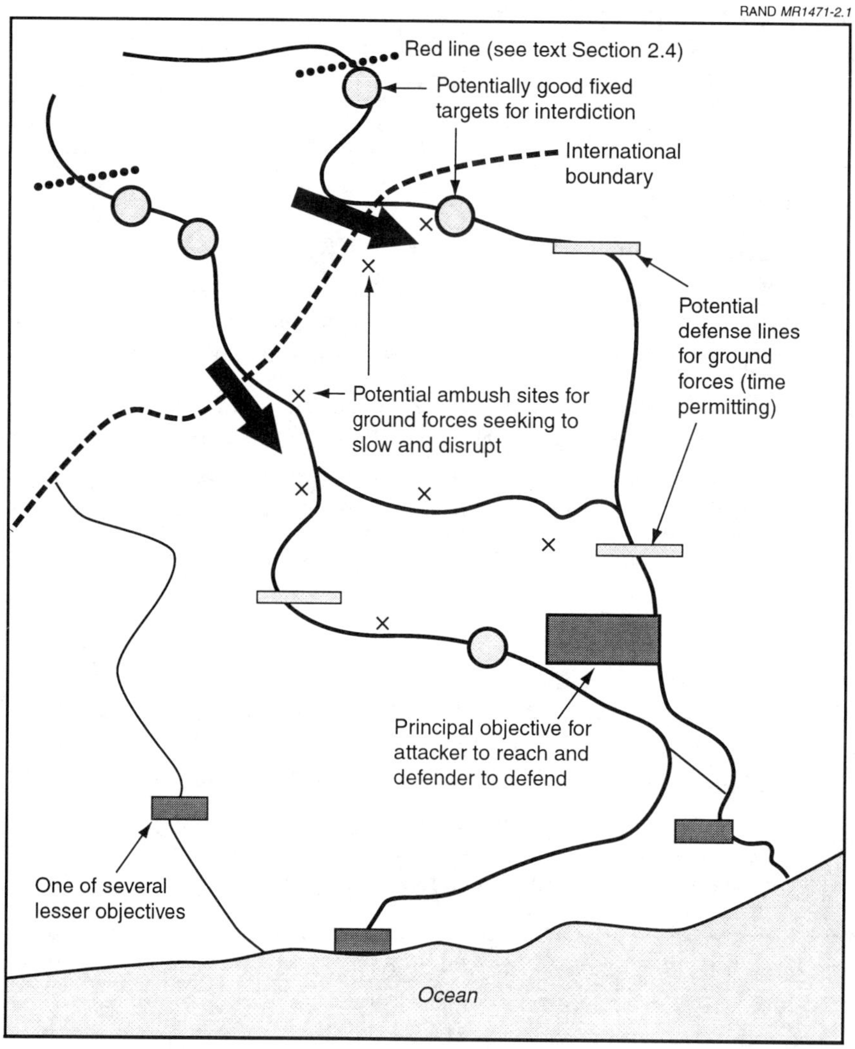

Figure 2.1—Generic Geography for Discussing the Halt Problem

lines—especially if joined early by U.S. forces. In this work, such ground forces at a defense line are represented in terms of how large a Red force the ground forces could stop if present at the given defense line, and how quickly they could reach that line. That is, we do not model close combat per se.[3]

[3]Adding a simple close-combat model would be trivial, but misleading. Actual combat would depend on more complex issues related to terrain, maneuver, C^4ISR, air forces, logistics, and preparations. Our approach is designed to accommodate, for example, assessments by the Army or Marine Corps of the capability of rapidly employable ground forces. Their assessments could reflect war gaming and expert judgment.

2.3 BASES: ACCESS AND VULNERABILITY

We assume that—in the best cases—the United States has early access to ample air bases (not shown in the figure) in the defended country. In other cases, the United States may need to operate from more distant bases, which may be outside the country or even outside the region. These bases may have reduced capacities and less developed infrastructures and weapon stockpiles for supporting operations, because of access restrictions, concerns about the use of mass-destruction weapons, or other factors. The result is to degrade sortie rates and other factors.[4]

2.4 THE CONCEPT OF RED LINES

Significance of the Red Line Concept

Figure 1.1 includes the concept of a red line (top of figure). The idea of a red line is that the parties involved recognize that the crossing of the line by major forces will be regarded as an indication of invasion intent.[5] Thus, that crossing may be regarded as a casus belli justifying immediate response. Red lines are old concepts. In modern times, Israel has used them in its planning for many years; and the United States has used a red line concept with Iraq since the Gulf War of 1990–1991. Even a simple analytical model should account for such a concept, since it can make a great deal of difference to war outcomes.

If red lines are sharply enough drawn, frequently enough emphasized, and built into a country's political and military doctrine, then they may increase the *likelihood* of a quick and strong response to strategic and tactical warning. That response could include preemptive strikes on the attacker's forces if, indeed, the crossing of the red line were regarded as a casus belli. As a data point, we should recall that in 1990 the United States did not deploy to the Persian Gulf until a week *after* Iraq invaded Kuwait. Why? Because until Iraq's invasion, the situation was highly ambiguous and there was no red line. Even after the invasion took place, Saudi Arabia had to be persuaded over the course of a week that its own security was in jeopardy before allowing U.S. forces to deploy. Today, in mid-2001, a similar Iraqi buildup would bring about an immediate U.S. response. Indeed, the United States has been vigilant in the region for the last decade. Whether that will be true in five years, however, is hard to know.[6] The value of red lines can be diminished substantially if, for example, they are violated repeatedly with innocuous exercises. That desensitizes the

[4]See Shlapak et al. (forthcoming). Whether the threat or reality of chemical- and biological-weapon attacks would cause U.S. air forces to deploy to more distant bases is controversial given the quality of modern protection gear and improved procedures for operations in such environments.

[5]Another use of "red line" is metaphorical, as when someone says that for a country to develop mass-destruction weapons is to cross a red line.

[6]A red line concept might also make sense as part of Korean arms control resulting in the North pulling many of its forces back from the border, which is extremely close to Seoul. A later movement back toward the border might then be considered basis for immediate response. See Han, Davis, and Darilek (2000).

observer and reduces the likelihood of response when response is in fact needed (when "exercises" could be cover for massing of invasion forces).

In any case, our models should allow for the possibility of red lines being exploited. Crossing a red line might hasten Blue's preparation for attack. In addition, it might make possible timely attacks on particularly good fixed targets such as the circular areas indicated in the upper part of Figure 2.1. Because mechanized armies typically are moved initially by trains or heavy-lift vehicles, invasions often involve assembly areas not far from the border. These may be good targets for strike operations. In addition, there may be subsequent targets of comparable vulnerability, such as bridges, tunnels, narrow roads surrounded by swamp or dense forest, and narrow mountain passes. If an *early* halt is desired, then the defender needs to exploit any such opportunities as far forward as possible—even on the enemy's side of the border.

Cautions

Red lines are useful concepts, but they have severe limitations. In particular, no law of nature guarantees that the defender will act decisively when the red line is violated. For example, an invader could violate a red line incrementally—avoiding until the last moment moving enough forces to cause a response. Or the invader could build up logistical networks near the border without involving combat forces. And, in the event of movement in force across red lines, an invader might fill the airwaves with propagandistic "explanations" such as needing to take defensive measures because of border incidents or to regain sovereignty. It might deny—until the crossing of the border itself—that any invasion was in progress. Any number of tactics are available (and historically precedented) to increase the likelihood of achieving a "surprise attack," which in practice has meant an attack against which adequate preparations have not been made. Ambiguities prior to the attack can go far in undercutting decisive actions by worried defenders, especially when decisionmaking is complex, as it often is in democracies. A red line, then, could mean nothing in the end. It all depends.

This said, defense and extended deterrence are difficult and red lines could be quite helpful.[7]

2.5 DEFENSE LINES AND GROUND FORCES

Figure 2.1 also shows potential defense lines at which Blue's ground forces might take stands—*if* the forces they could bring to bear quickly enough would be able to defeat—or at least substantially slow—Red's advance. A defense line that is far forward can only be used if a large ground force can be moved to it quickly. Even if small forces could move to such positions quickly enough to intercept Red, they would be overrun. On the other hand, a defense line too far to the rear might squan-

[7]For discussion of surprise attacks, red line concepts, and other matters in the context of conventional arms control, see Davis (1988). The context was the old European Central Region, but the concepts are generic.

der an opportunity to bring about an earlier halt—one made possible by the combination of interdiction and ground forces. As discussed later in the monograph, decisions on defense lines should be informed by quantitative assessments of risk, not just "best estimate" outcomes.

If an early halt cannot be achieved, then the defender may at least be able to halt the invasion before the entire country is overrun (farther south in Figure 2.1). However, for the purpose of this analysis, we assume that it is particularly important—if possible—to defend far forward. This raises the issue for Blue's commander of what price he should be willing to pay in losses to aircraft and risk to ground forces at defense lines.

Even in this schematic of an invasion scenario, then, there are numerous issues to be explored analytically. The models we develop will be simple but not simplistic for thinking about military capabilities and issues rather generically.

3. ANALYTICS OF THE ELEMENTARY HALT PROBLEM

In this chapter's first cut at the problem, the model is one of a simple race between a fast-moving invader and a defender attempting to stop the invader by destroying as many of his vehicles as possible with long-range fires from aircraft, missiles, and other sources. Here we ignore the effects of air defenses, ground forces, weapon exhaustion, and command-and-control factors. We treat such issues in subsequent chapters.

3.1 VIEWING THE PROBLEM AS A RACE

The attacking force moves with average speed V toward an objective at distance Obj.[1] The defending force seeks to destroy enough of the attacker's vehicles so that the invasion is halted. If the halt time T_{halt} is soon enough, then the invader's depth of penetration D will be tolerable. Blue might be able to compel withdrawal or mount a subsequent counteroffensive, but we are concerned here only with the halt phase.[2]

V
Obj
T_{halt}
D

We are interested here only in measures of effectiveness that relate to results—not detailed dynamics along the way. Thus, D and T_{halt} are the principal measures of interest. This focus allows us to use closed-form analytical models rather than simulations describing movement and losses over time as the invader traverses different types of terrain and undergoes close combat and air strikes.

The advancing army has N_{div} divisions, each of which has N_{vpd} armored fighting vehicles. The army is halted (and defeated) when a fraction H of its armored vehicles is killed; this is the halt fraction or break point. If the defender has some way to reduce the size of the attacking army at the outset (e.g., with a D-Day strike on assembly areas), then B denotes the vehicles killed by this effect. The number of vehicles to be killed by interdiction fires and other mechanisms is given by

N_{div}
N_{vpd}
H
B
ξ

$$\xi = (N_{div} N_{vpd} - B)H. \tag{3.1}$$

As Figure 3.1 suggests, ξ is a key parameter of higher-level analysis, whereas the other parameters of Eq. (3.1) affect the problem only indirectly, through ξ. Thus, one independent variable can be used instead of four—except when there is reason to "zoom in." This is the essence of multiresolution modeling (MRM) (Davis and Bigelow, 1998; Davis, 2000).

---

[1]Variables are indicated in the margin when they first occur. They are summarized in Appendix B.

[2]In describing a case with two or more axes of advance, as in Figure 2.1, D and T_{halt} may be seen as averages.

RANDMR1471-3.1

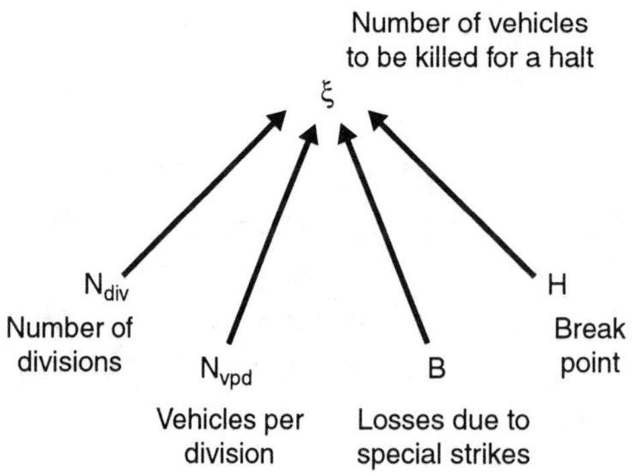

Figure 3.1—Goal: The Number of Vehicles to Be Killed

Blue's Employment Strategy and the Attacker's Resulting Movement Rate and Penetration

The war begins as the attacker mobilizes, maneuvers to assembly areas, assembles, and then invades. How long the pre-invasion activities take is reflected in the various warning times discussed later in the chapter. Here we are concerned with movement rate after D-Day. D-Day occurs when hostilities begin—when the invader crosses the border, or earlier if Blue preemptively attacks after the invader crosses a red line.

We consider two distinct strategies for Blue's employment of interdiction forces: "interdiction in depth" and "leading-edge interdiction." The first focuses strictly on attrition. The second is an example of what *effects-based planning* should consider: it seeks special slowing effects in addition to attrition. [3]

V **Interdiction in Depth.** When Blue interdicts in depth as called for in current doctrine and assumed in most studies, he has a larger set of potential targets to attack and greater operational space to exploit. The kills may be achieved anywhere along the axes of advance. For this case, let V represent an average rate of advance (km/day) over the period of the halt campaign, excepting periods when the attacker is stalled due to *special* delays, as discussed below. We treat V parametrically, rather than attempting to connect it to attrition, details of terrain, and so on, as would be done in a normal campaign model such as JICM, TACWAR, or THUNDER.

A real-world attacker may be slowed from time to time as the result of aircraft and missile strikes, sabotage, harassment from indigenous ground forces, weather effects, terrain, or problems in coordination and logistics. However, such normal delays are taken into account in the parameter V, which may be on the order of 20–100 km/day,

[3]"Effects-based planning" is defined in Air Force Doctrine Document AFDD 2, *Organization and Employment of Aerospace Power*. See also McCrabb (2001) and Davis (2001a).

even though a mechanized brigade could probably maneuver briefly for 30–60 km per *hour* and a sizable mechanized force could probably maneuver 100 km on the first day of an advance, if properly prepared.[4]

This said, it is possible that Blue could impose "special" delays from time to time. Obvious candidate periods would be during the assembly of the invasion force or as the force approaches critical bridges and tunnels that cannot be repaired quickly. Delays measured in days to a week are possible. However, the strikes would need to occur in certain windows of time. Further, they might be possible only at a few physical locations. More such natural choke points exist in some areas than in others. In the middle of a large desert, choke points may be hard to come by.

Choke-point targeting

For a simple and generic mathematical treatment, let T_{delay} denote the sum of "special" delays (in days) that can be accomplished between the beginning of hostilities and the time the attacker would either reach his objective or be halted. Implicitly, this assumes that the special delays occur, if at all, quite early. Otherwise, we could not be sure that they would occur before T_{halt}.

T_{delay}

It follows that we can usually estimate the distance moved by the invader before being halted as $D = V(T_{halt} - T_{delay})$. This is not correct, however, if the attacker reaches his objective Obj and stops (dispersing or otherwise hiding his forces from air attack), or if halt occurs within the delay time T_{delay}. The correct expression, then, is

$$D = \mathrm{Max}[\mathrm{Min}[V(T_{halt} - T_{delay}), \mathrm{Obj}], 0]. \qquad (3.2)$$

Leading-Edge Interdiction. The previous discussion used a constant value for V. However, as proposed in an earlier study (Ochmanek, Harshberger, Thaler, and Kent, 1998), a leading-edge strategy for Blue might systematically reduce *effective* movement rate over time. The idea is that Blue focuses interdiction assets on the fronts of advancing columns, disabling a large fraction of the forces attacked and thereby effectively destroying the units within which the attacked forces exist. For example, one might reasonably assume that if 50 percent of the armored fighting vehicles in a unit were killed by attrition, the remaining vehicles would be abandoned and, thus, effectively destroyed. One could argue about whether 50 percent is the correct number, but this is just a parameter of the model—one called the local break point H.[5]

H

In addition to the bonus attrition, the leading-edge attack would reduce the speed of the forward edge of surviving Red forces by the depth to which the interdiction destroys units. As Blue's interdiction capabilities build up and air defenses are suppressed, this depth would grow. Figure 3.2 describes the effect schematically.

---

[4]The discrepancy between hourly unit-level and daily army-level movement rates arises from the fact that ground forces plan their maneuvers to provide for rest, logistical operations, and problems that may occur (such as air attacks). As a result, movement rates have consistently been low for *major* formations. See, e.g., Dupuy (1979, p. 16) or McQuie (1988) for historical rates. See Savkin (1972, Ch. 3) for an interesting classic discussion of issues in achieving high-tempo operations.

[5]Elsewhere it is argued that H can be modeled qualitatively and would likely be much smaller except when dealing with heroic forces. See Davis (2001a).

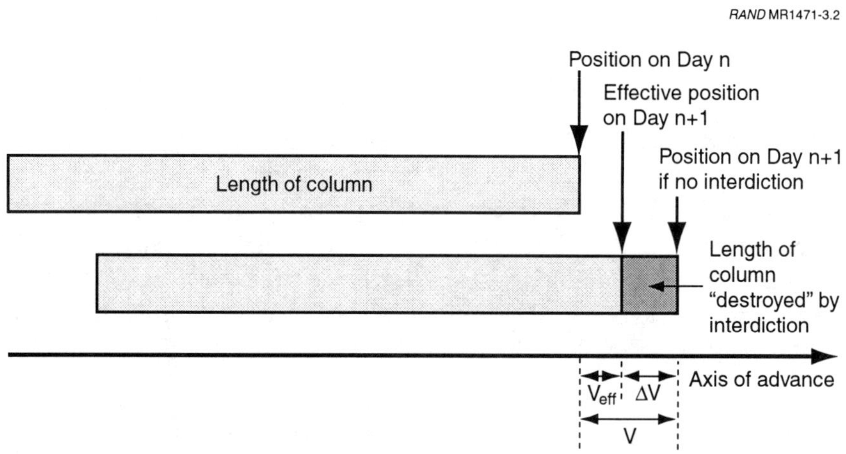

Figure 3.2—Leading-Edge Strategy Reduces Effective Movement Speed

Δ(t) The invader's net speed, then, would be given by V(t)= V – Δ(t), where Δ(t) might be small initially but would grow as additional shooters arrive and, more important, once a high fraction of shooters can be employed against armored vehicles. Conceivably, Δ(t) could become larger than V and, in at least a limited sense, interdiction forces could roll back Red forces.[6] We do not deal with that effect in this monograph.

Figure 3.3 shows the idea schematically. For the leading-edge strategy, the halt occurs at the earlier of two times—when a sufficiently large fraction of Red's total force is killed (as in the in-depth strategy) or when

$$\Delta(t = T_{halt}) = V. \tag{3.3}$$

In the example of Figure 3.3, it is assumed that the enemy's overall break point is achieved (i.e., ξ vehicles are killed) before the leading-edge strategy's slowing effect reduces movement rate to zero.

It is unclear how operationally realistic the leading-edge strategy is currently, because it is contrary to operational doctrine, requires careful management of air space and good C[4]ISR, and depends sensitively on the enemy's movement pattern. A sophisticated Red force would advance, if possible, on multiple fronts with multiple columns per front and with gaps between units. This would greatly reduce the effectiveness of the leading-edge strategy (Davis and Carrillo, 1997; Davis, Bigelow, and McEver, 1999), but it might also reduce movement rate and cause other problems for the invader as well (Ochmanek et al., 1998, p. 50). For example, the invader might

---

[6]This term is arguable, because the "disabled" forces could dismount and operate as infantry.

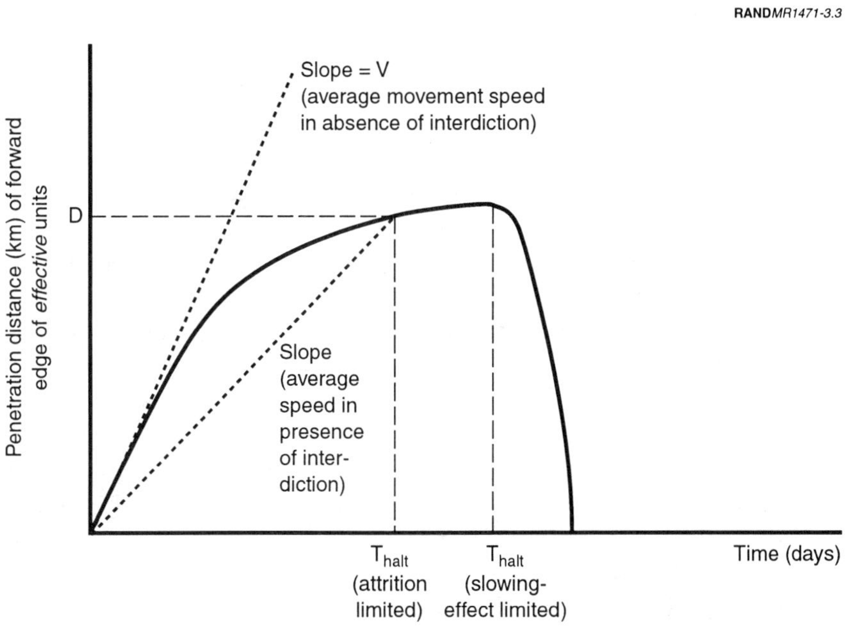

Figure 3.3—Distance Versus Time for the Leading-Edge Strategy

use secondary roads, but those would likely have lower capacities and might have more choke points exploitable by aircraft and missile strikes.[7]

Even though it has not been emphasized in DoD studies, the leading-edge strategy is an intriguing concept because many potential adversary forces are not highly competent and are constrained by geography and logistics. In some circumstances—especially if terrain, equipment limitations, or friendly ground-force opposition leads to channelization (i.e., concentrated movement along only a very few roads), if the immediate significance of a single axis is much higher than the others, if the attacker is highly dispersed along the axes of advance, or if the units in the nose of the advance can be shattered with less-than-usually-assumed fractional attrition—the strategy might be quite valuable. A factor-of-two reduction of movement rate is often possible (although the effect can be much larger or much smaller). This will be demonstrated analytically later in the chapter.

---

[7]The naïve imagery of the leading-edge strategy assumes that the attacker is moving on the road consistently. However, if movement is in spurts—with the average daily movement being the result of short fast movements, then it is possible that if one section of an advancing column were decimated during a given period, the invader would move ahead the schedule for other units and move them through or around the damaged units. What is possible here depends on terrain and other details of context and competence. In the desert terrain of Iraq, Kuwait, and Saudi Arabia, there are few hiding places for maneuver forces (although camouflage methods could be used). As a result, the "dash" tactic with its short spurts of maneuver may not be feasible. Nonetheless, the issue is an example of how tactical-level details may intrude in ways not intuitive to those reasoning only at an aggregate level.

One final observation about the leading-edge strategy. If the context is countering maneuver units on a smaller scale—as in suppressing maneuver forces while the United States or an ally is itself maneuvering forces and fires, or in interdicting formations en route to an immediate battle with U.S. or allied ground forces—the slowing effect would be even more plausible. Consider, for example, the problem of disrupting a very fast division-sized movement against friendly forces 50 km away. If the attacker moved in road-bound columns at 30 km/hour, interdiction might not only reduce the size of the force reaching the point of close combat, but also severely delay and disrupt the movement as a whole. It is not obvious that the attacker could "fill in" immediately with another division. Unfortunately, for the interdiction to be successful, a great deal of firepower would have to be applied precisely when needed—during the intended maneuver. Sorties scheduled for later in the day would not be present. For Blue to have the ability to concentrate firepower during the needed period would require either superb intelligence or a high degree of adaptiveness. More plausible solutions include maintaining orbiting CAP stations, but firepower would be quite limited with normal fighter aircraft and normal weapon loads. Weapon loads can be increased with the small smart munitions in development. Long-range bombers might have both large payloads and long times on station. In the longer run, unmanned combat aerial vehicles (UCAVs) could be used.

The Concept of Equivalent Shooters

N(t)
F(t)
A(t)

The defender's interdiction capability at time t depends on N(t), the number of shooters being used against armor. N(t), however, is shorthand for the number of "equivalent (anti-armor) shooters." The basic idea is that what matters is the product of sortie rate, fractional allocation of sorties to anti-armor missions, and kills per anti-armor sortie (or the equivalent for missiles). As allocations of aircraft across missions change, so also does the number of equivalent anti-armor shooters.[8] As an example, suppose that one has 100 standard aircraft (e.g., F-15Es) and 200 aircraft of a different type, and that the other type of aircraft has the same sortie rate but half the per-sortie effectiveness as the standard. The result is 200 equivalent aircraft. Suppose, however, that all of the standard aircraft but only 25 percent of the other aircraft are used for anti-armor missions during a particular phase of war. The others might be temporarily used for missions such as deep strike or suppression of air defenses, or might be withheld because of their vulnerability to air defenses. Then, during that phase, one has only 125 equivalent anti-armor aircraft, N(t). If F(t) denotes the fraction of available equivalent aircraft that are employed for anti-armor missions at time t, and A(t) is the number of aircraft physically present, then

$$N(t) = F(t)A(t). \tag{3.4}$$

[8]This approach can approximate results of much more detailed analysis if the only shooters counted in A(t) are those that are candidates for anti-armor attacks, thus excluding aircraft dedicated throughout the campaign to strategic bombing, suppression of air defenses, C^4ISR, air defense, and strategic or tactical mobility. To see the value of this procedure, consider the buildup curves shown in Ochmanek et al. (1998).

As discussed more fully in Appendix A, the equivalent-shooter concept can treat both Air Force and Navy aircraft and can be readily extended to include Army or Marine Corps attack helicopters. It can even reflect missile batteries or naval-gunfire systems characterized by a rate of shooting and an effectiveness per shot. A(T)

The equivalent-shooter concept is quite useful, but it can cause serious errors if applied sloppily. The root of the problem is the word "equivalent." Two systems that are equivalent in one respect (e.g., kills per day under ideal circumstances) may be very different with respect to their vulnerability, their dependence on airborne or spaceborne C^4ISR, or their ability to discriminate between military and nonmilitary targets moving along roads. Furthermore, different shooters may deploy at different rates over time, thus complicating the concept of an average deployment rate. To use the equivalent-shooter approach properly, one should break the campaign into phases, do the equivalency calculations separately for each phase, and adjust for circumstances. That may or may not be straightforward (Davis and Bigelow, 1998).

In any case, in what follows, the reader should interpret terms like "shooters" as "equivalent shooters." In this monograph for the Air Force, we largely have in mind aircraft, but the generalization is mostly straightforward (McEver et al., 2000a, and Appendix A).

Buildup of Shooters: Effects of Warning, Decision, and Access

As discussed above, N(t) anti-armor shooters are being employed at time t. Here N(t) is only a fraction F(t) of the number of shooters available, A(t). Again, F(t) may reflect the existence of other missions that use the same resources, or the withholding of some resources because of vulnerabilities to air defenses or the absence of critical C^4ISR. We need to distinguish N(t) from A(t) because the fraction F(t) may change discontinuously during the campaign as the result of the commander's decisions. As a result, there is no meaningful deployment rate for employed anti-armor shooters, but there is for overall shooters A(t)—i.e., for the physical systems.

A Canonical Buildup Curve. Figure 3.4 illustrates the buildup of shooters over time using a canonical case in which A_{00} aircraft are available in peacetime as the result of forward deployment. Further deployments occur at rate R_{strat} starting at the time of strategic warning W_{strat}.[9] Deployment rate increases to R_0 on C-Day, when full-scale deployment is ordered (but constrained by access), and moves to an even higher rate R_f when, in addition, access rights are granted at time T_{access} (including all the necessary permissions for in-theater bases, overflight, and en route basing). At D-Day, the number of shooters is A_0. All of this is a simplification, since deployment rates may vary in a more complicated way over time as a function of readiness, how reservists are used, which bases and en route permissions become available when, and so on. Nonetheless, this canonical view is both familiar and useful to planners. Figure 3.4 shows a leveling off of A(t) because the theater's capacity may be limited to A_{max}, as discussed later in the chapter.

A_{00}
W_{strat}
R_{strat}
R_0
C
A_0
T_{access}
R_f
A_{max}

[9]We assume R_{strat} is independent of access arrangements, since we have in mind movement of aircraft carriers and Air Force aircraft reinforcing bases to which they already have access.

More General Buildup Curves, for Diverse Time Orderings. Figure 3.4 assumes a particular time ordering, but many other combinations are possible, as illustrated in Figure 3.5. Depending on the time ordering, the character of the buildup curve changes also.[10]

To express the analytical forms for the buildup of shooters, it is convenient to have the inputs be C, ΔT_{strat}, and ΔT_{access}, where

ΔT_{strat}

$$\Delta T_{strat} \equiv C - W_{strat}; \quad \Delta T_{access} \equiv T_{access} - C. \tag{3.5}$$

ΔT_{access} The reason is that in exploratory analysis, it is often convenient to vary the single variable C while holding the deltas constant. Unless the deltas are used as inputs, one has to change W_{strat} and T_{access} also.

If we assume that strategic warning always appears first (i.e., warning occurs before or at the time full-scale deployment is ordered on C-Day, then there are six cases to distinguish among, depending on the relative positions of C, T_{access}, and time t (there are even more cases when we consider theater capacity limits later in the chapter). For each of the six cases, we can express A(t) in terms of the warning times and deployment rates (Table 3.1).

RANDMR1471-3.4

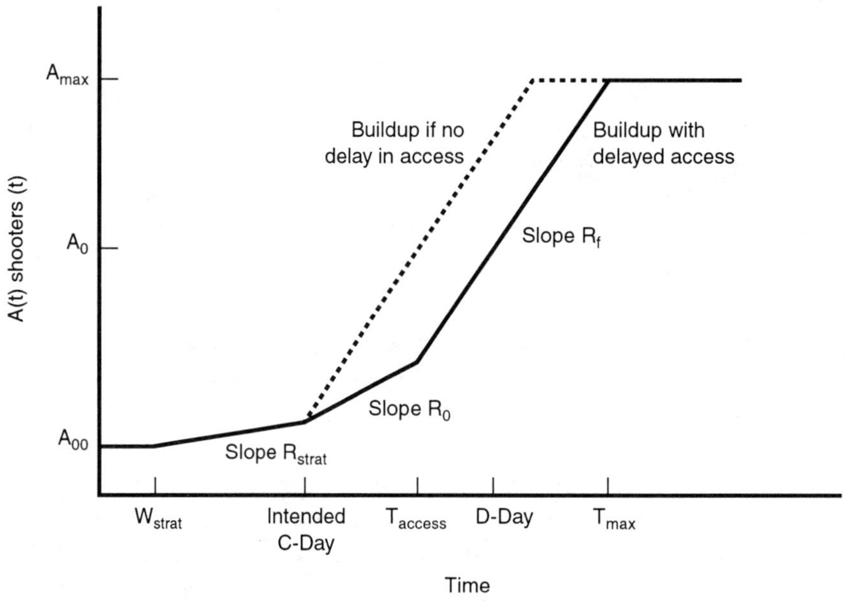

Figure 3.4—An Illustrative Buildup of Shooters

---

[10]Such complex time orderings have been demonstrated with plausible political-military scenarios for the Persian Gulf in work by colleague Bruce Narduli (Davis et al., 1997, unpublished).

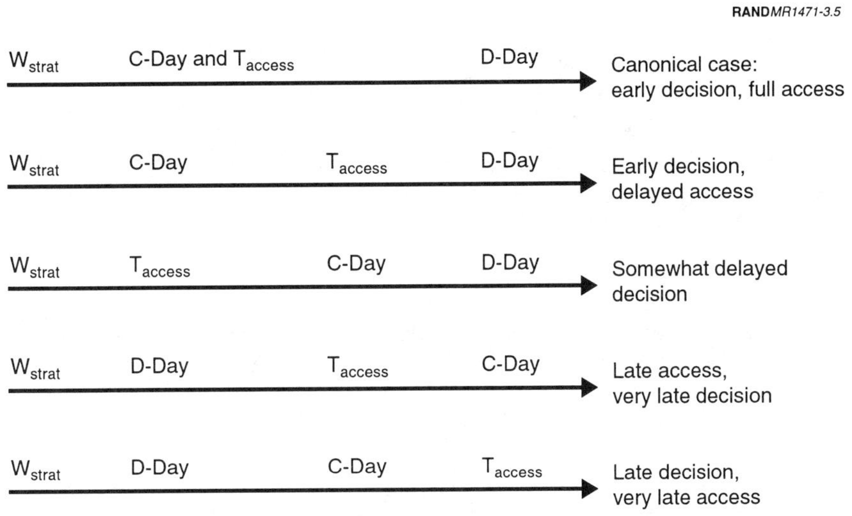

Figure 3.5—Some Alternative Orderings of Critical Times

Table 3.1

FORMULAS FOR SHOOTERS VERSUS TIME
(UNLIMITED THEATER CAPACITY)

Case	Formula for A(t)
$C \le T_{access} \le t$	$A(t) = A_{00} + R_{strat}\Delta T_{strat} + R_0\Delta T_{access} + R_f \vert t - (C + \Delta T_{access})\vert$
$T_{access} \le C \le t$	$A(t) = A_{00} + R_{strat}\Delta T_{strat} + R_f \vert t - C\vert$
$C \le t \le T_{access}$	$A(t) = A_{00} + R_{strat}\Delta T_{strat}$
$T_{access} \le t \le C$	$A(t) = A_{00} + R_{strat}\vert t - (C - \Delta T_{strat})\vert$
$t \le C \le T_{access}$	$A(t) = A_{00} + R_{strat}\vert t - (C - \Delta T_{strat})\vert$
$t \le T_{access} \le C$	$A(t) = A_{00} + R_{strat}\vert t - (C - \Delta T_{strat})\vert$

Solving for the Number of D-Day Shooters, A_0

It is convenient to work the halt problem using D-Day as time 0, in which case the number of D-Day shooters, A_0, is a natural input. We can then vary it parametrically without specifying the scenario that preceded D-Day or we can calculate A_0 based on the details of a particular scenario. Even if we wish to vary A_0 parametrically (it is, after all, extremely uncertain), we need to consider a range of scenarios to determine what "reasonable" values for A_0 might be considered. We can solve for A_0 by substituting $t = 0$ into Table 3.1. The result, after some simplification, is Table 3.2.

Figure 3.6 shows how A_0 depends on the more detailed variables. Figure 3.7 shows how introducing A_0 improves overall problem modularity and facilitates multiresolution modeling (MRM). The halt time can be expressed as a function of only A_0, R, and C (and variables from other parts of the problem), without worrying about warning times and the like. This requires that R be a suitable average of the deployment rate after D-Day, as discussed next.

Table 3.2

D-DAY SHOOTERS AS FUNCTION OF SCENARIO VARIABLES (UNLIMITED THEATER CAPACITY)

Case	Formula for A_0
$C \leq T_{access} \leq 0$	$A_0 = A_{00} + R_{strat}\Delta T_{strat} + R_0\lvert\Delta T_{access}\rvert + R_f\lvert t - (C + \Delta T_{access})\rvert$
$T_{access} \leq C \leq 0$	$A_0 = A_{00} + R_{strat}\Delta T_{strat} + R_f\lvert C\rvert$
$C \leq 0 \leq T_{access}$	$A_0 = A_{00} + R_{strat}\Delta T_{strat} + R_0\lvert C\rvert$
$C > 0$	$A(t) = A_{00} + R_{strat}\lvert C - \Delta T_{strat}\rvert$

NOTE: This table is to be implemented with "if-then-else" statements. There are 3! or 6 orderings of C, T_{access}, and D-Day (0). The last row covers three of those.

RANDMR1471-3.6

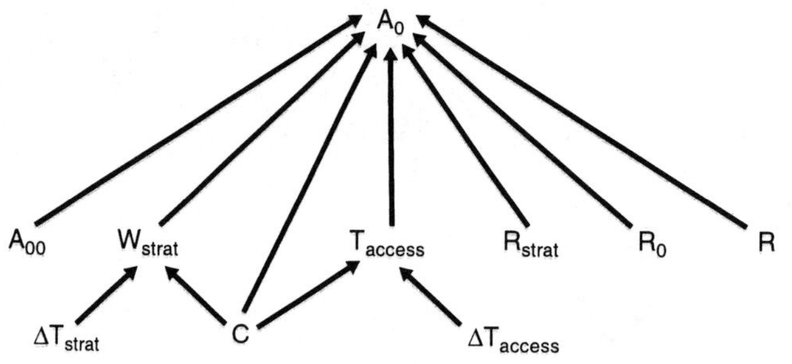

Figure 3.6—Dependence of D-Day Shooters on Scenario Variables

RANDMR1471-3.7

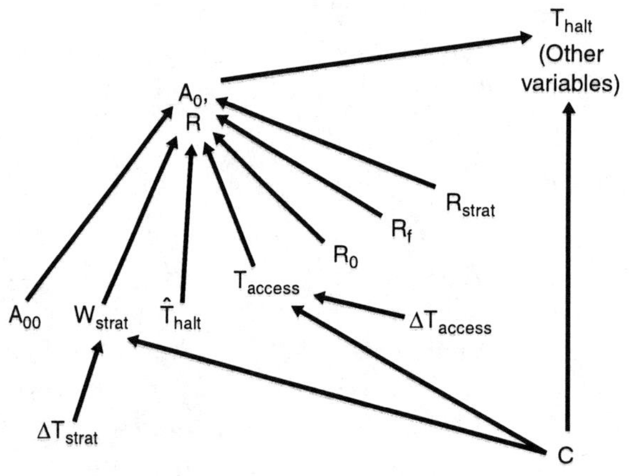

Figure 3.7—Improving Problem Modularity

Shooters Versus Time After D-Day: Average Deployment Rate

For times greater than 0, A(t) is given by

$$A(t) = A_0 + \int_0^t R(s)ds, \tag{3.6}$$

where R(s) has values of R_{strat}, R_0, or R_f depending on the value of s in comparison with the times of strategic warning, deployment decision, and access permission. As anticipated earlier, it is convenient to work the halt problem treating post–D-Day R as a constant, even though the actual value of R may vary if full-scale deployment is not ordered at D-Day (or if access rights are not fully available). Thus, we need to think of R as an appropriate average value. As with A_0, we can just vary it parametrically, but we should know from scenario-based work what values are reasonable and how R depends on scenario. Unfortunately, a good "estimator" for R depends on having an estimator $\hat{T}_{halt}$ for the halt time itself. Table 3.3 gives the relevant equations. We then use the result in

R

$\hat{T}_{halt}$

$$A(t) = A_0 + Rt \qquad \text{for } t \geq 0. \tag{3.7}$$

Figure 3.8 shows how R depends on more detailed variables, if one wishes to use them rather than specifying R directly.

The error caused by using an a priori estimate of R rather than a more carefully calculated value depends, of course, on all the lower-level variables—i.e., on scenario. It also depends on the quality of the estimate of halt time. The estimate, however, does not need to be very good. Figure 3.9 illustrates the issues.[11] It shows the fractional error in estimating shooters over time as the result of using the average value of deployment rate. For actual halt times of 10 days or more, the error is fairly small (i.e., 0–30 percent) if the estimated halt time is 10–20 days. Such an error is arguably a good deal less than the uncertainty in actual deployment rates because of factors such as decision times, readiness, and quality of prior planning. On the other hand, guessing that a halt would take only 5 days would have a significant error if the halt time were 10 days or so.

When the halt time is, in fact, on the order of a few days, the fractional error in the estimate of halt time or halt distance would usually be smaller yet. These "good" outcomes tend to occur when the number of D-Day shooters is fairly large (and thus the precise amount of post–D-Day deployment is relatively less important). In summary, using an average value of deployment rate is usually reasonable—especially when varying R parametrically, but even when one estimates its value exogenously.

Shooter Effectiveness

Having discussed the buildup of shooters, let us next consider shooters' effectiveness. When air defenses are suppressed and command and control is efficient,

[11]This and many subsequent figures in the manuscript are direct "screen dumps" from model calculations performed in Analytica, which will be discussed more fully later.

Table 3.3

FORMULAS FOR AVERAGE POST–D-DAY DEPLOYMENT RATE R AS FUNCTION OF DETAILED SCENARIO VARIABLES

T_{halt}	C, T_{access}, D	C, T_{access}, and T_{halt}	Formula for R
≤ 0	—	—	0
>0	$C \leq 0$	$T_{access} \leq 0$	R_f
>0	$C \leq 0$	$0 < T_{access} \leq \hat{T}_{halt}$	$\frac{T_{access}}{\hat{T}_{halt}} R_0 + \frac{\hat{T}_{halt} - T_{access}}{\hat{T}_{halt}} R_f$
>0	$C \leq 0$	$\hat{T}_{halt} < T_{access}$	R_0
>0	$C > 0$ $T_{access} > 0$	$C \leq T_{access} \leq \hat{T}_{halt}$	$\frac{C}{\hat{T}_{halt}} R_{strat} + \frac{T_{access} - C}{\hat{T}_{halt}} R_0 + \frac{\hat{T}_{halt} - T_{access}}{\hat{T}_{halt}} R_f$
>0	$C > 0$ $T_{access} > 0$	$C \leq \hat{T}_{halt} \leq T_{access}$	$\frac{C}{\hat{T}_{halt}} R_{strat} + \frac{\hat{T}_{halt} - C}{\hat{T}_{halt}} R_0$
>0	$C > 0$ $T_{access} > 0$	$\hat{T}_{halt} \leq T_{access} \leq C$	R_{strat}
>0	$C > 0$ $T_{access} > 0$	$\hat{T}_{halt} \leq C \leq T_{access}$	R_{strat}
>0	$C > 0$ $T_{access} > 0$	$T_{access} \leq C \leq \hat{T}_{halt}$	$\frac{C}{\hat{T}_{halt}} R_{strat} + \frac{\hat{T}_{halt} - C}{\hat{T}_{halt}} R_f$
>0	$C > 0$ $T_{access} > 0$	$T_{access} \leq \hat{T}_{halt} \leq C$	R_{strat}
>0	$C > 0$ $T_{access} \leq 0$	$C \leq \hat{T}_{halt}$	$\frac{C}{\hat{T}_{halt}} R_{strat} + \frac{\hat{T}_{halt} - C}{\hat{T}_{halt}} R_f$
>0	$C > 0$ $T_{access} \leq 0$	$\hat{T}_{halt} \leq C$	R_{strat}

NOTE: This table should be implemented with "If-then-else" statements. Each case is defined not only by the condition stated in its line, but by the requirement that the earlier cases do not apply. For those checking completeness, the table covers the 24 cases generated by different orderings of the four times. Half are covered by the first, trivial case in which the halt is estimated to occur before D-Day. The next row covers two cases, since the order of T_{access} and C does not matter to results.

RANDMR1471-3.8

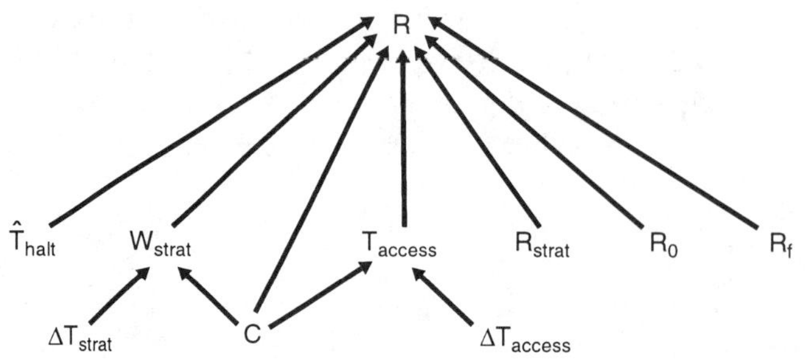

Figure 3.8—Estimating Buildup of Available Shooters

RANDMR1471-3.9

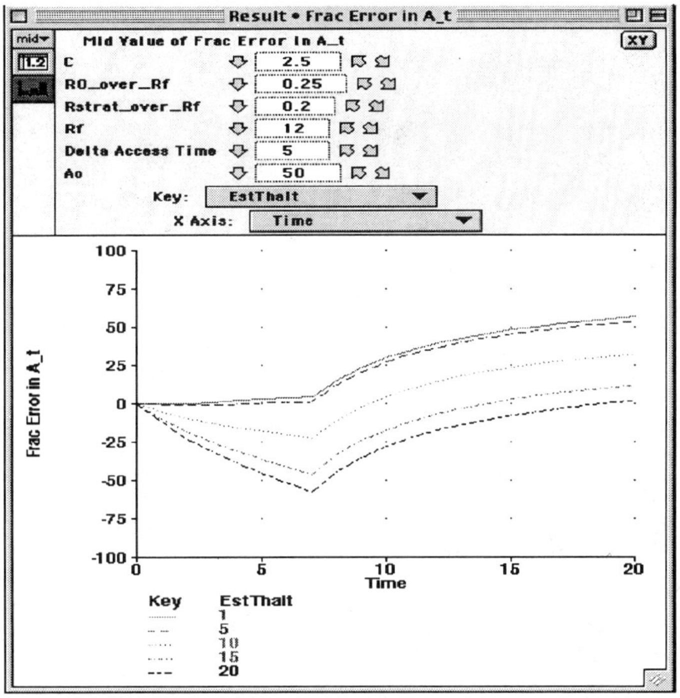

Figure 3.9—Error in Estimating Shooters Versus Time

$$\delta = KS. \tag{3.8}$$

shooter effectiveness is determined by the product of sortie rate S and kills per sortie K, using nominal values for both. We can define δ, the nominal number of kills per aircraft day, as follows:

In simplified cases, this is a key measure of capability. More generally (see later chapters), however, these coefficients may be time dependent because command-control efficiencies and other factors are time dependent and the best weapons may be used up. Thus, we can denote them as δ(t), K(t), and S(t). In this monograph, they are assumed to be at piecewise constant, which simplifies the mathematics.

δ
K
S

We are now in position to solve the halt problem analytically. Let us do so first for interdiction in depth and then for the leading-edge strategy.

3.2 SOLVING THE HALT PROBLEM FOR INTERDICTION IN DEPTH (NO CAPACITY LIMITS)

Basic Features of Solution

The key to solution here is a simple integral equation[12] that equates the number of vehicles that must be killed ξ, which can be expressed in terms of more elementary

[12] Shooters actually arrive at discrete times, but the continuous approximation is a good approximation for our purposes.

variables as shown in Figure 3.1, to the sum of the kills on successive days from 0 to $T_{halt.}$ In this simplest of cases, δ and FR, the product of allocation fraction F and deployment rate R, are constants and we have

$$\xi = \int_0^{T_{halt}} N(s)\delta ds$$
$$\xi = \int_0^{T_{halt}} \{FA_0 + FRs\}\delta ds \qquad (3.9)$$
$$\xi / \delta = F\left\{A_0 T_{halt} + \frac{1}{2} R T_{halt}^2\right\}.$$

Let us define α, the number of shooter days required to accomplish a simple halt, by

$$\alpha \equiv \frac{\xi}{\delta}, \qquad (3.10)$$

then, after some rearranging,

$$\frac{1}{2} T_{halt}^2 + \frac{A_0}{R} T_{halt} - \frac{\alpha}{FR} = 0. \qquad (3.11)$$

The quadratic equation of elementary algebra is

$$aX^2 + bX + c = 0, \qquad (3.12)$$

which has solutions $X = \dfrac{-b \pm \sqrt{b^2 - 4ac}}{2a}$,

of which only the solution with the positive root is physically meaningful. It follows that the solution to our simple halt problem is

$$T_{halt} = \sqrt{\frac{A_0^2}{R^2} + 2\frac{\alpha}{FR}} - \frac{A_0}{R}. \qquad (3.13)$$

Anticipating more complex versions of the model, let us reexpress Eq. (3.12) and Eq. (3.13) by introducing the composite parameters ζ and ψ:

$$\zeta(\text{zeta}) \equiv \frac{A_0}{R}, \quad \psi(\text{psi}) \equiv \frac{\alpha}{FR}. \qquad (3.14)$$

The original equation is then

$$\frac{1}{2} T_{halt}^2 + \zeta T_{halt} - \psi = 0, \qquad (3.15)$$

with the solution being

$$T_{halt} = \sqrt{\zeta^2 + 2\psi} - \zeta. \tag{3.16}$$

The definitions of ζ and ψ will change as complications are added to the model, but most of the solutions will continue to have this form.

We can now solve for the halt distance—i.e., the distance from the international border at which halt occurs. The expression for the interdiction–in-depth case is

$$D = \mathrm{Max}[\mathrm{Min}[V(T_{halt} - T_{delay}), \mathrm{Obj}], 0], \tag{3.17}$$

with T_{halt} calculated from Eq. (3.16).

Limiting Forms

Even this trivial version of the halt problem generates some useful insights. The equation for T_{halt} is nonlinear and it is difficult to see immediately how the different factors affect results. We can, however, look at some limiting cases.

Small Deployment Rates. If R is small, or more rigorously if

$$\frac{\left[\dfrac{\alpha}{FA_0}\right]}{\left[\dfrac{A_0}{R}\right]}$$

or $R\alpha / (FA_0^2)$ is small,[13] then the limiting form is[14]

$$\lim_{\frac{R\alpha}{FA_0^2} \to 0} T_{halt} = \mathrm{Lim}\left\{\frac{A_0}{R}\left[\sqrt{1 + 2\frac{\alpha R}{FA_0^2}} - 1\right]\right\} = \frac{\alpha}{FA_0} = \frac{\xi}{\delta FA_0} \tag{3.18}$$

This is consistent with intuition: When the outcome depends on the D-Day shooters rather than subsequent deployments, the halt time grows in proportion to the size of the threat and inversely with the number of initial anti-armor shooters being employed (N_0) and their effectiveness.

Small Number of D-Day Shooters. If N_0 is small, results are not so intuitive. The limiting form is obvious from inspection:

---

[13]The condition requires a certain ratio to be small: the ratio of the number of days it would take the D-Day anti-armor shooters to kill the requisite number of Red AFVs, divided by the number of days it would take to deploy, at rate R, the D-Day shooters. If this is small, then what matters is the number of D-Day shooters.

[14]This follows from the general relationship that, for small values of x, $\sqrt{1+x} \approx 1 + (1/2)x$.

$$\lim_{A_0/R \to 0} T_{halt} = \sqrt{\frac{2\alpha}{FR}} = \sqrt{\frac{2\xi/\delta}{FR}} \quad (3.19)$$

Without D-Day shooters, T_{halt} shrinks only as the square root of deployment time and per-sortie effectiveness.

That is, if there are no shooters available on D-Day, the halt time grows with the square root of the threat and, more troublesome, shrinks only as the square root of shooter effectiveness and deployment rate. To reduce T_{halt} by a factor of two, we might have to double both shooter effectiveness and deployment rates, or quadruple one of them. Figure 3.10 shows some parametrics. It indicates that for short halt times—if they are feasible at all—very high deployment rates and effectiveness are necessary if shooters are not available already on D-Day.[15] Success would depend on substantially unprecedented performance levels.

Figure 3.11 illustrates calculations with the simple model of Eq. (3.16) (not just the limiting cases). Here we assume that 1500 AFVs must be killed and that each anti-armor shooter kills 4 vehicles per day. We then solve for halt time. Suppose that we start with no forward presence or warning time (and, therefore, no D-Day shooters), but have the ability to deploy a half squadron (12 shooters) per day, half of which are used against moving armor (top curve). The halt time is 11 days (point A). Now suppose that we seek a halt time of 4 days. According to the figure, we can achieve this by increasing deployment rates eightfold (point B) or increasing D-Day anti-armor shooters to about 180 (point C). Doing either is difficult, but recall that long-range bombers can be considered as D-Day shooters with very large payloads (but small sortie rates). Also, aircraft carriers have 60 or so aircraft. Thus, increasing D-

RANDMR1471-3.10

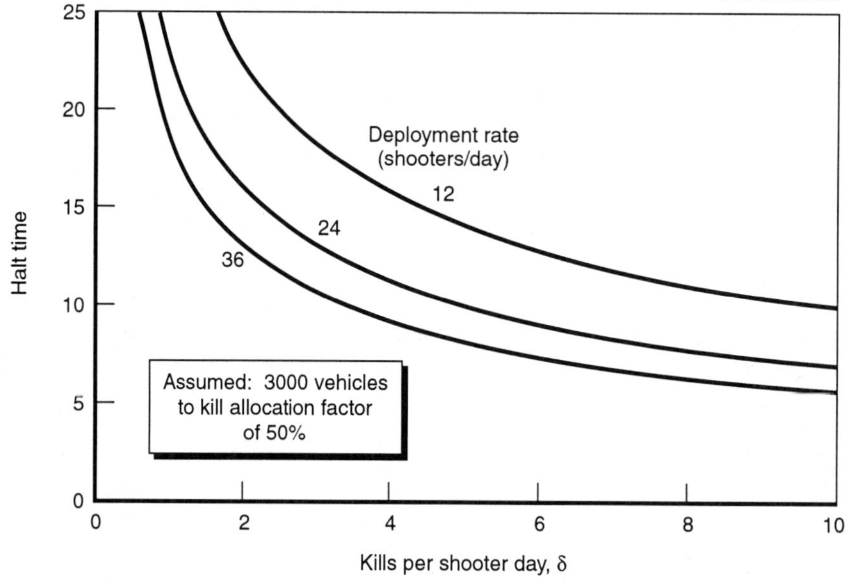

Figure 3.10—Halt Time for Zero D-Day Shooters

15The deployment rate in Desert Shield was about 12, counting not only aircraft potentially usable in the anti-armor role, but others as well. Higher deployment rates are feasible.

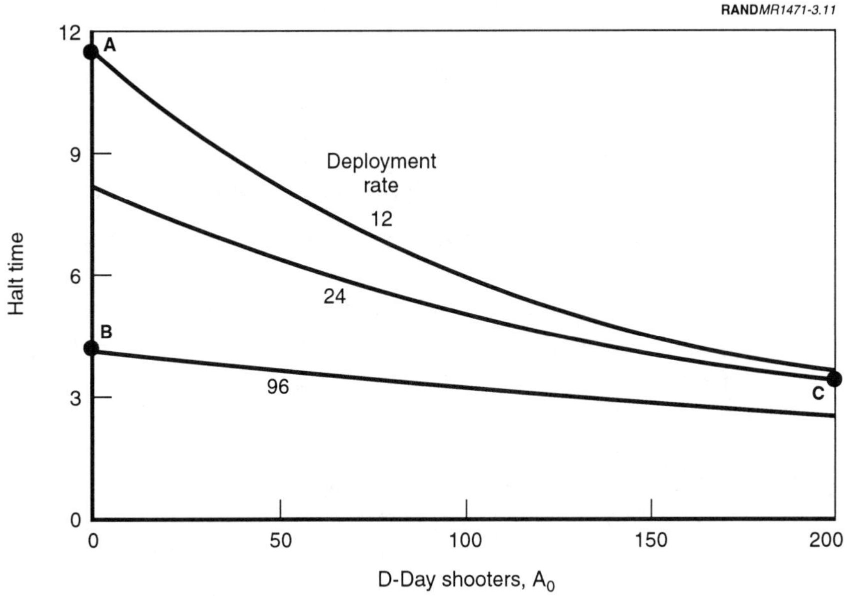

Figure 3.11—Relative Impact of Deployment Rates and D-Day Shooters

Day shooters significantly is often possible with even ambiguous warning. Although R is important mathematically, it is difficult to make dramatic improvements. Thus, D-Day shooters is a critical factor.

3.3 SOLVING THE HALT PROBLEM FOR LEADING-EDGE INTERDICTION (NO CAPACITY LIMITS)

Solution Based on Slowing Effect Alone

Halt Time and Halt Distance for the Slowing Effect. Let us now rework the problem assuming a leading-edge strategy and—for now—that halt occurs only when net movement is reduced to zero by the slowing effect described in Chapter 2. Later we allow for instances in which halt occurs as the result of aggregate attrition before the movement rate is reduced to zero by the slowing effect.

Assume that if the nose of a column suffers fractional attrition H_{local}, all of the vehicles within that nose can be considered to be disabled. Then assume N_{axes} of advance, N_{col} columns per axis, ρ vehicles per km, and δ_{edge} kills per sortie, which may be different from δ for interdiction in depth. It is usually convenient to use $A_{spacing}$, the distance between armored fighting vehicles, which is the inverse of ρ. The slowing of the advance's nose due to interdiction is then given by

N_{axes}
N_{col}
ρ
$A_{spacing}$
δ_{edge}
γ

$$\Delta(t) = \frac{N(t) A_{spacing} \delta_{edge}}{N_{axes} N_{col} H_{local}} \equiv N(t)\gamma . \qquad (3.20)$$

This defines γ, which has units of km/shooter-day. We can decompose γ into a factor that Blue controls, δ_{edge}, and a factor that Red controls, Ω:

Ω

$$\gamma = \delta_{edge}\Omega$$
$$\Omega = \frac{A_{spacing}}{N_{axes}N_{col}H_{local}}. \tag{3.21}$$

This decomposition into more detailed variables is shown in Figure 3.12.[16]

δ_{edge}

δ_{edge}^{nom}

We see that γ is a measure of the effectiveness of the leading-edge strategy. As Eq. (3.21) indicates, it varies in proportion to Ω—i.e., inversely with the number of axes of advance, the number of columns per axis, and the local break point—and in proportion to the spacing between armored vehicles in the march. Thus, the attacker may decrease his vulnerability to this tactic by concentrating his forces (small AFV distances). That, however, will tend to increase substantially his vulnerability to area munitions. Increasing axes and columns may be easier.[17] This implies a modest complication in the analytics: δ_{edge} is a function of AFV spacing. The dependence varies with the specific munition and is therefore beyond the scope of this treatment to specify in general. Within this monograph, we distinguish between use of area weapons (e.g., sensor-fuzed weapons) or point weapons (e.g., Maverick). For area weapons, we assume that

$$\delta_{edge} = \delta_{edge}^{nom}\frac{0.05}{A_{spacing}}, \tag{3.22}$$

RANDMR1471-3.12

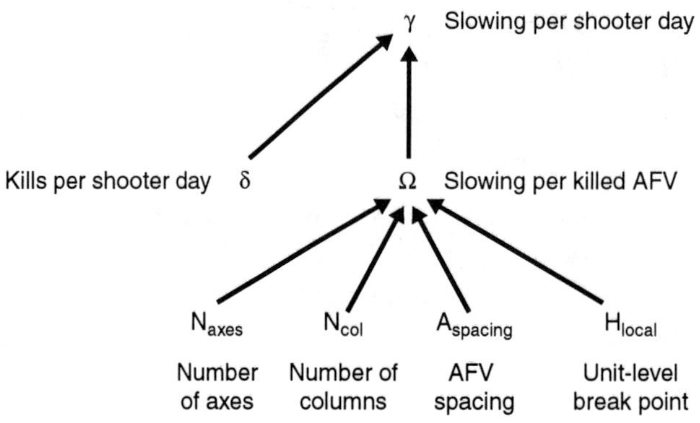

Figure 3.12—Decomposition of γ

---

[16]The effectiveness δ could be further reduced by countermeasures, which are not treated explicitly here.

[17]What constitutes a column in the context of these equations is ambiguous. From afar, an axis of advance looks like one massive column. Microscopically, however, there might be mini columns moving in parallel along different lanes of a highway, on secondary roads going in the same direction, or even along off-road tracks. Analytically, the number of columns must be calculated with due account taken of the weapon characteristics. Two columns that are so close together as to be simultaneously vulnerable to a single area munition count as only one column. However, the effective density (AFVs per km) of vehicles in that "effective column" will be twice as high as in a physical column.

where the standard input δ_{edge}^{nom} is to be for a spacing of 50 m (0.05 km).[18] The effectiveness of point weapons is assumed independent of AFV spacing.

The net result is that the net movement is given by

$$V(t) = V - N(t)\gamma, \tag{3.23}$$

subject to the constraint that we do not permit it to be negative.

We can now solve for T_{halt}:

$$N(T_{halt})\gamma = V. \tag{3.24}$$

For the simple case of interest in this chapter, the number of anti-armor shooters is simply $A_0 + FRt$. Thus, we obtain[19]

$$\begin{aligned} FA_0 + FRT_{halt} &= \frac{V}{\gamma} \\ T_{halt} &= \left\{\frac{V}{FR\gamma} - \frac{A_0}{R}\right\} = \left\{\frac{V}{FR\gamma} - \zeta\right\}, \end{aligned} \tag{3.25}$$

where ζ has the same meaning as before (A_0/R, or N_0/RF). In this case, T_{halt} is independent of threat size, but dependent on its maneuver scheme.

Letting D_a denote the distance the attacker could move without regard to his objective, we have (except for $T_{halt} < T_{delay}$, when D is 0):

$$\begin{aligned} D_a &= \int_{T_{delay}}^{T_{halt}} \{V - \gamma N(s)\} ds \\ D_a &= \int_{T_{delay}}^{T_{halt}} \{V - \gamma[FA_0 + FRs]\} ds \\ D_a &= V(T_{halt} - T_{delay}) - \gamma\left\{FA_0(T_{halt} - T_{delay}) + \frac{1}{2}FR(T_{halt}^2 - T_{delay}^2)\right\}. \end{aligned} \tag{3.26}$$

The actual penetration depth is the minimum of this and the attacker's objective:

$$D = Max[Min[D_a, Obj], 0]. \tag{3.27}$$

---

[18]This is consistent with conclusions from detailed work by colleague Glenn Kent (Ochmanek et al., 1998), and with assumptions in McEver, Davis, and Bigelow (2000a). Kent also notes an interesting game-theory aspect to AFV spacing. The attacker benefits from increasing AFV spacing, in that area weapons kill fewer AFVs per sortie. However, the length of column affected per AFV killed does not change and the slowing effectiveness of point weapons increases. If command-control considerations and the time required to complete the march are not issues, then in the game-theory calculation, attacker should increase AFV spacing until area weapons and point weapons are equally effective and the defender should have a mix of area and point weapons. The "optimum spacing," according to this calculation, can be found straightforwardly if one specifies performances of the area and point weapons.

[19]Again, recall that these formulas assume that the halt is brought about by the slowing effect of the leading-edge attack rather than overall attrition. In a later section we shall consider both mechanisms.

The implications of this are summarized as in Table 3.4.

Table 3.4

FORMULAS FOR HALT TIME AND HALT DISTANCE

Case	$V(T_{halt} - T_{delay}) \leq Obj$	$V(T_{halt} - T_{delay}) > Obj$
$T_{halt} \geq T_{delay}$	$V(T_{halt} - T_{delay})$	Obj
$T_{halt} < T_{delay}$	0	0

Sensitivity of Slowing-Effect Results for Zero Delay Time. Several observations are possible if we view the above equations in more detail. For simplicity, assume zero delay time (i.e., there is no early strike delaying Red's invasion). Then, using T_h for T_{halt},

$$D_a = VT_h - \gamma\left\{FA_0T_h + \frac{1}{2}FRT_h^2\right\} = (V - \gamma FA_0)T_h - \frac{1}{2}\gamma FRT_h^2.$$

Consider first the case in which the number of D-Day shooters is small, so that we can drop the A_0 term. Substituting in the expression for T_{halt} from Eq. (3.25) (and again simplifying for small A_0), we obtain for small A_0

$$D_a \approx V\left(\frac{V}{FR\gamma}\right) - \frac{1}{2}\gamma FR\left(\frac{V}{FR\gamma}\right)^2 = \frac{1}{2}\frac{V^2}{FR\gamma}. \quad (3.28)$$

In this case, we see a very strong (quadratic) dependence on speed and an inverse dependence on R and γ. The general case is more complex.

In contrast, the interdiction–in-depth results for small A_0 had halt distance scaling only with the inverse square root of interdictor effectiveness and deployment rate, and linearly with V. Thus, the outcome for leading-edge attack can be much more sensitive to operational factors.

Another observation is that, at least for small A_0, the leading-edge strategy depends sensitively on the threat's maneuver strategy: number of axes, number of columns per axis, and dispersion of vehicles along the march. On the other hand, more generally, *the slowing effect is independent of the threat's size.*[20] This said, if the threat is small enough, halt will occur when the overall halt fraction of the threat has been killed—before the slowing effect draws the movement rate to zero. Nonetheless, the slowing effect can have a big impact on halt distance.

The relative dependence of the two strategies on the threat's speed is more difficult to infer from the formula because it depends on the other parameter values. However, *we would expect the leading-edge strategy to be most attractive when the number of axes is small and the threat large.*

[20]This will not be true if the top-quality weapons are exhausted prior to the time of halt. That complication is introduced in subsequent chapters.

Combined Solutions and Optimal Strategies

If Blue chooses a leading-edge strategy, Red may still be halted by attrition before he would be by the slowing effect alone. Thus, the halt time for the leading-edge strategy is the smaller of the halt time for the slowing effect and the halt time for the attrition calculation. The attrition halt time will be given by the same formulas as for the in-depth strategy except that the effectiveness of Blue shooters may be different. That is, δ and α vary with Blue's strategy. We shall refer to δ_{edge} and α_{edge} when referring to the values for the leading-edge strategy.

Red's halt distance under the leading edge strategy may be substantially smaller than in the in-depth strategy even if halt times are similar because Red's movement rate will have been slowed. It might seem that Blue should automatically choose a leading-edge strategy. That is not so, however, because—as mentioned above—choice of strategy might affect Blue's per-sortie effectiveness rate; it might also affect loss rates. In particular, command and control problems might be worse for the leading-edge strategy because of the more limited battle space. Similarly, the air defenses might be better able to predict Blue's ingress routes and timings. If so, there would be some penalty for the leading-edge strategy. Whether the value obtained (an earlier halt) would be greater than the penalty paid would depend on details.

Let us assume, for analytical purposes, that Blue's strategy holds throughout the simulated war.[21] As suggested in Table 3.5, it is then convenient to implement the model to permit results to be shown for four cases. Having Case 2 is useful if one wishes to generate displays showing clearly where the slowing effect is important.

Table 3.5

CASES TO BE REPRESENTED IN MODEL IMPLEMENTATION

Case	Blue Strategy	When Halt Occurs
1 (In depth)	In depth	When attrition exceeds H
2 (Slowing effect)	Leading edge	When slowing effect reduces V to 0
3 (Leading edge)	Leading edge	When slowing effect reduces V to 0 or when attrition exceeds H, whichever comes first
4 (Optimal)	Optimal (either in depth or leading edge)	As in Case 1 or 3, depending on which minimizes the halt distance.

[21]More complicated possibilities exist. Blue might, for example, want to maximize Red's daily attrition and minimize its own command and control problems and losses by using the in-depth strategy until the number of shooters had reached a level permitting a leading-edge attack to bring about a halt. That dynamically adaptive strategy would come at the expense of permitting Red somewhat greater gain of territory prior to the halt than would be obtained if the leading-edge strategy had been pursued from the outset.

The formulas for the leading-edge strategy are then as follows:

$$T_{halt} = \mathrm{Min}\left[\sqrt{\frac{A_0^2}{R^2} + 2\frac{\alpha_{edge}}{FR}} - \frac{A_0}{R}, \frac{V}{FR\gamma} - \frac{A_0}{R}\right] \tag{3.29}$$

$$D_a = V(T_{halt} - T_{delay}) - \gamma F\left\{A_0 + \frac{1}{2}R(T_{halt}^2 - T_{delay}^2)\right\} \tag{3.30}$$

$$D = \mathrm{Max}[\mathrm{Min}[D_a, Obj], 0]. \tag{3.31}$$

Figure 3.13 illustrates this, making the point that which of the two interdiction strategies is superior depends on the size of the threat force to be killed.[22] In Figure 3.13, halt distance is plotted against the size of the threat to be killed (i.e., the number of armored fighting vehicles that must be killed to bring about an attrition-based halt). The horizontal graph corresponds to the leading-edge strategy, but with the halt distance calculated considering only the slowing effect. The steep curve corresponds to the in-depth strategy, with results dictated by overall attrition to Red. For threats less than about 2000 AFVs, the optimal strategy is the in-depth strategy, but for larger threats the leading-edge strategy is superior. Finally, the results for the optimal

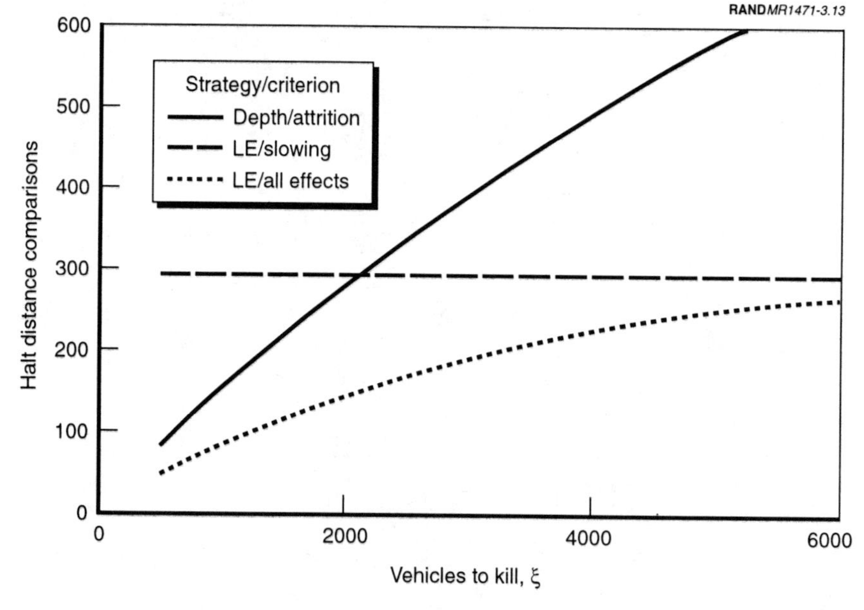

Figure 3.13—Comparative Advantage of the Interdiction Strategies

[22]This relatively dramatic cross-over occurs in only certain cases. Figure 3.13 assumes one axis of advance with two columns, a local break point of 0.75, a nominal speed of 70 km/day, 200 D-Day shooters, a deployment rate of 24 shooters per day, the use of only half of the shooters in an anti-armor role, an AFV spacing of 100 meters, eight kills per shooter day, no delay time, area weapons, and no penalty for use of the leading-edge strategy (i.e., $\delta_{edge} = \delta$).

strategy (dotted line) starts (left side, moving rightward) following the in-depth strategy results, but then follows results for the leading-edge strategy for threats (vehicles to kill) greater than about 2000 AFVs.

Implementation Notes

Although the conceptual model so far is relatively simple, implementing it as computer code can be somewhat tricky and the problems become much more acute when the embellishments of later chapters are added. It is therefore useful to have a clear overview of the data flow. Figure 3.14 provides an overview, which may be useful to users either in implementing the model themselves or in understanding the EXHALT-CF program, which is written in Analytica.

On the one hand, the problems for the leading-edge and in-depth strategies may seem largely independent. In the figure, they are shown on the left and right sides, respectively. Upon reflection, however, one realizes that the modeling is simplified by using array mathematics with components in the strategy dimension of in-depth and leading edge. Some of the calculations apply to both strategies—notably, the buildup of Blue shooters and attrition. Others (e.g., calculation of Red's movement

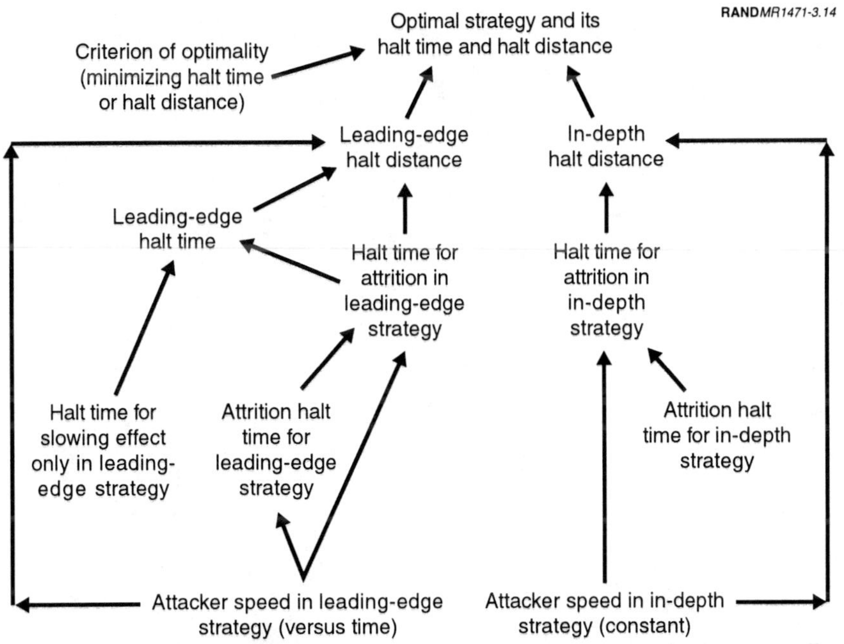

Input Variables (most aggregated versions)

- Threat size
- Threat's basic movement rate
- Threat's maneuver strategy (axes, columns, dispersion)
- Delay due to special strikes by defender
- Defender's buildup (initial shooters, deployment rate)
- Commitment of shooters to anti-armor mission by phase
- Defender's basic per-shooter-day effectiveness (by strategy)

Figure 3.14—Overview of Model

rate over time) are significantly different in character for the two strategies. Red's halt distance is just a constant times the halt time in the case of the in-depth strategy. For the leading-edge strategy, it is the time integral of movement rate over time.

3.4 SIGNIFICANCE OF DELAY TIME (NO CAPACITY LIMITS)

At this point it is appropriate to indicate the significance quantitatively of the special delay times that may be caused by aircraft and missile strikes, especially in the context of red lines and early actions. Figure 3.15 shows this sensitivity as a function of number of D-Day anti-armor shooters. The left panel assumes an in-depth strategy; the right panel assumes a leading-edge strategy.[23] These results are merely illustrative. In a later chapter we shall discuss and illustrate exploratory analysis, which enables us to see results for a myriad of cases in which the various parameters are varied simultaneously. For now, the main point is that a delay of 2–4 days caused by early strikes, barriers, etc., would have major effects. This also suggests the value of red lines in making early strikes possible.

3.5 EFFECTS OF ACCESS CONSTRAINTS AND MAXIMUM THEATER CAPACITY

If the Air Force found it necessary to conduct a theater campaign from secondary bases or, even worse, ad hoc bases, the theater's effective capacity might well be

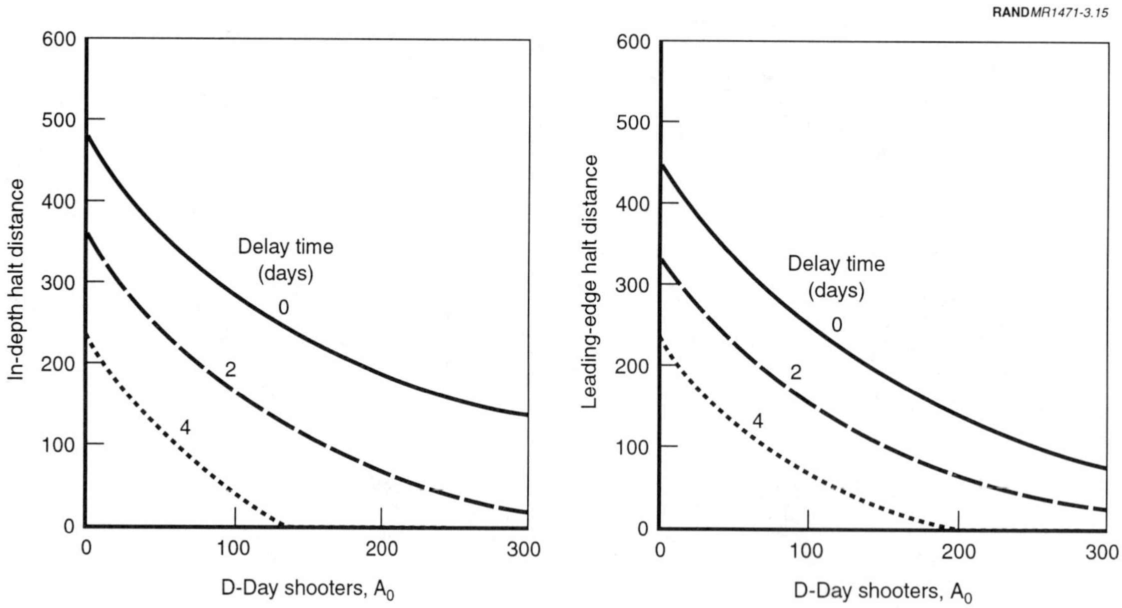

Figure 3.15—Significance of Delay Time for Interdiction In-Depth and Leading-Edge Strategies

---

[23]This particular set of results assumes area weapons, an AFV spacing of 100 m (irrelevant in the in-depth strategy), up to 6000 AFVs to be killed (e.g., 12 divisions with 1000 AFVs each and a break point of 0.5), a speed of 70 km/day, allocation of 50 percent of shooters to the anti-armor mission with all shooters counted, a deployment rate of 24 shooters per day, and eight kills per shooter day, one axis of advance, two columns per axis, no penalty for the leading-edge strategy, and a local halt fraction of 0.75.

quite limited because of shortages in (1) ramp space, (2) pump stations, (3) relevant fuel storage, and (4) other infrastructure such as buildings in which to rest and plan.

This problem could certainly arise if use of mass-destruction weapons were credible. In addition, it would arise if some of the key regional states delayed granting access rights—perhaps because of ambiguities in strategic warning, threats regarding attacks by mass-destruction weapons, or doubts about U.S. capabilities. Although access would likely be granted eventually, it might be limited during the critical period of the intended halt campaign.

This monograph is not the place to work through particular political-military scenarios nor the implications of having one or another set of bases. In the spirit of our work here, we merely note that there might be a limit A_{max} on the number of shooters that the theater could handle. In that case, the model formulas would need to be somewhat different.

Determining A_{max} is not entirely straightforward. The principal subtlety is that neither aircraft carriers nor long-range Air Force bombers would be affected by the problems we are referring to. Thus, A_{max} should be seen as the sum of the equivalent aircraft from those sources, missiles, and such tactical aircraft as could be handled by the theater. A second subtlety is that analysts should be cautious not to double-count effects. If, for example, Air Force tactical fighters were able to operate from some of the more-distant but well-developed bases (e.g., in Israel and Turkey), sortie rates might be reduced although capacity would not be a problem. On the other hand, if the tactical fighters operated from relatively austere bases within the Persian Gulf, both sortie rates and theater capacity might be affected. Such issues are scenario dependent. For our purposes here, we merely recognize that there might be an A_{max}. A_{max}

Interdiction In Depth with a Theater Capacity

To calculate the effects of limited theater capacity A_{max}, let T_{max} denote the time at which A(t) reaches A_{max}. Since we are concerned only with positive times when computing attrition to the attacker, we can define T_{max} as a nonnegative variable,

$$T_{max} = \text{Max}\left[\frac{A_{max} - A_0}{R}, 0\right] \quad (3.32)$$

The max function occurs because it might be that A_0 is A_{max}. That is, the theater may be saturated by D-Day.

Figure 3.16 shows the essence of the analytics. Recall that α is the number of anti-armor shooter days to halt the invasion. If we take a dynamic look at the problem, plotting anti-armor shooter days versus time, then the result is the solid curve. This curve grows with time, initially with a linear component, proportional to the number of D-Day shooters, and a quadratic component, proportional to the rate of new deployments. When the theater capacity is reached, from which time onward the number of shooters is constant, the number of shooter days grows only linearly. Had there been no constraint, the top curve would apply.

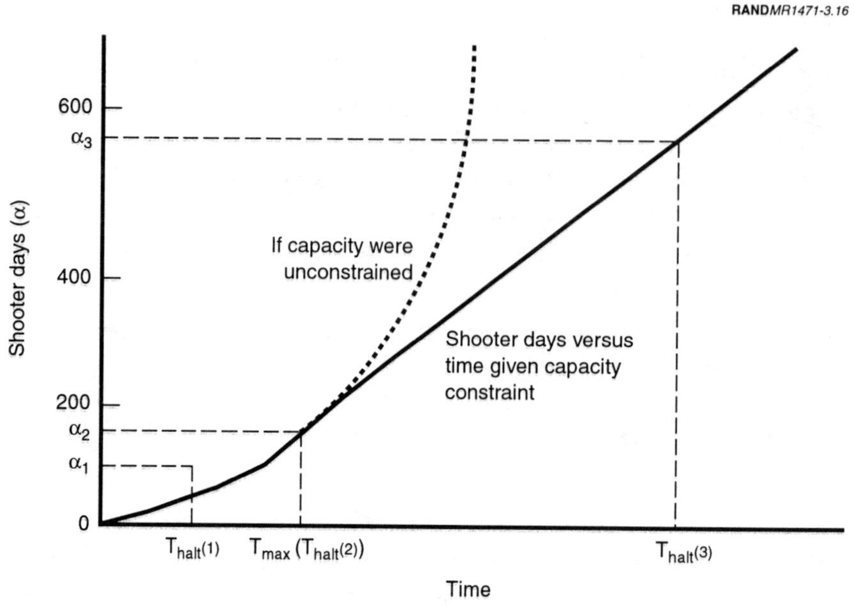

Figure 3.16—Analytics of Capacity Constraints

Recall that the halt time depends on the number of shooter days required to kill the halt fraction of forces. The three horizontal dashed lines show results for three possible requirements—i.e., three values of α. We see that the first illustrative halt time occurs before T_{max}, the second at T_{max}, and the third later than T_{max}.

The transition point is α_2, which is the number of shooter days achieved at the time the theater's capacity for shooters, A_{max}, is reached:

$$\alpha_2 \equiv FA_0 T_{max} + \frac{1}{2} FRT_{max}^2 . \tag{3.33}$$

There is another transition not shown on the figure. If the number of shooters on D-Day already is at or above the maximum level A_{max}, i.e., if $T_{max} \leq 0$, then the shooter days by the time of halt will be simply $FA_0 T_{halt}$ and Figure 3.16 will not apply. In all other cases it does.

If $A_0 < A_{max}$, the halt time is determined differently depending on whether α exceeds α_2.

For $\alpha \geq FA_0 T_{max} + \left(\frac{1}{2}\right) FRT_{max}^2$

$$\alpha = FA_0 T_{max} + \left(\frac{1}{2}\right) FRT_{max}^2 + FA_{max}(T_{halt} - T_{max}).$$

If we combine the first and last terms—those with T_{max}—and if we invoke Eq. (3.33), there is some cancellation and we can solve for T_{halt}.

$$\alpha = (FA_0 - FA_{max})T_{max} + \left(\frac{1}{2}\right)RT_{max}^2 + FA_{max}T_{halt}$$
$$T_{halt} = T_{max} + \frac{\alpha - \alpha_2}{FA_{max}}. \quad (3.34)$$

Finally, if $\alpha \le \alpha_2$,

$$\alpha = FA_0T_{halt} + (1/2)RT_{halt}^2$$
$$T_{halt} = \sqrt{\zeta^2 + 2\psi} - \zeta. \quad (3.35)$$

Table 3.6 summarizes the results for all cases.

The equation for halt distance D is as before, Eq. (3.27). That is,

$$D = MAX\{MIN[V(T_{halt} - T_{delay}), 0], Obj\}. \quad (3.36)$$

Table 3.6

HALT TIMES FOR IN-DEPTH INTERDICTION WITH CAPACITY CONSTRAINTS

Case Conditions		T_{halt}	ζ	ψ
$A_0 \ge A_{max}$ (i.e., $T_{max} = 0$)	Any value of α	$\frac{\alpha}{FA_{max}}$	n.a.	n.a.
$A_0 < A_{max}$ (i.e., $T_{max} \ge 0$)	$\alpha > \alpha_2$	$T_{max} + \frac{\alpha - \alpha_2}{FA_{max}}$	n.a.	n.a.
$A_0 < A_{max}$ (i.e., $T_{max} \ge 0$)	$\alpha \le \alpha_2$	$\sqrt{\zeta^2 + 2\psi} - \zeta$	$\frac{A_0}{R}$	$\frac{\alpha}{FR}$

Leading-Edge Interdiction with Theater Capacity

So long as the effectiveness per sortie is constant, as it is in this chapter, the slowing-induced halt time cannot exceed T_{max}. Either the number of shooters at T_{max} is sufficient to bring about a halt or there is no halt due to the leading-edge effect because, after T_{max}, the slowing power is not further increased.

Thus, the previous leading-edge results, Eqs. (3.30–3.31), still apply if there is a theater capacity issue. Table 3.7 gives the results. T_{halt}(attrition) denotes the value of halt time determined by when the attacker's overall attrition exceeds its break point—i.e., when all the ξ armored fighting vehicles that must be killed have been killed.

As mentioned earlier, the overall halt time for the leading-edge strategy will be the lesser of that due to slowing (Table 3.7) and the halt time due to attrition. The latter is given by the in-depth formulas, but with effectiveness δ_{edge}.

In either case,

Table 3.7

SLOWING-INDUCED HALT TIMES FOR LEADING-EDGE INTERDICTION WITH A THEATER CAPACITY

Case Condition	T_{halt} (slowing only)
$FA_{max}\gamma < V$	$Min[\infty, T_{halt}(attrition)]$
$FA_{max}\gamma \geq V$	$Min\left[\left\{\frac{V}{FR\gamma} - \zeta\right\}, T_{halt}(attrition)\right]$

$$D = Max\left[Min[V(T_{halt} - T_{delay}) - \gamma\left\{FA_0(T_{halt} - T_{delay}) + \frac{1}{2}FR(T_{halt}^2 - T_{delay}^2)\right\}Obj], 0\right]. \quad (3.37)$$

Effects of a Theater Capacity Constraint

Figure 3.17 shows the consequences of the theater-capacity constraint for a particular case of attrition in depth in which these constraints have a significant effect.[24] The

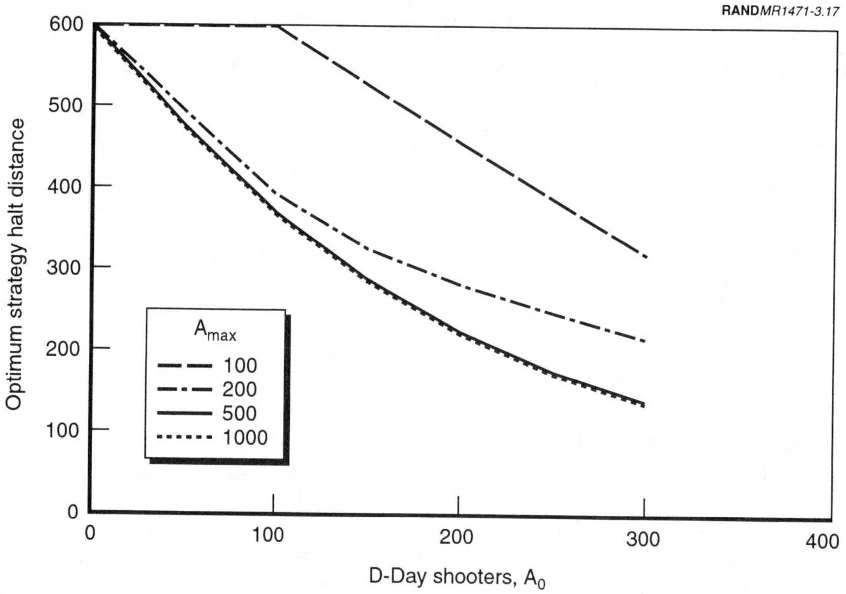

Figure 3.17—Effects of Theater-Capacity Constraint (access or WMD-related)

[24] The case assumes one axis of advance, two columns per axis, 50 percent of shooters are allocated to anti-armor missions, the local break point is 0.75, the AFV spacing is 100 m, 2000 AFVs are to be killed (e.g., 4000 AFVs as threat, with halt occurring if half are killed), an advance rate of 70 km/day, deployment rate of 24 shooters per day, an effectiveness of eight kills per shooter day (for both strategies), an optimal strategy, and no strike-imposed delays.

several curves represent results for different theater capacities: 100, 200, 500, and 1000 (effectively unconstrained). Clearly, theater capacity matters in this case.

3.6 INDIRECT EFFECTS OF MASS-DESTRUCTION WEAPONS

Let us now enrich the model—not by adding additional variables, but rather by associating the case in which the defender must deal with mass-destruction weapons in the form of chemical or biological ordnance, with values of the input parameters of the simple model.

The threat or actual use of WMD might have no effect on the halt problem if Blue is able to intercept the attacking weapons or if Blue is sure that they will be ineffective.[25] At the other extreme, however, Blue commanders might choose not to use forward air bases. They might then be driven to distant air bases, which might have substantially poorer logistical infrastructure and substantially less capacity. Table 3.8, then, suggests a mapping.

The first adjustment is to assume that the effectiveness of regional aircraft would be reduced by longer flight times to target and poorer logistics—primarily through effects on sortie rate. A related phenomenon occurred in the Kosovo operation, where decision delays often forced air forces to loiter for lengthy periods of time. This reduced overall sortie rates significantly even though logistics were good. For a theater such as the Persian Gulf or Korea, factors of two effects are easily plausible.

The second adjustment is to deployment rates. Although the deploying aircraft would not be directly affected, the deployment rate might well be reduced because of base-capacity problems and the confusion created by shifting operations. A factor of two effect is surely possible, as suggested by analysis of possible disruptions to deployments of even a single air expeditionary force (Shlapak, forthcoming). Much larger effects are plausible, depending on prior preparations.

Naval air forces and long-range air forces would likely not be affected in the same way. Moreover, these reductions in effectiveness could be mitigated or avoided by prior preparations to use the more-distant bases (or more adequately protect the forward bases). Thus, anyone using the models (or other, much more complex models) to investigate effects of mass-destruction weapons should vary the effects parametrically and relate the values to postulated mitigation efforts.

---

[25]Detailed studies conducted by RAND in the 1980s indicated that chemical attacks against large air bases can be tolerated, assuming that crews have and use appropriate suits, that the attacking missiles are not accurate or frequent, and that the chemicals are not lethal or persistent. However, there are many uncertainties in thinking about such matters more generally: missile accuracies are increasing, the biological and chemical agents that might be used would be more lethal and persistent than in the past, the number of flight suits is limited, and the civilians conducting logistical operations would probably not be as well protected as U.S. personnel. In view of the problems encountered with Gulf War syndrome, we remain unconvinced that U.S. commanders (including the President) would continue operating from bases vulnerable to mass-destruction weapons—especially when the stakes are less than vital to the United States itself. Others are more sanguine, at least with respect to near-term chemical weapons.

Table 3.8

EFFECTS OF MASS-DESTRUCTION WEAPONS

Input	Possible Multiplier of Normal Value (for Tactical Air Force Fraction of Overall Force)	Comments
Kills per shooter day, δ	0.5 (e.g., for reduced sortie rates due to longer ranges and poor logistics at alternative bases)	Effect could be mitigated by developing and stocking the alternative bases and, in some cases, by using ship-based prepositioning. Degradation applies only to Air Force tactical fighters.
Deployment rate, R	0.5 (e.g., because of reduced base capacity)	Sortie-generation rates can be improved generally by arranging for increased crew and support-team ratios. Degradation applies only to Air Force tactical fighters.
D-Day shooters, A_0	Reduce 10–25% to reflect possible need to transfer aircraft to other bases, disrupting operations temporarily	Effect would not exist if the transfers had been planned in advance.
Theater capacity		Very scenario dependent, but early limits of about 200 may be appropriate unless efforts are made to improve the infrastructure of bases outside of the range of missiles armed with chemical and biological warheads. The 200 figure would allow for a carrier battle group, some long-range bombers based outside the immediate region, and a wing of tactical fighters.

3.7 SUMMARY INSIGHTS

With this first set of models on the halt problem, we have focused strictly on interdiction and ignored such complications as air defenses, limited supplies of top-quality weapons, and time-dependent effects on command-control, reconnaissance and surveillance, and overall system effectiveness. Those issues will be taken up in subsequent chapters. However, even this first cut reveals a number of points and suggests appropriate measures of effectiveness. These include:

- Outcome, as measured by either halt time or halt distance, is in general a nonlinear function of the principal inputs. For interdiction in depth—the baseline strategy most likely to be employed—improving outcomes by a factor of two may require a factor of four improvement in Blue's capabilities (i.e., kills per sortie, sorties per day, or a combination).
- Having substantial forces available on D-Day is important for an early halt, especially for the modest deployment rates that have been demonstrated to date. This has major implications for forward deployment of forces, prompt use of strategic warning, and the ability to convince regional allies to grant full access to key bases early.

- The capability to exploit a red line for early warning and to accomplish early strikes very early, when they might have substantial delay effects, is important to an early halt. This capability, however, depends sensitively on political preparations and continued vigilance. Analysis—especially when presented simply—might be a persuasive factor in convincing allies of the need to create or maintain the red line concept. Although not shown here, the value of a red line strategy becomes even more apparent when one accounts for the possibility of faster-than-average first-day enemy movements.
- Although a leading-edge strategy does not improve results in cases using highly conservative assumptions,[26] it may be attractive—and even essential—to an *early* halt for some realistic cases. In particular, it can be highly effective if the most worrisome attack is restricted to a single axis with only one or two major columns, if shooters are able to use large-footprint area weapons that see the multiple columns as one, or if the local break point turns out to be much smaller than is often assumed. Effectiveness shrinks as the number of axes or columns per axis increase, although in some cases this could be offset by the attacker moving more slowly on poorer roads or by the defender attacking the axes sequentially (Davis, 2001a).
- The use or credible threatened use of weapons of mass destruction could seriously undercut plans for an *early*-halt campaign. It might force Blue to operate from much more distant and austere bases, reducing sortie rates and deployment rates, and quite possibly imposing a severe limit on the number of shooters that could be effectively operated in the theater. These problems could be mitigated by preparing now for operations from the more distant bases (improving the bases, stocking weapons, etc.), and by maximizing the early effectiveness of long-range Air Force bombers and naval systems. Another approach is to prepare to fight from the more forward bases even in a chemical or biological-weapon environment. That approach, however, is intrinsically brittle. Policymakers should ask whether—in the event of a future crisis—a U.S. president and theater commanders would be willing to expose U.S. personnel to unknown toxic agents. Any decision to count on making the forward-basing approach work for such circumstances should follow careful full-system analysis that accounts for the effects of mass-destruction weapons on local forces and support personnel, and on the ability to maintain operations for more than a few days. Realistic experimentation with benign but persistent chemicals might be valuable.[27]

---

[26] Here we assume that the halt time for a leading-edge strategy would be assessed as the smaller of the times at which the leading-edge movement rate is reduced to zero or the time at which the overall halt fraction of the invading force has been destroyed. That is, in terms of Figure 3.13, we use the adaptive strategy rather than the "pure" leading-edge strategy.

[27] At the risk of overdoing caveats, we note that this aggregate-level analysis does not deal *explicitly* with many complications of detail. For example, the nature of targets in advancing forces changes as strikes occur because dead targets may attract weapons and forces may disperse off-road. Also, weapon effectiveness can be much degraded if the delay between initial targeting and sortie arrival is large—especially for small-footprint weapons or in mixed terrain. Some of these issues are dealt with elsewhere (Davis, Bigelow, and McEver, 2000a). In this monograph, it is assumed that such considerations are reflected implicitly in the range of values chosen for parameters such as δ.

4. LOSSES TO AIR DEFENSE AND TRADEOFFS BETWEEN LOSSES AND HALT TIME

This chapter considers the effects of air defenses. We define two times: T_{SEAD} and T_{wait}. T_{SEAD} is the time by which air defenses have been essentially suppressed, Blue recognizes this, and Blue allocates air forces to anti-armor missions accordingly—e.g., by increasing the sortie rate of aircraft that would previously have been vulnerable. Suppression of enemy air defenses (SEAD) operations may continue throughout the campaign, but some aircraft may shift from SEAD missions to anti-armor missions.

In the more detailed simulation model, EXHALT (McEver, Davis, and Bigelow, 2000a), loss rates to air defense are assumed to decay exponentially from an initial loss rate per sortie, L_0. Loss rate drops by a factor of e (about 2.7) in time $T_{SEAD}/2$. T_{wait} is the time that a portion of the shooters is withheld because of vulnerability concerns. T_{wait} is between 0 and T_{SEAD}. The effect of having some of the shooters wait is reflected in the factor F(t) introduced in Chapter 3.[1] For example, if half the shooters are withheld during the wait period, and only half of those are allocated to anti-armor missions, then F(t) will be 1/4 during that period. We shall also need to account for T_{max} (the time at which the theater's capacity is reached).[2]

T_{SEAD}
T_{wait}

4.1 SOLUTIONS FOR IN-DEPTH INTERDICTION (IGNORING LOSSES)

Basic Analytics

To solve the problem, we proceed by analogy with expressions in Chapter 3. We again have

$$\xi = \int_0^{T_{halt}} N(s)\delta(s)\,ds, \tag{4.1}$$

where ξ is the number of armored fighting vehicles that we assume must be killed to bring about a halt.

---

[1]Using fewer aircraft could also reduce loss rates per sortie if those sorties that were flown were directed along particularly safe routes or had an unusual number of escort aircraft for jamming and the like.

[2]Some subtleties are worth mentioning. Blue may mistakenly believe SEAD has been accomplished when Red in fact has maintained additional air defenses in reserve. That can be represented by assuming that Blue allocates more shooters to anti-armor missions at $t = T_{wait}$ than if the true status was understood. Alternatively, Blue may mistakenly believe that air defenses remain active and may withhold some shooters longer than necessary. That can be represented by increasing the assumed value of T_{SEAD}, but doing so will cause some error: Blue's losses will be overestimated if Blue operates some shooters before what it believes is T_{SEAD}. A larger problem is that air-defense-related parameters like T_{SEAD} should not properly be treated as exogenous. After all, if A_0 is very small, SEAD operations could not begin in earnest until enough shooters deployed to the theater. EXHALT-CF provides a simple correction for this: It treats the true T_{SEAD} as the inputted value plus any extra time required to deploy a minimum number of shooters enabling SEAD operations.

If we consider air defenses and related phasing of operations, we must break the integral up into several terms to reflect the various time periods. As in the previous chapter, the precise form of the equations depends on the partition of the input domain.

Another complication is losses of shooter (primarily nonstealthy aircraft). This introduces a more complex time dependence into N(s):

$$N(s) = F(s)A_0 + F(s)\int_0^s \{R - L(q)S(q)A(q)\}dq, \quad (4.2)$$

L(q)
S(q)

where L(q) is the time-dependent per-sortie fractional loss rate for vulnerable aircraft and S(q) is the sortie rate of the vulnerable aircraft. Note that F(s) appears ahead of the integral. This is because the buildup is a buildup of shooters, not of employed anti-armor shooters. The fraction of shooters that is employed against armor at time s is a multiplier of the accumulated shooters.

Note that A(q) appears in the second term of integrand, thereby complicating the equation. That is, the number of shooters appears on both sides of the equation. We shall develop an approximation later in the chapter.

Figure 4.1 illustrates the analytical issues schematically by showing the separate phases of the campaign for an illustrative case in which the relevant times are the wait time, the SEAD time, and the time at which the theater reaches capacity (T_{wait}, T_{SEAD}, and T_{max}, respectively). The y axis is the number of (accumulated) shooter days accomplished as of time t. For a given threat and a given level of per-shooter-day effectiveness, the requirement is to achieve α shooter days. This corresponds to

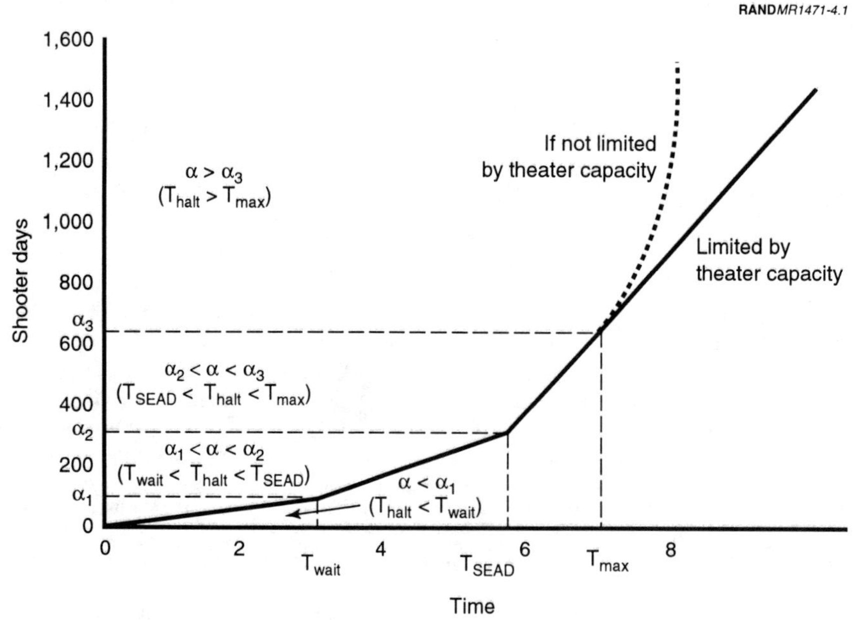

Figure 4.1—Illustrative Buildup of Shooter Days Employed Against Armor

drawing a horizontal line, which intercepts the curve at the time T_{halt}. Note that the solution curve is different in the several time regimes. That is, it is different in the periods before T_{wait}, between T_{wait} and T_{SEAD}, between T_{SEAD} and T_{max}, and the period after T_{max}. This is equivalent to saying that the solution forms are different for α values less than α_1, between α_1 and α_2, between α_2 and α_3, and larger than α_3. Since α is an input of the problem, whereas halt times are outputs, it is better to express the cases in terms of α values.

The equation expressing halt time in terms of inputs can be either quadratic (as in most of Chapter 3) or linear, depending on whether halt time occurs before or after T_{max}. Let us first work through the illustrative case corresponding to Figure 4.1 and then return to the more general instances.

An Illustrative Case

Working with the illustrative time ordering of Figure 4.1, let us use the subscripts pre, post, and final to indicate values of F(t) applicable prior to the wait time, between the wait time and SEAD time, and after the SEAD time. If no subscript is used, it means the same as "final."

The curve shown in Figure 4.1 is, for large t,

$$\alpha[t(t > T_{max})] = \int_0^{T_{wait}} F_{pre}(A_0 + Rs)ds + \int_{T_{wait}}^{T_{SEAD}} F_{post}(A_0 + Rs)ds + \int_{T_{SEAD}}^{T_{max}} F_{final}(A_0 + Rs)ds + \int_{max}^{T_{halt}} F_{final}(A_0 + Rs)ds. \tag{4.3}$$

If $\alpha > \alpha_3$, we can work out the integrals, insert $\alpha = \xi/\delta$, and switch sides to obtain

$$\begin{aligned} &\left[F_{pre}A_0T_{wait} + \frac{1}{2}F_{pre}RT_{wait}^2\right] \\ &+\left[F_{post}A_0(T_{SEAD} - T_{wait}) + \frac{1}{2}F_{post}R(T_{SEAD}^2 - T_{wait}^2)\right] \\ &+\left[F_{final}A_0(T_{max} - T_{SEAD}) + \frac{1}{2}F_{final}R(T_{max}^2 - T_{SEAD}^2)\right] \\ &+\left[F_{final}A_0(T_{halt} - T_{max})\right] \\ &= \alpha. \end{aligned} \tag{4.4}$$

Next, we can rearrange to solve for the halt time. Since the solution is in the linear regime (i.e., T_{halt} occurs after T_{max}),

$$T_{halt} = \frac{\alpha - \{\} + F_{final}A_0T_{max}}{F_{final}A_0}, \tag{4.5}$$

where

$$\{\} = \left[F_{pre}A_0T_{wait} + \frac{1}{2}F_{pre}RT_{wait}^2\right]$$
$$+\left[F_{post}A_0(T_{SEAD} - T_{wait}) + \frac{1}{2}F_{post}R(T_{SEAD}^2 - T_{wait}^2)\right] \qquad (4.6)$$
$$+\left[F_{final}A_0(T_{max} - T_{SEAD}) + \frac{1}{2}F_{final}R(T_{max}^2 - T_{SEAD}^2)\right].$$

The bracketed quantity { } is the number of shooter days accomplished as of the last discontinuity in Blue's effectiveness; in this case, that is the number of shooter days as of T_{max}.

A Second Illustrative Case

As a second example, suppose halt time is less than T_{max} but larger than the other critical times. We would then be in the quadratic regime and, by analogy with the derivations in Chapter 3, we would have

$$\left[F_{pre}A_0T_{wait} + \frac{1}{2}F_{pre}RT_{wait}^2\right]$$
$$+\left[F_{post}A_0(T_{SEAD} - T_{wait}) + \frac{1}{2}F_{post}R(T_{SEAD}^2 - T_{wait}^2)\right] \qquad (4.7)$$
$$+\left[F_{final}A_0(T_{halt} - T_{SEAD}) + \frac{1}{2}F_{final}R(T_{halt}^2 - T_{SEAD}^2)\right]$$
$$= \alpha.$$

In this case, we could rearrange to obtain the standard quadratic form. We would obtain, in steps:

$$\frac{1}{2}F_{final}RT_{halt}^2 + F_{final}A_0T_{halt} + \{\} = 0, \qquad (4.8)$$

where

$$\{\} = \alpha - \left[F_{pre}A_0T_{wait} + \frac{1}{2}F_{pre}RT_{wait}^2\right]$$
$$-\left[F_{post}A_0(T_{SEAD} - T_{wait}) + \frac{1}{2}F_{post}R(T_{SEAD}^2 - T_{wait}^2)\right] \qquad (4.9)$$
$$-\left[F_{final}A_0T_{SEAD} + \frac{1}{2}F_{final}RT_{SEAD}^2\right].$$

Here the bracketed quantity { } is the number of shooter days needed after the last discontinuity at T_{SEAD}.

If we divide by RF_{final} and define ψ as $(-1/RF)\{\ \}$, we obtain

$$\frac{1}{2}T_{halt}^2 + \frac{A_0}{R}T_{halt} - \psi = 0. \tag{4.10}$$

Again solving the quadratic equation and ignoring the nonphysical negative root, we obtain:

$$T_{halt} = \left\{\sqrt{\zeta^2 + 2\psi_{depth}} - \zeta\right\}, \tag{4.11}$$

where

$$\zeta = \frac{A_0}{R}$$

$$\psi = \frac{1}{RF_{final}} \left\{ \begin{array}{l} +\alpha - \left[F_{pre}A_0T_{wait} + \frac{1}{2}F_{pre}RT_{wait}^2\right] \\ -\left[F_{post}A_0(T_{SEAD} - T_{wait}) + \frac{1}{2}F_{post}R(T_{SEAD}^2 - T_{wait}^2)\right] \\ + \left[F_{final}A_0T_{SEAD} + \frac{1}{2}F_{final}RT_{SEAD}^2\right] \end{array} \right\}. \tag{4.12}$$

And, as before, D is a simple function of T_{halt} and T_{delay},

$$D = Max[Min[V(T_{halt} - T_{delay}), Obj], 0]. \tag{4.13}$$

Solutions Covering All Time Orderings

The above derivations were for particular orderings of times, but many combinations are possible. For each, a variant of Figure 4.1 applies, as shown in Figure 4.2. Figure 4.2a describes a case like the one above, where $T_{max} > T_{SEAD}$. Figure 4.2b describes a case where T_{max} lies between T_{wait} and T_{SEAD}. And Figure 4.2c describes the case where T_{max} lies between 0 and T_{wait}. Each figure indicates the transition-point values of α, where the derivative of shooter days versus time changes. These occur at the wait, SEAD, or maximum-capacity times. Since T_{wait} must be less than T_{SEAD}, there are only three time orderings—those represented by the three panels.

There is, however, another time involved—the halt time T_{halt}. This is determined by the value of α (i.e., if one specifies the threat to be killed and the effectiveness per shooter day, that determines the halt time). Given the other three times, the halt time may occur before the first, between the first and second, between the second and third, or after the third. For each ordering of the four times, there exists a distinct analytical solution.

Figure 4.2 shows the 12 solution regimes. In Figure 4.2a, for example, the regimes are for α's greater than α_3 (i.e., halt times greater than T_{max}), α's between α_2 and α_3, etc.

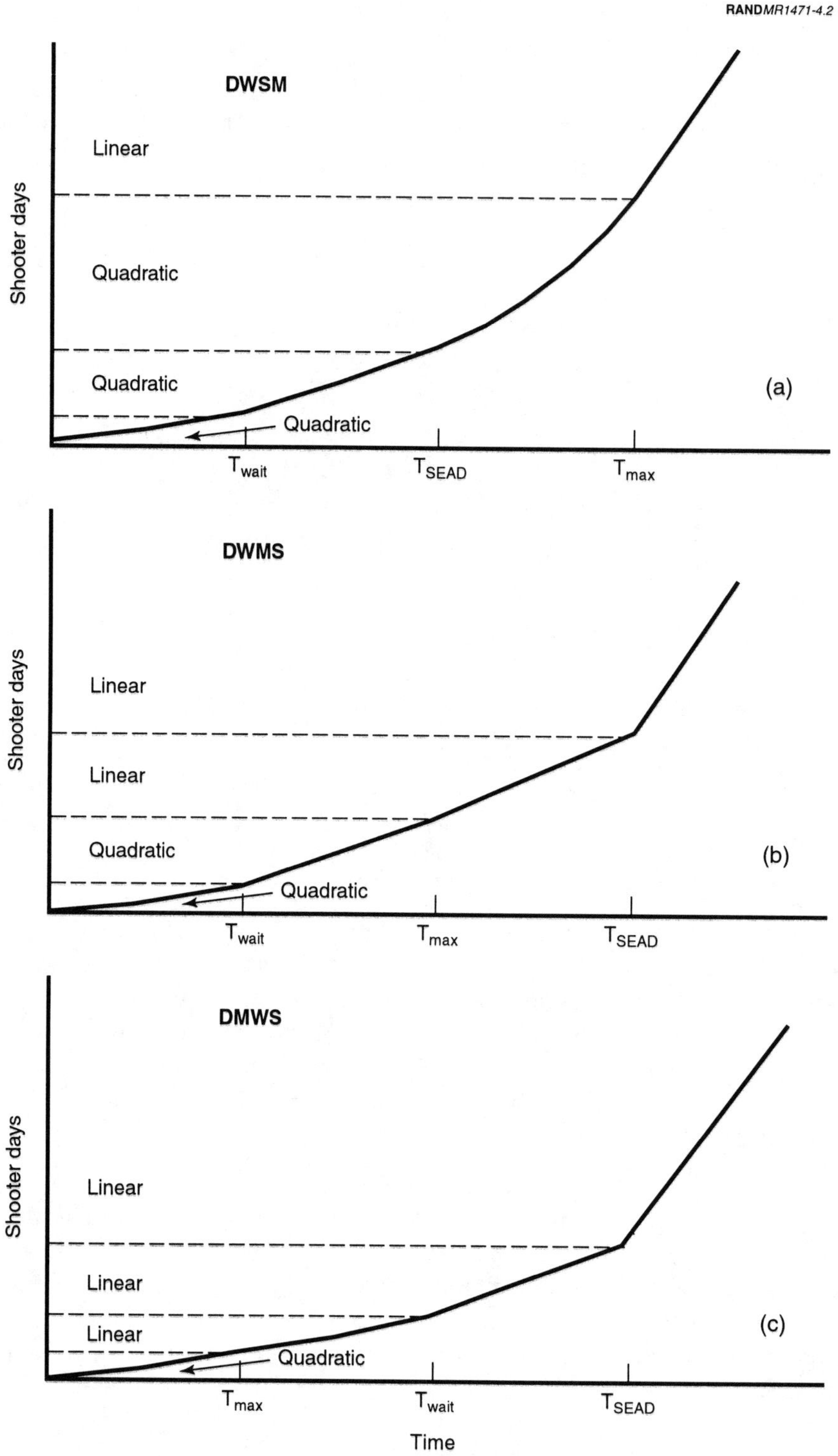

Figure 4.2—Schematic Showing Effects of Phasing and Theater Capacity (with different timings D, W, S, M = D-Day, T_{wait}, T_{SEAD}, T_{max})

There are four solution zones shown in Figure 4.2a, and four more in each of the other panels.

Figure 4.2 also highlights the fact that the governing equation shifts from quadratic to linear as one crosses the border between halt times less than or greater than T_{max}.

Fortunately, the solutions for the 12 cases can be expressed in only two forms. The solutions for the various quadratic cases can all be expressed in the form

$$T_{halt} = \sqrt{\zeta^2 + 2\psi} - \zeta, \quad \text{(quadratic cases)} \tag{4.14}$$

and

$$D = Max[Min[V(T_{halt} - T_{delay})], 0], \tag{4.15}$$

but the composite parameters ζ and ψ may be different in the various cases. ψ can be thought of as having the form

$$\psi = \frac{1}{F_{now}R}\left\{\alpha - \alpha_{prev} + F_{now}A_0T_{prev} + \frac{1}{2}RT_{prev}^2\right\}, \tag{4.16}$$

where this means that if halt occurs in the time period called "now" (i.e., α exceeds the previous threshold), then ψ is—aside from the multiplicative factor—α minus the shooter days accomplished up until the previous threshold time, plus the shooter days accomplished between then and halt. Understanding this form makes it possible to work out the various cases systematically and to review formulas implemented in computer code.

In the cases in which halt occurs after T_{max} (i.e., α is greater than the transition point associated with T_{max}), the solution is instead linear. We can find the general solution

$$\alpha = \alpha_{prev} + F_{now}A_{max}(T_{halt} - T_{prev})$$

$$\therefore T_{halt} = \frac{\alpha - \alpha_{prev} + F_{now}A_{max}T_{prev}}{F_{now}A_{max}} \quad \text{(linear cases).} \tag{4.17}$$

To summarize, it is useful to precompute several transition points (Table 4.1). The solution formulas are then given in Table 4.2 using those transition points.[3] The second set of transition points applies if the number of shooters on D-Day equals or exceeds the theater's capacity.

---

[3]Some simplification of algebra is possible, as can be seen by expanding all of the intermediate variables and then looking for cancellations. However, as expressed, the formulas bear an understandable relationship to one another.

Table 4.1

THRESHOLDS OF THE SHOOTER-DAY PARAMETER FOR IN-DEPTH STRATEGY

Ordering[a]	Threshold	Value (Number of Shooter Days at the Threshold)
DWSM	α_1 (at T_{wait})	$F_{pre}A_0T_{wait} + \frac{1}{2}F_{pre}RT_{wait}^2$
DWSM	α_2 (at T_{SEAD})	$\alpha_1 + F_{post}A_0(T_{SEAD} - T_{wait}) + \frac{1}{2}F_{post}R(T_{SEAD}^2 - T_{wait}^2)$
DWSM	α_3 (at T_{max})	$\alpha_2 + FA_0(T_{max} - T_{SEAD}) + \frac{1}{2}FR(T_{max}^2 - T_{SEAD}^2)$
DWMS	α_4 (at T_{wait})	$F_{pre}A_0T_{wait} + \frac{1}{2}F_{pre}RT_{wait}^2$
DWMS	α_5 (at T_{max})	$\alpha_4 + F_{post}A_0(T_{max} - T_{wait}) + \frac{1}{2}F_{post}R(T_{max}^2 - T_{wait}^2)$
DWMS	α_6 (at T_{SEAD})	$\alpha_5 + F_{post}A_{max}(T_{SEAD} - T_{max})$
DMWS	α_7 (at T_{max})	$F_{pre}A_0T_{max} + \frac{1}{2}F_{pre}RT_{max}^2$
DMWS	α_8 (at T_{wait})	$\alpha_7 + F_{pre}A_{max}(T_{wait} - T_{max})$
DMWS	α_9 (at T_{SEAD})	$\alpha_8 + F_{post}A_{max}(T_{SEAD} - T_{wait})$
MDWS	α_{10} (at T_{wait})	$F_{pre}A_{max}T_{wait}$
MDWS	α_{11} (at T_{SEAD})	$\alpha_{10} + F_{post}A_{max}(T_{SEAD} - T_{wait})$

[a]DWSM is an abbreviation indicating the order of the critical times: D-Day, T_{wait}, T_{SEAD}, and T_{max}, respectively.

4.2 SOLUTIONS FOR THE LEADING-EDGE STRATEGY (IGNORING LOSSES)

General Comments

The generalization to the case of phasing to deal with air defenses also changes the solutions for the leading-edge strategy. As before,

$$\gamma \equiv \frac{\delta_{edge}A_{spacing}}{N_{axes}N_{col}H_{local}}, \tag{4.18}$$

and, so long as the attack has not been halted by attrition rather than slowing,

$$V(t) = V - N(t)\gamma .$$

To distinguish clearly among phases, we write:

$$V(t) = V - F(t)A(t)\gamma. \tag{4.19}$$

To find T_{halt} is a bit complicated, but Figure 4.3 explains what is going on. Here we are interested not in accumulated shooter days but in accumulated shooters. The plot of $F(t)A(t)\gamma$—i.e., of $\Delta V(t)$—is discontinuous. That is, the reduction of invader speed increases abruptly when the allocation of shooters increases. These transitions occur at the points indicated as V_1, V_2, and V_3 (so marked because the units are those of speed).

Table 4.2

SOLUTIONS FOR ALL OF THE INPUT DOMAIN (IN-DEPTH STRATEGY)[a]

Ordering[b]	Conditions of Case	ψ (quadratic case) or T_{halt} (linear case)
DHWSM	$\alpha \le \alpha_1$	$\psi = \dfrac{\alpha}{F_{pre}R}$
DWHSM	$\alpha_1 < \alpha \le \alpha_2$	$\psi = \dfrac{1}{F_{post}R}\left[\alpha - \alpha_1 + F_{post}A_0T_{wait} + \dfrac{1}{2}F_{post}RT_{wait}^2\right]$
DWSHM	$\alpha_2 < \alpha \le \alpha_3$	$\psi = \dfrac{1}{FR}\left[\alpha - \alpha_2 + FA_0T_{SEAD} + \dfrac{1}{2}FRT_{SEAD}^2\right]$
DWSMH	$\alpha > \alpha_3$	$T_{halt} = \dfrac{1}{FA_{max}}[\alpha - \alpha_3 + FA_{max}T_{max}]$
DHWMS	$\alpha \le \alpha_4$	$\psi = \dfrac{\alpha}{F_{pre}R}$
DWHMS	$\alpha_4 < \alpha \le \alpha_5$	$\psi = \dfrac{1}{F_{post}R}\left[\alpha - \alpha_4 + F_{post}A_0T_{wait} + \dfrac{1}{2}F_{post}RT_{wait}^2\right]$
DWMHS	$\alpha_5 < \alpha \le \alpha_6$	$T_{halt} = \dfrac{1}{F_{post}A_{max}}[\alpha - \alpha_5 + F_{post}A_{max}T_{max}]$
DWMSH	$\alpha > \alpha_6$	$T_{halt} = \dfrac{1}{FA_{max}}[\alpha - \alpha_6 + FA_{max}T_{SEAD}]$
DHMWS	$\alpha \le \alpha_7$	$\psi = \dfrac{\alpha}{F_{pre}R}$
DMHWS	$\alpha_7 < \alpha \le \alpha_8$	$T_{halt} = \dfrac{1}{F_{pre}A_{max}}[\alpha - \alpha_7 + F_{pre}A_{max}T_{max}]$
DMWHS	$\alpha_8 < \alpha \le \alpha_9$	$T_{halt} = \dfrac{1}{F_{post}A_{max}}[\alpha - \alpha_8 + F_{post}A_{max}T_{wait}]$
DMWSH	$\alpha > \alpha_9$	$T_{halt} = \dfrac{1}{FA_{max}}[\alpha - \alpha_9 + FA_{max}T_{SEAD}]$
MDHWS	$\alpha \le \alpha_{10}$	$T_{halt} = \dfrac{\alpha}{F_{pre}A_{max}}$
MDWHS	$\alpha_{10} \le \alpha \le \alpha_{11}$	$T_{halt} = \dfrac{\alpha - \alpha_{10} + F_{post}A_{max}T_{wait}}{F_{post}A_{max}}$
MDWSH	$\alpha > \alpha_{11}$	$T_{halt} = \dfrac{\alpha - \alpha_{11} + FA_{max}T_{SEAD}}{FA_{max}}$

[a]This should be understood as an if-then-else table.

[b]This indicates the order of critical times, including the halt time H. Note that the location of the halt time is actually an output; the input is the size of α in comparison with the various threshold levels. However, it is easier to orient oneself mathematically by discussing everything in terms of the ordering of critical times.

The question is when the slowing effect $F(t)A(t)\gamma$ reaches the initial speed V so that the net speed is zero.

If the speed V intercepts the curve during one of the periods in which the curve is rising, then we can solve for halt time and obtain (again, so long as the problem is limited by the slowing effect rather than overall attrition):

$$F(t)[A_0 + RT_{halt}]\gamma = V$$

$$T_{halt} = \frac{1}{R}\left[\frac{V}{F(T_{halt})\gamma} - A_0\right]. \qquad (4.20)$$

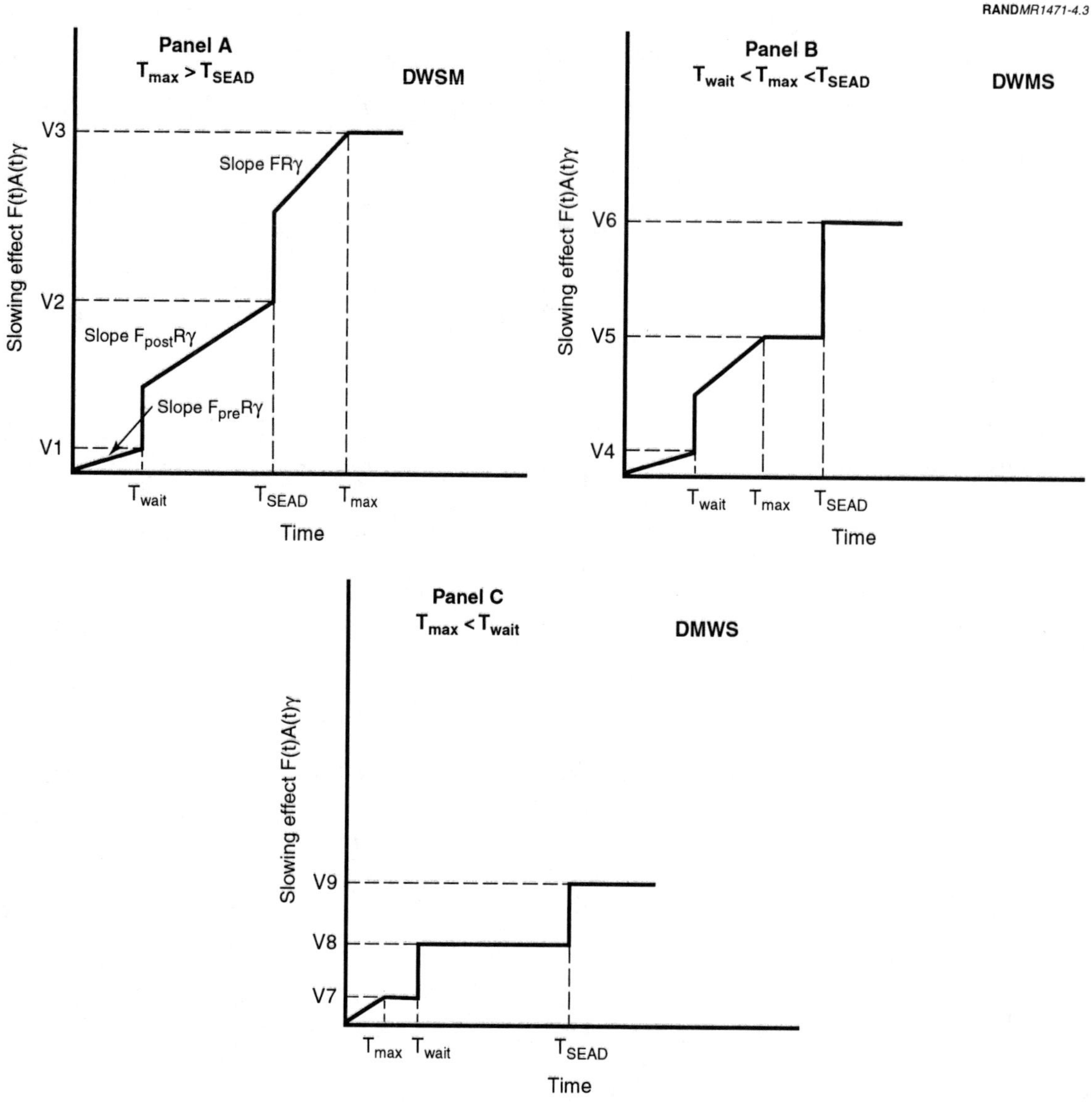

Figure 4.3—Schematic Showing Effects of Phasing and Theater Capacity on Slowing Effect Versus Time

If T_{halt} occurs at a discontinuity, F is to be evaluated at its lower value. For example, in Figure 4.3, if V =V_2, then T_{halt} is evaluated using Eq. (4.17) with F(t) = F_{post}.

If the speed V has a value just above a transition point, and F(t)A(t) is flat because it is limited by the theater's capacity A_{max}, the intercept and halt time is at the next transition of F—i.e., at either T_{wait} or T_{SEAD}.

By analogy with the previous section, we can calculate the transition points (the speeds indicated in Figure 4.3) and use them to express solutions. These are shown in Tables 4.3 and 4.4.

Table 4.3

TRANSITION POINTS FOR LEADING-EDGE PROBLEM

Ordering	Threshold	Formula
DWSM	V_1 (at T_{wait})	$F_{pre}(A_0 + RT_{wait})\gamma$
	V_2 (at T_{SEAD})	$F_{post}(A_0 + RT_{SEAD})\gamma$
	V_3 (at T_{max})	$FA_{max}\gamma$
DWMS	V_4 (at T_{wait})	$F_{pre}(A_0 + RT_{wait})\gamma$
	V_5 (at T_{max})	$F_{post}A_{max}\gamma$
	V_6 (at T_{SEAD})	$FA_{max}\gamma$
DMWS	V_7 (at T_{max})	$F_{pre}A_{max}\gamma$
	V_8 (at T_{wait})	$F_{post}A_{max}\gamma$
	V_9 (at T_{SEAD})	$FA_{max}\gamma$

Table 4.4

HALT TIMES FOR LEADING-EDGE STRATEGY (SLOWING EFFECT ONLY)

Ordering	Condition	Halt Time (ignoring overall attrition)[a]
D<u>H</u>WSM	$V \le V_1$	$\frac{1}{R}\left[\frac{V}{F_{pre}\gamma} - A_0\right]$
DW<u>H</u>SM	$V_1 < V \le V_2$	$\frac{1}{R}\left[\frac{V}{F_{post}\gamma} - A_0\right]$
DWS<u>H</u>M	$V_2 < V \le V_3$	$\frac{1}{R}\left[\frac{V}{F\gamma} - A_0\right]$
DWSM<u>H</u>	$V > V_3$	∞
D<u>H</u>WMS	$V \le V_4$	$\frac{1}{R}\left[\frac{V}{F_{pre}\gamma} - A_0\right]$
DW<u>H</u>MS	$V_4 < V \le V_5$	$\frac{1}{R}\left[\frac{V}{F_{post}\gamma} - A_0\right]$
DWM<u>H</u>S	$V_5 < V \le V_6$	T_{SEAD}
DWMS<u>H</u>	$V > V_6$	∞
D<u>H</u>MWS	$V \le V_7$	$\frac{1}{R}\left[\frac{V}{F_{pre}\gamma} - A_0\right]$
DM<u>H</u>WS	$V_7 < V \le V_8$	T_{wait}
DMW<u>H</u>S	$V_8 < V \le V_9$	T_{SEAD}
DMWS<u>H</u>	$V > V_9$	∞

[a]In many cases, overall halt time will be limited by attrition: The attacker's break point H will be reached.

Halt Distance

The halt distance is given by

$$D = \mathrm{Max}\left[\int_0^{T_{halt}} [V(s)ds, Obj], 0\right],$$

where

$$V(s) = V - \Delta(s) = V - F(s)A(s)\gamma, \tag{4.21}$$

and T_{halt} is the smaller of the value from Table 4.4 or the value found by using the in-depth formulas, but with δ = edge.

Exact or approximate solutions for D can be found for each case in Table 4.4 (i.e., DHWSM, etc.). Since this is tedious, however, we defer doing so until Chapter 6 and Appendix E, which include effects of exhaustion, theater capacity, delays, and so on.

4.3 SOLUTIONS THAT INCLUDE LOSSES TO AIR DEFENSES

General Comments

The equations of Section 4.2 ignored losses of shooters per se. As discussed earlier, however, the correct equation is

$$N(s) = F(s)A_0 + F(s)\int_0^s \{R - L(q)S(q)A(q)\}dq. \tag{4.22}$$

Fortunately, the previous equations apply with only simple changes if losses are fairly small. Approximations are appropriate for several reasons. First, losses to air defenses will likely be small because commanders will withhold aircraft—or channel them to particular areas rather than others—so as to control losses. Second, losses are assumed to occur only for a limited period of time, between T_{wait} and T_{SEAD} (only stealth aircraft or missiles would be used before T_{wait}); they are assumed to have negligible loss rates. It now follows that we can make some approximations:

L_{avg}
$L_{dailyavg}$

L(q) (a per-sortie loss rate) can be approximated by a constant L_{avg} to estimate the integral from T_{wait} to T_{SEAD}. We let $L_{dailyavg}$ be the per-day loss rate. It is just the product of the per-sortie average, L_{avg}, and the sortie rate of vulnerable aircraft. L(q) is zero for values of q outside the range T_{wait} to T_{SEAD}.[4]

N(q) in the integrand, or FA(q), can be approximated by N_{avg}, which is a bit different depending on the time-ordering cases. Remembering that this is to be used only for integrating, in Eq. (4.26), between the wait time and the SEAD time, we could approximate N_{avg} by

$$N_{avg} \approx \mathrm{Max}[F_{post}[A_0 + RT_{wait} + \frac{1}{2}R(T_{SEAD} - T_{wait})], F_{post}A_{max}]. \tag{4.23}$$

---

[4]In a more microscopic treatment, per-sortie defense effectiveness would depend on sortie rate.

For the purposes of integrating from T_{SEAD} onward, the effect of losses can be approximated by replacing the constant term, A_0, with A_0 – Losses, where

$$\text{Losses} \approx L_{dailyavg} N_{avg} (T_{SEAD} - T_{wait}). \tag{4.24}$$

The above discussion depends on $L_{dailyavg}$. It can be estimated using the exponential decay assumption, as in EXHALT (McEver, Davis, and Bigelow, 2000a). Remembering that L_{avg} is the average during the period T_{wait} to T_{SEAD} of the *per-sortie* loss rate, we obtain:

$$L_{avg} = \frac{L_0}{T_{SEAD} - T_{wait}} \int_{T_{wait}}^{SEAD} e^{-\frac{2s}{T_{SEAD}}} F_{post} ds \tag{4.25}$$

$$L_{dailyavg} \approx \frac{L_0 F_{post} S_{avg}}{T_{SEAD} - T_{wait}} \int_{T_{wait}}^{SEAD} e^{-\frac{2s}{T_{SEAD}}} ds$$

$$L_{dailyavg} \approx \frac{-F_{post} S_{avg}}{T_{SEAD} - T_{wait}} \frac{T_{SEAD}}{2} \left[e^{-2} - e^{-2\frac{T_{wait}}{T_{SEAD}}} \right] L_0 \tag{4.26}$$

$$L_{dailyavg} \approx \frac{F_{post} S_{avg}}{T_{SEAD} - T_{wait}} \frac{T_{SEAD}}{2} \left[e^{-2\frac{T_{wait}}{T_{SEAD}}} - 0.135 \right] L_0,$$

where S_{avg} is the nominal sortie rate of vulnerable aircraft in the absence of air defenses. In the absence of other information, it can be the nominal sortie rate for an equivalent aircraft. $L_{dailyavg}$ will typically be perhaps 1/3 of the initial daily loss rate, or less. S_{avg} L_0

As Figure 4.4 indicates, we could choose to treat the average number of losses per day, $N_{avg}L_{dailyavg}$, as an independent parameter, rather than calculate it from per-sortie loss rate and the average sortie rate of vulnerable aircraft. That would reduce the number of independent parameters to be varied and improve the modularity of analysis. Such simplifications are useful in first-cut exploratory analysis. Obviously, however, $N_{avg}L_{dailyavg}$ is not really an independent exogenous parameter. Thus, in analyses in which estimating losses is important, it is better to include the detail (i.e., to calculate $N_{avg}L_{dailyavg}$). On the other hand, if one knows that losses are small enough so that calculating them is unimportant, or if one believes that the range of plausible values for $N_{avg}L_{dailyavg}$ can be estimated directly as well as or better than by calculating the range with the formulas involving L_0 etc. (after all, L_0 is typically not well known and is dependent on detailed aspects of employment planning as well as the threat's air defense systems and tactics), then the simplification is appropriate.

RANDMR1471-4.4

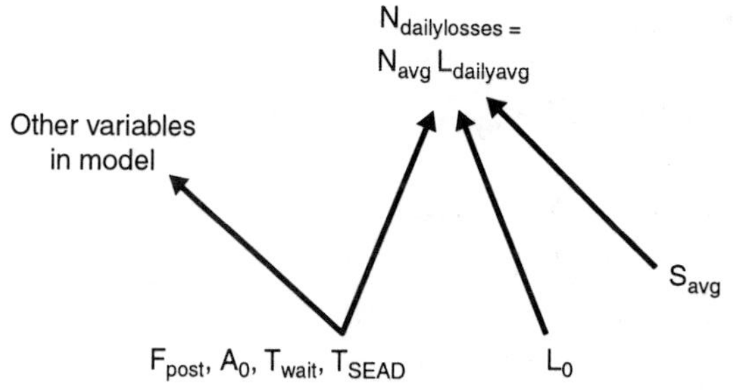

Figure 4.4—Convenient Variables for Treating Losses

One further set of approximations is quite important at this point. So long as daily losses are no greater than the deployment rate R, and so long as overall losses are no greater than A_0, the total number of shooters will increase monotonically with time (i.e., it will never decrease). In contrast, if we consider cases where shooters can decrease with time in certain periods, the result is a further proliferation of integration intervals and a further increase in model complexity. To avoid this, we introduce approximations for $L_{dailyavg}$ and Losses. They are to be used only in computing other variables, such as the time theater capacity is reached, halt time, and halt distance. The approximations ensure that certain terms in the related computations are never negative. The approximations are

$$\begin{aligned} \Delta R &\equiv \text{Min}[L_{dailyavg}, R - .001] \\ \text{ALosses} &\equiv \text{Min}[\text{Losses}, A_0 - .001]. \end{aligned} \tag{4.27}$$

The .001 terms are to avoid division by zero. We shall use these approximations in what follows.

Effects on the Time Maximum Theater Capacity Is Reached

Losses increase the time at which theater capacity is reached. T_{max} was tentatively defined in Chapter 3 as $(A_{max} - A_0)/R$, with a minimum of 0. That was actually a "nominal" value, so let us henceforth use T_{max} to indicate the time theater capacity is reached if there are losses. As in the larger halt problem, a clean solution for T_{max} can be found by first identifying thresholds and then writing different solutions for the different regimes. Figure 4.5 shows the issues. It plots *potential* shooters versus time—i.e., the shooters that would be available if unconstrained by theater capacity. The drop in slope that occurs at the wait time signals the period of attrition. As mentioned above, attrition is assumed to be no larger than the deployment rate. After SEAD is complete, the buildup returns to the original slope. The horizontal dashed lines indicate some alternative values of A_{max}. Each of the illustrative values of T_{max} could be solved with a simple linear equation, but the equations are different in the different regions. There is a limiting case (not shown) in which theater capacity obtains at the outset. We then assume that $T_{max} = 0$ and that losses are replaced

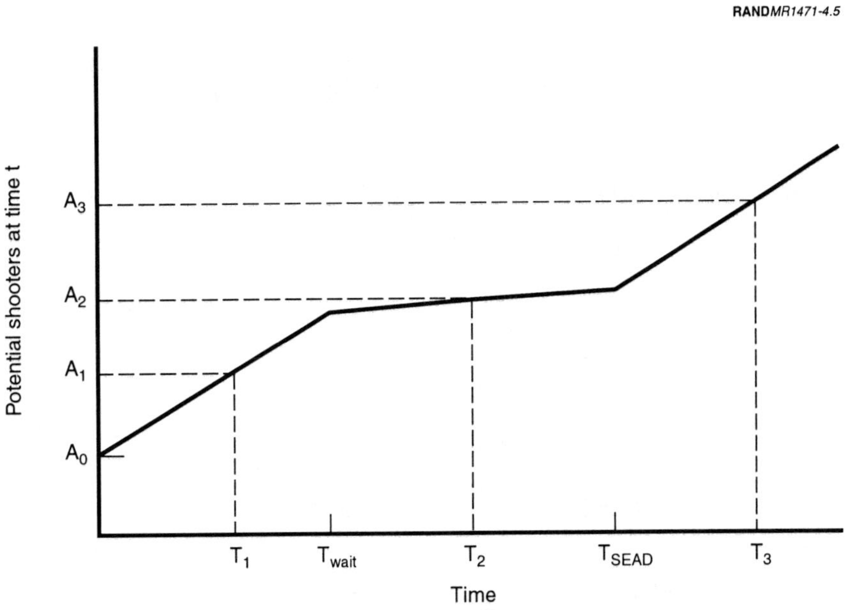

Figure 4.5—Solution Regimes for T_{max}

as they occur, without diminution in number of shooters. Table 4.5 summarizes the formulas. Although just using the nominal value of A_{max} is often a fair approximation when calculating T_{halt}, the resulting errors can cause distracting peculiarities in graphs. The formulas of Table 4.5 do much better.

Table 4.5

TIMES THEATER CAPACITY IS REACHED

Case	T_{max}
$A_{max} = 0$	0
$A_{max} \le A_0 + RT_{wait}$	$\frac{A_{max} - A_0}{R}$
$A_0 + RT_{wait} < A_{max} \le A_0 + RT_{SEAD} - ALosses$	$\frac{A_{max} - (A_0 + \Delta RT_{wait})}{R - \Delta R}$
$A_{max} > A_0 + RT_{SEAD} - ALosses$	$\frac{A_{max} - (A_0 - ALosses)}{R}$

In-Depth and Leading-Edge Interdiction with Losses

The earlier formulas of Tables 4.1–4.5 can now be adjusted to account approximately for losses. If we assume that losses are replaced when theater capacity is the limiting factor, then the in-depth interdiction results are as shown in Tables 4.6–4.7, and those for the leading-edge strategy are shown in Tables 4.8–4.9.

We use the following definitions:

Table 4.6

THRESHOLDS OF THE SHOOTER-DAY PARAMETER (IN-DEPTH STRATEGY, WITH EXPLICIT LOSSES)

Ordering	Threshold	Value
DWSM	α_1 (at T_{wait})	$F_{pre}A_0T_{wait} + \frac{1}{2}F_{pre}RT_{wait}^2$
	α_2 (at T_{SEAD})	$\alpha_1 + F_{post}A_0(T_{SEAD} - T_{wait}) + \frac{1}{2}F_{post}(R - \Delta R)(T_{SEAD}^2 - T_{wait}^2)$
	α_3 (at T_{max})	$\alpha_2 + F\,(A_0 - ALosses)(T_{max} - T_{SEAD}) + \frac{1}{2}FR(T_{max}^2 - T_{SEAD}^2)$
DWMS	α_4 (at T_{wait})	$F_{pre}A_0T_{wait} + \frac{1}{2}F_{pre}RT_{wait}^2$
	α_5 (at T_{max})	$\alpha_4 + F_{post}A_0(T_{max} - T_{wait}) + \frac{1}{2}F_{post}(R - \Delta R)(T_{max}^2 - T_{wait}^2)$
	α_6 (at T_{SEAD})	$\alpha_5 + F_{post}A_{max}(T_{SEAD} - T_{max})$
DMWS	α_7 (at T_{max})	$F_{pre}A_0T_{max} + \frac{1}{2}F_{pre}RT_{max}^2$
	α_8 (at T_{wait})	$\alpha_7 + F_{pre}A_{max}(T_{wait} - T_{max})$
	α_9 (at T_{SEAD})	$\alpha_8 + F_{post}A_{max}(T_{SEAD} - T_{wait})$

$$
\begin{aligned}
\zeta &= \zeta_2 = \frac{A_0 - ALosses}{R} \quad \text{if } T_{halt} \geq T_{SEAD} \\
\zeta &= \zeta_1 = \frac{A_0}{R - \Delta R} \quad \text{if } T_{wait} \leq T_{halt} < T_{SEAD} \\
\zeta &= \zeta_{base} = \frac{A_0}{R} \quad \text{if } T_{halt} < T_{wait}.
\end{aligned} \tag{4.28}
$$

Halt distances in the leading-edge strategy are more complex to express (see Chapter 6 and Appendix D).

Results for an Optimum Strategy

As before, we can solve for the better solution for a given set of assumptions, shifting strategies as necessary as we change assumptions. The better strategy is the one that gives the smaller value of the halt distance (not necessarily the smaller halt time).

4.4 OPTIMIZING THE WAIT TIME

The solutions in this chapter depend on the parameters T_{wait}, F_{pre}, and F_{post}, which are special inputs because they represent command decisions about when to commit relatively vulnerable aircraft. In exploratory analysis, they can be varied to find "optimum" wait times. However, to do this, one needs to have an explicit representation of the tradeoff between halt distance and losses. A simple utility function that treats both losses of territory and losses of aircraft as quite painful is a product of exponentials:

Table 4.7

SOLUTIONS FOR IN-DEPTH STRATEGY WITH EXPLICIT LOSSES

Ordering	Conditions of Case	ψ (quadratic cases) or T_{halt} (linear cases)
D<u>H</u>WSM	$\alpha \le \alpha_1$	$\psi = \frac{\alpha}{F_{pre}R}$, $\zeta = \zeta_{base}$
DW<u>H</u>SM	$\alpha_1 < \alpha \le \alpha_2$	$\psi = \frac{1}{F_{post}R}\left[\alpha - \alpha_1 + F_{post}A_0T_{wait} + \frac{1}{2}F_{post}(R - \Delta R)T_{wait}^2\right]$ $\zeta = \zeta_1$
DWS<u>H</u>M	$\alpha_2 < \alpha \le \alpha_3$	$\psi = \frac{1}{FR}\left[\alpha - \alpha_2 + F(A_0 - ALosses)T_{SEAD} + \frac{1}{2}FRT_{SEAD}^2\right]$ $\zeta = \zeta_2$
DWSM<u>H</u>	$\alpha > \alpha_3$	$T_{halt} = \frac{1}{FA_{max}}[\alpha - \alpha_3 + FA_{max}T_{max}]$
D<u>H</u>WMS	$\alpha \le \alpha_4$	$\psi = \frac{\alpha}{F_{pre}R}$, $\zeta = \zeta_{base}$
DW<u>H</u>MS	$\alpha_4 < \alpha \le \alpha_5$	$\psi = \frac{1}{F_{post}R}\left[\alpha - \alpha_4 + F_{post}A_0T_{wait} + \frac{1}{2}F_{post}(R - \Delta R)T_{wait}^2\right]$ $\zeta = \zeta_1$
DWM<u>H</u>S	$\alpha_5 < \alpha \le \alpha_6$	$T_{halt} = \frac{1}{F_{post}A_{max}}[\alpha - \alpha_5 + F_{post}A_{max}T_{max}]$
DWMS<u>H</u>	$\alpha > \alpha_6$	$T_{halt} = \frac{\alpha - \alpha_6 + FA_{max}T_{SEAD}}{FA_{max}}$
D<u>H</u>MWS	$\alpha \le \alpha_7$	$\psi = \frac{\alpha}{F_{pre}R}$ $\zeta = \zeta_{base}$
DM<u>H</u>WS	$\alpha_7 < \alpha \le \alpha_8$	$T_{halt} = \frac{1}{F_{pre}A_{max}}[\alpha - \alpha_7 + F_{pre}A_{max}T_{max}]$
DMW<u>H</u>S	$\alpha_8 < \alpha \le \alpha_9$	$T_{halt} = \frac{1}{F_{post}A_{max}}[\alpha - \alpha_8 + F_{post}A_{max}T_{wait}]$
DMWS<u>H</u>	$\alpha > \alpha_9$	$T_{halt} = \frac{1}{FA_{max}}[\alpha - \alpha_9 + FA_{max}T_{SEAD}]$

$$U = 100\, e^{(-K_{distance})(D)} e^{(-K_{losses})(Fractional\_losses)}. \tag{4.29}$$

The values of the constants d and s must be set for a particular theater, since distances of valuable assets from the border vary a good deal, as would U.S. interests. Figure 4.6 illustrates what the result might look like. It uses $K_{distance} = 1/250$, $K_{losses} = 5$. Figure 4.7 shows the same tradeoffs, but in the form of equal-utility curves. These are straight lines because of the assumed exponential form of both factors. Suppose that we consider utilities of 80–100 as very good, 60–80 as tolerable, 40–60 as marginal, and anything less as quite poor. Looking at either Figure 4.6 or 4.7, we see, for example, that 10 percent losses is considered barely tolerable (utility of 60) only if the hold distance is less than 100 km. To do well, the hold distance must be quite short and losses must be small. For example, 5 percent losses and zero hold distance generate a utility of about 90.

Table 4.8

TRANSITION POINTS FOR LEADING-EDGE PROBLEM, INCLUDING LOSSES

Ordering	Threshold	Formula
DWSM	V_1 (at T_{wait})	$F_{pre}(A_0 + RT_{wait})\gamma$
	V_2 (at T_{SEAD})	$F_{post}[A_0 + RT_{SEAD} - ALosses]\gamma$
	V_3 (at T_{max})	$FA_{max}\gamma$
DWMS	V_4 (at T_{wait})	$F_{pre}(A_0 + RT_{wait})\gamma$
	V_5 (at T_{max})	$F_{post}A_{max}\gamma$
	V_6 (at T_{SEAD})	$FA_{max}\gamma$
DMWS	V_7 (at T_{max})	$F_{pre}A_{max}\gamma$
	V_8 (at T_{wait})	$F_{post}A_{max}\gamma$
	V_9 (at T_{SEAD})	$FA_{max}\gamma$

NOTE: The speed thresholds are set at the lower end of discontinuities. V_1, for example, is the lower of the two speeds "at" time T_{wait}. Thus, criteria will be expressed in terms such as If $V > V_1$.

Implementation

To implement this concept, one could use the average daily loss rate from Eq. 4.26 and multiply it by ($T_{SEAD} - T_{wait}$) to estimate the fractional losses as a function of the wait time chosen. Since this is calculated after T_{halt}, we can develop formulas in terms of T_{halt} as shown in Table 4.10.

4.5 SUMMARY INSIGHTS

Accounting for SEAD and wait times leads to a complex set of analytic solutions—a reminder that a closed-form model is not necessarily a simple model. Still, the functional forms of the solutions are in many cases the same as in the simpler cases of Chapter 3. Thus, some insights from the simpler treatments carry over, but it is difficult to infer implications of air-defense issues from staring at equations: Numerical calculations and graphical depiction of results become preferable. This trend will continue as we add further embellishments in subsequent chapters and prepare for exploratory analysis.

Table 4.9

SLOWING-EFFECT HALT TIMES FOR LEADING-EDGE STRATEGY, INCLUDING LOSSES

Ordering	Condition	Halt Time (if limited by slowing effect)[a]
DHWSM	$V \le V_1$	$\frac{1}{R}\left[\frac{V}{F_{pre}\gamma} - (A_0 + \Delta R\, T_{wait})\right]$
DWHSM	$V_1 < V \le V_2$	$\frac{1}{R - \Delta R}\left[\frac{V}{F_{post}\gamma} - A_0\right]$
DWSHM	$V_2 < V \le V_3$	$\frac{V}{FR\gamma} - \frac{A_0 - ALosses}{R}$
DWSMH	$V > V_3$	∞
DHWMS	$V \le V_4$	$\frac{1}{R}\left[\frac{V}{F_{pre}\gamma} - A_0\right]$
DWHMS	$V_4 < V \le V_5$	$\frac{1}{R - \Delta R}\left[\frac{V}{F_{post}\gamma} - (A_0 + \Delta R\, T_{wait})\right]$
DWMHS	$V_5 < V \le V_6$	T_{SEAD}
DWMSH	$V > V_6$	∞
DHMWS	$V \le V_7$	$\frac{1}{R}\left[\frac{V}{F_{pre}\gamma} - A_0\right]$
DMHWS	$V_7 < V \le V_8$	T_{wait}
DMWHS	$V_8 < V \le V_9$	T_{SEAD}
DMWSH	$V > V_9$	∞

[a]If overall attrition is considered, then the halt time and halt distance should be considered to be those calculated for the strategy (in-depth or leading-edge) that minimizes halt distance. See Chapter 3 for discussion.

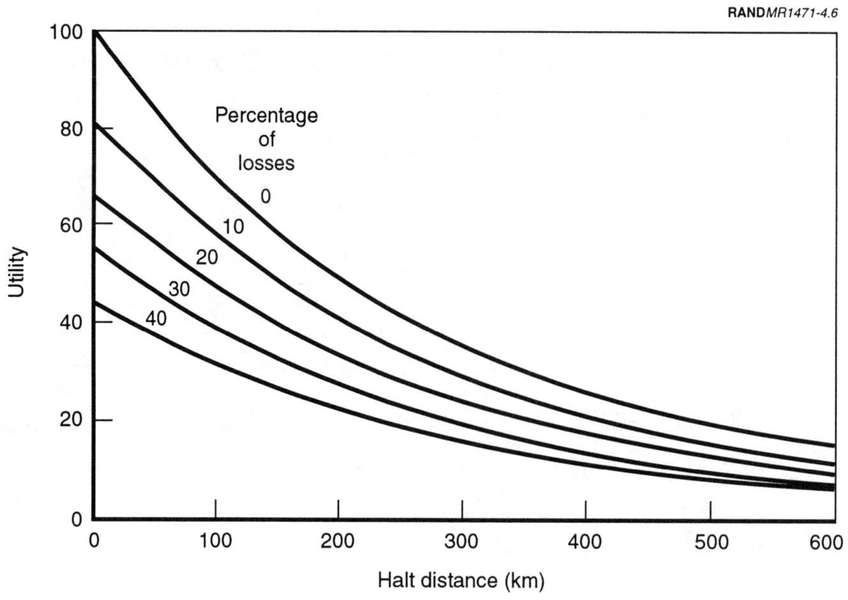

Figure 4.6—A Set of Simple Tradeoff Curves

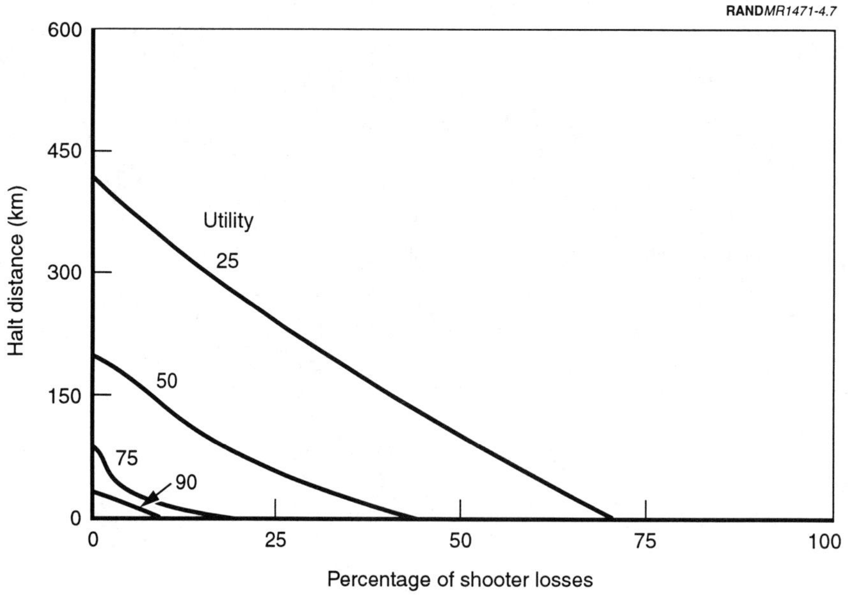

Figure 4.7—Equal-Utility Curves

Table 4.10

CALCULATING FRACTIONAL LOSSES

Condition	A_{halt}	Fractional Losses
$T_{halt} < T_{wait}$	$A_0 + RT_{halt}$	0
$T_{wait} \leq T_{halt} < T_{SEAD}$	$A_0 + RT_{wait} + (R - N_{avg}L_{dailyavg})(T_{halt} - T_{wait})$	$\frac{N_{avg}L_{dailyavg}(T_{halt} - T_{wait})}{A_{halt}}$
$T_{halt} > T_{SEAD}$	$A_0 + RT_{SEAD} - Losses$	$\frac{Losses}{A_{halt}}$

5. GROUND FORCES AT A DEFENSE LINE

5.1 OVERVIEW

This chapter defines easy ways to account for the most important contributions of ground forces in bringing about an early halt in the kind of idealized, capabilities-measuring scenario used in this monograph. The first method suggested is a trivial modification of previous expressions that accounts crudely for attrition caused by "miscellaneous" ground forces able to cause difficulties and modest attrition, but not able to hold ground. We mention it here but do not discuss it further. The more important second method focuses on defense lines, asking under what circumstances such lines could be held.

5.2 GROUND FORCES AS A SMALL SOURCE OF DAILY ATTRITION AND DISRUPTION

If Blue lacks substantial ground forces, it may still have the capacity to cause a modest amount of attrition to advancing forces and, as a result, slow their movement. The slowing of movement rate would be the more important effect in this case, but the attrition could be accounted for approximately by merely introducing an assumed daily rate of losses to the advancing army of b AFVs per day. If one wished to bother with such a correction (I do not in this monograph), it could be reflected by generalizing the composite parameter ζ as follows:[1]

$$\begin{aligned}
&\text{If } T_{halt} \le T_{wait},\ \zeta^1 = \frac{A_0}{R} + \frac{b}{\delta} \\
&\text{If } T_{wait} < T_{halt} \le T_{SEAD},\ \zeta^1 = \frac{A_0}{R - L_{dailyavg} N_{avg}} + \frac{b}{\delta} \qquad (5.1) \\
&\text{If } T_{halt} > T_{SEAD},\ \zeta^1 = \frac{A_0 - \text{Losses}}{R} + \frac{b}{\delta}.
\end{aligned}$$

5.3 GROUND FORCES AT A DEFENSE LINE

Motivations and Concerns

A much more useful and insightful way to represent the effects of ground forces semi-explicitly, and to show how defending ground forces and long-range fires could work together, is to postulate a defense line at which ground forces would attempt to hold. We can then assess whether interdiction forces could reduce the approaching invader forces sufficiently and quickly enough to make such a defense line feasible.

[1] Alternatively, the effect could be represented as an adjustment to δ, but the adjustment term would be time dependent through the number of shooters.

The answer would depend on (1) the defense line's location, (2) the size of the attacking force that the defending force could stop, and (3) the time at which the defending force could be in place.

In more comprehensive war games and simulations such as the Joint Integrated Contingency Model (JICM), such issues are handled automatically and the deployment, maneuver, and employment of ground forces are treated explicitly. In Persian Gulf scenarios, a key issue may turn out to be whether warning time is sufficient to permit U.S. Army and Marine Corps forces to fall in on prepositioned equipment (both land-based and sea-based), and then maneuver to the desired defense lines before the attacker reaches them. In some scenarios, they can do so; in other cases, they must instead maneuver to much deeper defense lines; in still other scenarios, forward-located prepositioned equipment must be abandoned because it would be overrun before it could be used. In the more realistic games and simulations, the effectiveness of the defending ground forces depends not just on force ratio (an inherently ambiguous term), but also on force-to-space considerations and the ability of the attacker to maneuver around the defending units in the particular terrain and defense line, or even to insert unconventional forces behind the defender.

Researchers have devised a number of methods for attempting to represent ground forces crudely. Perhaps the most common amounts to assuming a straightforward attrition battle at the defense line, one governed by standard equations of close combat such as the famous (or infamous) Lanchester equations. Such representations are misleading in the present context because the principal issues are not those of simple head-on-head attrition, but rather of maneuver. Understanding the defensibility of particular defense lines requires in-depth war gaming, preferably informed by professional ground-force officers familiar with the terrain and circumstances.

Moreover, even to represent the attrition battle intelligently (i.e., even if maneuver is ignored), one needs to account for classes of weapons, command and control asymmetries, and the true qualitative distinctions between comparably sized American and third-world units. It is of interest to note that in Desert Storm, a number of M-1/A-1 tanks were hit by Iraqi T-72s, but not killed: not only were the M-1's superior in terms of range and lethality, they also had very low vulnerabilities. If one wants to use straightforward score-based attrition models, then, what scores should be used to represent U.S. and enemy units?[2]

A Modularization That More Fully Respects the Subtleties of Close Combat

With this background, we have chosen to treat ground forces in an unusual way that modularizes the problem without introducing much complexity or trivializing the ground battle by assuming simplistic equations for close combat. The essence of the approach is to recognize that separately conducted war games and simulations can

[2]These issues were researched by Daryl Press and discussed in an interesting debate about lessons learned from Desert Storm in the journal *International Security*. See Biddle (1996, 1997), Press (1997), and Mahnken and Watts (1997). RAND colleague Carl Jones is currently working with the U.S. Army's Concepts Analysis Agency to incorporate modern killer-victim scoreboards, based on weapon-level simulation, into the JICM theater model.

realistically characterize how quickly candidate ground forces could be in place at alternative defense lines (Gritton et al., 2000) and the size of enemy forces that they could be expected to stop. Such a characterization can be specific to a theater, defense line, defense units (indigenous, Army, or Marine Corps), the extent of U.S. air supremacy, and so on. As a result, we can treat the ground-force capabilities as inputs.

Our procedure, then, is as follows:

We consider as inputs the size of the enemy ground force that the defending ground force can deal with effectively at a given defense line and the time at which the defense line can be ready. Interdiction might cause a halt before the attacker reaches that line, but, if it does not, then halt occurs at the defense line if (1) it is manned in time and (2) the attacker's strength has been reduced by the time it reaches the defense line to a level that can be handled by the ground force. If these conditions are not met, the halt time occurs later, when it would result from interdiction alone (or the attacker reaching his objective). Consistent with the purposes of our model, we do not attempt to represent close combat per se.[3] Thus, if ground forces would be overrun, they are not employed. As a result, there is no attrition to the attacker caused by ground forces that it overruns.

A variant of this procedure is instead to solve for the ground-force capability that would be needed to achieve halt at a given defense line, for a particular threat and interdiction capabilities, or to solve for the defense line that could be held for specified levels of threat, interdiction, and ground-force capability. Looking to the former, we can measure the value of interdiction in reducing the requirement for ground forces. The point here is that one has some choices about what to treat as input rather than output.

The Mathematics of the Defense-Line Calculations

With this background, we can now express the approach mathematically. The key inputs are

G: Capability of the ground force to be used at the defense line, as measured by the size of the attacking force (measured in armored fighting vehicles) that it could halt.

D_{line}: The defense line itself (km).

$T_{defense}$: The time (days) at which the defense line can be manned and ready.

D_{line}
G
$T_{defense}$

It now follows that we have some important calculated variables:

[3]Aside from simplifying the model, this is also reasonable. In war games, Blue players are loath to attempt to man a defense line unless they believe it is viable. Real Blue commanders would be no less conservative: if a forward line were too risky, they would consider a deeper alternative or rely upon air interdiction alone. Moreover, if the ground forces are not really attempting to hold a line, but rather to cause delays, then that can be represented by considering smaller values of the movement rate V. One can estimate the magnitude of such delays as well directly (based on war gaming and historical results) as by running existing simulation models of close combat.

ξ': The number of AFVs that must be killed by interdiction if the defense line is to be viable

$$\xi' = \xi - G \qquad (5.2)$$

T_{toline}: The time (days) at which the attacker reaches the defense line. For the in-depth attack strategy, this is

$$T_{toline} = \frac{D_{line}}{V} + Delay \qquad (5.3)$$

$T^{(1)}_{halt}$: The halt time (days) calculated without any ground forces

$T^{(2)}$: The time (days) at which interdiction can reduce the attack size to G; this can be expressed as the time by which interdiction alone would kill ξ' AFVs:

$$T^{(2)} = T^{(1)}_{halt}(\xi') \qquad (5.4)$$

$D^{(1)}$: The halt distance (km) in the absence of ground forces.

$T^{(2)}_{halt}$: The time (days) at which the attacker's forces have been reduced to G, which is equal to $T^{(2)}$ if ground forces are present in time, is given by:

$$T^{(2)}_{halt} = \sqrt{\zeta^2 - 2\psi'} - \zeta. \qquad (5.5)$$

Solutions

The solutions to the halt problem are then given by Table 5.1.

Table 5.1

HALT TIMES AND DISTANCES GIVEN GROUND FORCES AT A DEFENSE LINE

$T^{(1)}_{halt} \le T_{toline}$	$T_{toline} < T_{defense}$	$T^{(2)} > T_{toline}$	Halt Time	Halt Distance
Yes	—[a]	—	$T^{(1)}_{halt}$	$D^{(1)}$
No	Yes	—	$T^{(1)}_{halt}$	$D^{(1)}$
No	—	Yes	$T^{(1)}_{halt}$	$D^{(1)}$
No	No	No	$T^{(2)}$	D_{line}

[a]The — means "any value." Thus, the first line below the header row is read as "If the halt time for interdiction alone is less than the time for the attacker to reach the defense line, then—regardless of the values of T_{toline} and $T^{(2)}_{halt}$—the halt time and halt distance are those based on interdiction alone."

This is equivalent to the if-then-else logic of the following:

$$\begin{aligned}
&\text{If } T_{halt}^{(1)} \le T_{toline}, \text{ then } T_{halt} = T_{halt}^{(1)} \text{ and } D = D^{(1)}.\\
&\text{Else, if } T_{halt}^{(2)} \le T_{toline} \text{ and } T_{halt}^{(2)} \le T_{defense},\\
&\text{then, } T_{halt} = T_{halt}^{(2)} \text{ and } D = D_{line}.\\
&\text{Else, } T_{halt} = T_{halt}^{(1)} \text{ and } D = D^{(1)}.
\end{aligned} \tag{5.6}$$

Figure 5.1 provides an overview of the data flow relating to halt time and halt distance for the two strategies—taking into account the several mechanisms for bringing about a halt, including ground forces at a defense line.

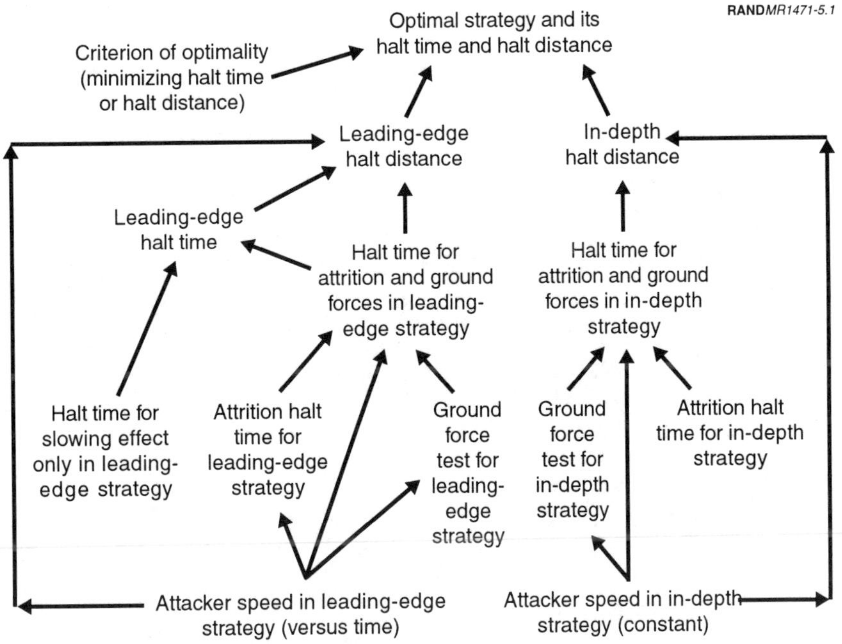

Input Variables (most aggregated versions)

- Threat size
- Threat's basic movement rate
- Threat's maneuver strategy (axes, columns, dispersion)
- Delay due to special strikes by defender
- Defender's buildup (initial shooters, deployment rate, losses to air defense)
- Commitment of shooters to anti-armor mission by phase
- Defender's basic per-shooter-day effectiveness (by strategy)
- Wait time
- SEAD time
- Number of good weapons
- Ground-force line
- Time line is defended
- Capability of ground forces at defense line

Figure 5.1—Overview of Model Flow

As discussed elsewhere (Davis, Gompert, Hillestad, and Johnson, 1998), one should not take such calculations too seriously without extensive uncertainty analysis, including a recognition of stochastic factors. In particular, the United States would ordinarily man a defense line only if it had a rather high confidence that it were viable: "best estimates" would not be good enough. We shall see more of this issue in the last chapter.

6. FACTORS REFLECTING WEAPONS SUPPLY, C^2, C^4ISR, TERRAIN, AND ENEMY MANEUVER TACTICS

6.1 REPRESENTING LIMITED SUPPLIES OF BEST WEAPONS

δ_A
δ_B
N_{Awpns}
ξ_A
α_A

Despite numerous studies noting the high cost effectiveness of buying more high-quality weapons, procurement of the better precision-guided munitions continues to lag and inventories are periodically depleted as the result of contingencies such as that in Kosovo. As a result, real-world halt capabilities are likely to be a good deal lower than would otherwise be possible. Representing the effects of running out of good weapons is easily simulated, but it can also be represented approximately in closed-form models. Assume that the inventory can be approximately represented in terms of two weapon classes, A and B. Each of these has an associated δ (for fixed platform and avionics). Suppose that A-weapons are much superior and will be used first. Suppose further that there are N_{Awpns} A-weapons, which is sufficient to kill ξ_A armored fighting vehicles when the weapons are employed in standard fashion with K_A kills per sortie and S_A sorties per day, each using n_A A-weapons per sortie. That is, ξ_A AFVs can be shooter days of shooters with A-weapons. The mathematical expressions are

$$\delta_A = S_A K_A \tag{6.1}$$

$$\xi_A = [N_{Awpns}/(Frac)(n_A)]K_A \tag{6.2}$$

$$\alpha_A = \xi_A/\delta_A = [N_{Awpns}/(Frac)(n_A)]K_A, \tag{6.3}$$

where Frac is the fraction of a sortie's weapons that are used (the remainder return to base).

Figure 6.1 shows these relationships hierarchically, making the point visually that we have a choice of levels of detail when discussing the exhaustion-effect problem.

This expression of good-weapon inventory in terms of shooter days of supply is analogous to measures long used in other domains. For example, theater-level ground-force calculations often assume that the ground forces have some specified number of days of supply.

Calculating Exhaustion Time

To reflect the limited supply of A-weapons, we can calculate an "exhaustion time," T_{exh} at which point the defender would run out of A-weapons and drop in effectiveness to δ_B. We can do this simply by using the halt-problem formulas already derived in Chapter 4 (assuming no constraint on the number of good weapons), but using α_A or ξ_A as the input, rather than α. Or we may use the formulas that follow, but

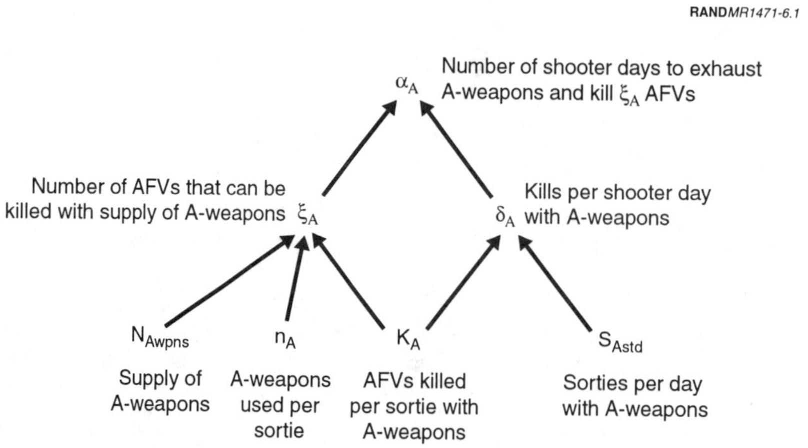

Figure 6.1—Multiresolution Relationship of Variables for Type-A Weapons

substitute infinite exhaustion time and use α_A for α. The resulting value of T_{exh} may be smaller, the same, or greater than the ultimate halt time.

Treating Exhaustion Time T_{exh} as an Exogenous Input

In some computer languages, it is relatively tedious to implement the prescription given above for calculating T_{exh}. An alternative is to treat T_{exh} as an independent input. Because of complicated interactions, however, the observed behavior of the estimated halt time and halt distance will show confusing and nonsensical behavior for small values of T_{exh} or large values of A_0. We prefer to calculate T_{exh} using some combination of the inputs suggested in Eqs. (6.1)–(6.3). The most meaningful to most users will probably be N_{Awpns}, n_A, and S_A. Here S_A should be seen as the *nominal* sortie rate of shooters with A-weapons. The actual sortie rate may be reduced in WMD situations, as discussed in earlier chapters.

6.2 CALCULATING HALT TIME AND HALT DISTANCE WITH LIMITED BEST WEAPONS

An Approximation to Reduce Dimensionality

We are now ready to find solutions for T_{halt}, but to avoid the potential combinatorial explosion we introduce approximations. Consider that there exist 120 (i.e., 5!) orderings of D-Day, T_{wait}, T_{SEAD}, T_{max}, and T_{exh}. Fortunately, many seldom or never make sense. In particular, $T_{wait} \le T_{SEAD}$, and both T_{wait} and T_{SEAD} exceed 0 (i.e., they occur after D-Day, even if by a tiny amount). Furthermore, there is usually little point in working out formulas for instances in which $T_{exh} < T_{wait}$. Doing so would add a great deal of additional complexity to cover cases that are seldom of interest.[1]

[1]Exhaustion could occur before the wait time if, for example, there were a small number of exceptionally effective weapons usable on stealthy aircraft used to attack moving columns from the outset. In

In what follows, we assume that the calculated value of T_{exh} has been artificially constrained to be no less than T_{wait}.

Identifying the "Chunks": The Cases for Which Separate Formulas Are Needed

Having constrained away the cases in which exhaustion occurs prior to the wait time, the residual combinations for which we need to develop formulas are, with the notation D, W, S, M, and E for D-Day, T_{wait}, T_{SEAD}, T_{max}, $T_{exhaust}$, respectively:

DWSME

DWSEM

DWMSE

DWMES

DWEMS

DWESM

DMWSE

DMWES

MDWSE

MDWES

For each of these, the formulas may differ depending on the number of targets to be killed. Or, equivalently, the formulas will differ depending on where the halt time turns out to be relative to the other times. For the eight orderings that begin with D, the halt time H may occur in any of five slots (after D, or after the successive times). For the two orderings that begin with M, there are only four slots for H. It follows that there are 48 cases.

Solutions for the In-Depth Strategy

The results for the in-depth strategy are shown in Tables 6.1–6.2.[2]

For compactness we use abbreviations. The first column in Table 6.1 shows the order of the critical input times and is to be interpreted, for example, as: DWSME means $D \le T_{wait} \le T_{SEAD} \le T_{max} \le T_{exh}$.

The second column of Table 6.1 gives the name of the threshold and indicates where it occurs, with, for example, "(at W)" meaning "at T_{wait}." This is unambiguous for

---

that instance, it is best to do side calculations to estimate T_{exh} and use it as an input—but taking care not to plot results for excessively large values of A_0.

[2]These do *not* include the usually-marginal effect of small harassing ground forces denoted by the constant daily attrition b mentioned in Chapter 5. If one wants to include those effects, then the formulas in Tables 6.1 and 6.2 should be reworked with A_0 and A_{max} replaced everywhere by primed versions, where the prime versions are the originals plus b/δ. The leading-edge strategy's formulas (Tables 6.3–6.4) do not change, since we cannot reasonably assume that the ground-force effects in question could be focused on the leading edge of the attack.

Table 6.1

THRESHOLDS FOR IN-DEPTH STRATEGY, INCLUDING EXHAUSTION OF GOOD WEAPONS

Ordering[a]	Threshold[b]	Value of Threshold (Shooter Days)
DWSME	α_1 (at W)	$F_{pre}A_0T_{wait} + \frac{1}{2}F_{pre}RT_{wait}^2$
	α_2 (at S)	$\alpha_1 + F_{post}A_0(T_{SEAD} - T_{wait}) + \frac{1}{2}F_{post}(R - \Delta R)(T_{SEAD}^2 - T_{wait}^2)$
	α_3 (at M)	$\alpha_2 + F(A_0 - ALosses)(T_{max} - T_{SEAD}) + \frac{1}{2}FR(T_{max}^2 - T_{SEAD}^2)$
	α_4 (at E)	$\alpha_3 + FA_{max}(T_{exh} - T_{max})$
DWSEM	α_5 (at W)	$F_{pre}A_0T_{wait} + \frac{1}{2}F_{pre}RT_{wait}^2$
	α_6 (at S)	$\alpha_5 + F_{post}A_0(T_{SEAD} - T_{wait}) + \frac{1}{2}F_{post}(R - \Delta R)(T_{SEAD}^2 - T_{wait}^2)$
	α_7 (at E)	$\alpha_6 + F(A_0 - ALosses)(T_{exh} - T_{SEAD}) + \frac{1}{2}FR(T_{exh}^2 - T_{SEAD}^2)$
	α_8 (at M)	$\alpha_7 + \frac{\delta_B}{\delta}F(A_0 - ALosses)(T_{max} - T_{exh}) + \frac{1}{2}\frac{\delta_B}{\delta}FR(T_{max}^2 - T_{exh}^2)$
DWMSE	α_9 (at W)	$F_{pre}A_0T_{wait} + \frac{1}{2}F_{pre}RT_{wait}^2$
	α_{10} (at M)	$\alpha_9 + F_{post}A_0(T_{max} - T_{wait}) + \frac{1}{2}F_{post}(R - \Delta R)(T_{max}^2 - T_{wait}^2)$
	α_{11} (at S)	$\alpha_{10} + F_{post}A_{max}(T_{SEAD} - T_{max})$
	α_{12} (at E)	$\alpha_{11} + FA_{max}(T_{exh} - T_{SEAD})$
DWMES	α_{13} (at W)	$F_{pre}A_0T_{wait} + \frac{1}{2}F_{pre}RT_{wait}^2$
	α_{14} (at M)	$\alpha_{13} + F_{post}A_0(T_{max} - T_{wait}) + \frac{1}{2}F_{post}(R - \Delta R)(T_{max}^2 - T_{wait}^2)$
	α_{15} (at E)	$\alpha_{14} + F_{post}A_{max}(T_{exh} - T_{max})$
	α_{16} (at S)	$\alpha_{15} + \frac{\delta_B}{\delta}F_{post}A_{max}(T_{SEAD} - T_{exh})$
DWEMS	α_{16b} (at W)	$F_{pre}A_0T_{wait} + \frac{1}{2}F_{pre}RT_{wait}^2$
	α_{16c} (at E)	$\alpha_{16b} + F_{post}A_0(T_{exh} - T_{wait}) + \frac{1}{2}F_{post}(R - \Delta R)(T_{exh}^2 - T_{wait}^2)$
	α_{16d} (at M)	$\alpha_{16c} + \frac{\delta_B}{\delta}F_{post}A_0(T_{max} - T_{exh}) + \frac{1}{2}\frac{\delta_B}{\delta}F_{post}(R - \Delta R)(T_{max}^2 - T_{exh}^2)$
	α_{16e} (at S)	$\alpha_{16d} + \frac{\delta_B}{\delta}F_{post}A_{max}(T_{SEAD} - T_{max})$

Table 6.1 (continued)

Ordering[a]	Threshold[b]	Value of Threshold (Shooter Days)
DWESM	α_{16f} (at W)	$F_{pre}A_0T_{wait} + \frac{1}{2}F_{pre}RT_{wait}^2$
	α_{16g} (at E)	$\alpha_{16f} + F_{post}A_0(T_{exh} - T_{wait}) + \frac{1}{2}F_{post}(R - \Delta R)(T_{exh}^2 - T_{wait}^2)$
	α_{16h} (at S)	$\alpha_{16g} + \frac{\delta_B}{\delta}F_{post}A_0(T_{SEAD} - T_{exh}) + \frac{1}{2}\frac{\delta_B}{\delta}F_{post}(R - \Delta R)(T_{SEAD}^2 - T_{exh}^2)$
	α_{16i} (at M)	$\alpha_{16h} + \frac{\delta_B}{\delta}F(A_0 - ALosses)(T_{max} - T_{SEAD}) + \frac{\delta_B}{2\delta}FR(T_{max}^2 - T_{SEAD}^2)$
DMWSE	α_{17} (at M)	$F_{pre}A_0T_{wait} + \frac{1}{2}F_{pre}RT_{wait}^2$
	α_{18} (at W)	$\alpha_{17} + F_{pre}A_{max}(T_{wait} - T_{max})$
	α_{19} (at S)	$\alpha_{18} + F_{post}A_{max}(T_{SEAD} - T_{wait})$
	α_{20} (at E)	$\alpha_{19} + FA_{max}(T_{exh} - T_{SEAD})$
DMWES	α_{21} (at M)	$F_{pre}A_0T_{wait} + \frac{1}{2}F_{pre}RT_{wait}^2$
	α_{22} (at W)	$\alpha_{21} + F_{pre}A_{max}(T_{wait} - T_{max})$
	α_{23} (at E)	$\alpha_{22} + F_{post}A_{max}(T_{exh} - T_{wait})$
	α_{24} (at S)	$\alpha_{23} + \frac{\delta_B}{\delta}F_{post}A_{max}(T_{SEAD} - T_{exh})$

[a]The abbreviations are D for D-Day, W for T_{wait}, S for T_{SEAD}, M for T_{max}, and E for T_{exh}.

[b]The formulas cover the cases in which the exhaustion time exceeds the wait time. For lesser exhaustion times, the problem can be solved approximately by setting δ to δ_B and using infinite T_{exh}.

Table 6.1 (the in-depth strategy's thresholds) because there are no discontinuities. When implementing the formulas, the blocks shown in the first column are natural modules.

In Table 6.2, the first column shows the input-determined case in terms of the thresholds established in Table 6.1. The second column is useful in understanding the formulas. It shows where the halt time occurs for the condition specified in the first column. It does this by using the same blocks (e.g., DWSME) as in Table 6.1, but by inserting H to indicate where the halt occurs. In implementing the formulas, the conditions of the first column may be expressed in if-then-else terms within each block such as WSME.

The third column of 6.2 provides *either* the values of ψ and ζ needed in the quadratic formula solution,

$$T_{halt} = \sqrt{\zeta^2 + 2\psi} - \zeta$$

Table 6.2

SOLUTIONS FOR IN-DEPTH STRATEGY, INCLUDING WEAPON EXHAUSTION EFFECTS (b = 0)

Case[a]	Ordering[b]	Value of Threshold (Shooter Days Achieved)[c]
$\alpha \le \alpha_1$	$\mathrm{D\underline{H}WSME}$	$\psi = \dfrac{\alpha}{F_{pre}R}$ $\zeta = \zeta_{base}$
$\alpha_1 < \alpha < \alpha\alpha$	$\mathrm{DW\underline{H}SME}$	$\psi = \dfrac{1}{F_{post}R}\left[\alpha - \alpha_1 + F_{post}A_0T_{wait} + \dfrac{1}{2}F_{post}(R - L_{dailyavg}N_{avg})T_{wait}^2\right]$ $\zeta = \zeta_1$
$\alpha_2 \le \alpha < \alpha_3$	$\mathrm{DWS\underline{H}ME}$	$\psi = \dfrac{1}{FR}\left[\alpha - \alpha_2 + F_{post}A_0T_{SEAD} + \dfrac{1}{2}F_{post}(R - L_{dailyavg}N_{avg})T_{SEAD}^2\right]$ $\zeta = \zeta_2$
$\alpha_3 \le \alpha \le \alpha_4$	$\mathrm{DWSM\underline{H}E}$	$T_{halt} = \dfrac{1}{FA_{max}}[\alpha - \alpha_3 + FA_{max}T_{max}]$
$\alpha > \alpha_4$	$\mathrm{DWSME\underline{H}}$	$T_{halt} = \dfrac{1}{\frac{\delta_B}{\delta}FA_{max}}\left[\alpha - \alpha_4 + \dfrac{\delta_B}{\delta}FA_{max}T_{exh}\right]$
$\alpha \le \alpha_5$	$\mathrm{D\underline{H}WSEM}$	$\psi = \dfrac{\alpha}{F_{pre}R}$ $\zeta = \zeta_{base}$
$\alpha_5 < \alpha \le \alpha_6$	$\mathrm{DW\underline{H}SEM}$	$\psi = \dfrac{1}{F_{post}R}\left[\alpha - \alpha_5 + F_{post}A_0T_{wait} + \dfrac{1}{2}F_{post}(R - L_{dailyavg}N_{avg})T_{wait}^2\right]$ $\zeta = \zeta_1$
$\alpha_6 < \alpha \le \alpha_7$	$\mathrm{DWS\underline{H}EM}$	$\psi = \dfrac{1}{FR}\left[\alpha - \alpha_6 + F(A_0 - \text{Losses})T_{SEAD} + \dfrac{1}{2}FRT_{SEAD}^2\right]$ $\zeta = \zeta_2$
$\alpha_7 < \alpha \le \alpha_8$	$\mathrm{DWSE\underline{H}M}$	$\psi = \dfrac{1}{\frac{\delta_B}{\delta}FR}\left[\alpha - \alpha_7 + \dfrac{\delta_B}{\delta}F(A_0 - \text{Losses})T_{exh} + \dfrac{1}{2}\dfrac{\delta_B}{\delta}FRT_{exh}^2\right]$ $\zeta = \zeta_2$
$\alpha > \alpha_8$	$\mathrm{DWSEM\underline{H}}$	$T_{halt} = \dfrac{1}{\frac{\delta_B}{\delta}FA_{max}}\left[\alpha - \alpha_8 + \dfrac{\delta_B}{\delta}FA_{max}T_{max}\right]$
$\alpha \le \alpha_9$	$\mathrm{D\underline{H}WMSE}$	$\psi = \dfrac{\alpha}{F_{pre}R}$ $\zeta = \zeta_{base}$
$\alpha_9 < \alpha \le \alpha_{10}$	$\mathrm{DW\underline{H}MSE}$	$\psi = \dfrac{1}{F_{post}R}\left[\alpha - \alpha_9 + F_{post}A_0T_{wait} + \dfrac{1}{2}F_{post}(R - L_{dailyavg}N_{avg})T_{wait}^2\right]$ $\zeta = \zeta_1$
$\alpha_{10} < \alpha \le \alpha_{11}$	$\mathrm{DWM\underline{H}SE}$	$T_{halt} = \dfrac{1}{F_{post}A_{max}}[\alpha - \alpha_{10} + F_{post}A_{max}T_{max}]$
$\alpha_{11} < \alpha \le \alpha_{12}$	$\mathrm{DWMS\underline{H}E}$	$T_{halt} = \dfrac{1}{FA_{max}}[\alpha - \alpha_{11} + FA_{max}T_{SEAD}]$

Table 6.2 (continued)

Case	Ordering	Value of Threshold (Shooter Days Achieved)
$\alpha > \alpha_{12}$	DWMSE<u>H</u>	$T_{halt} = \frac{1}{\frac{\delta_B}{\delta} FA_{max}}\left[\alpha - \alpha_{12} + \frac{\delta_B}{\delta} FA_{max} T_{exh}\right]$
$\alpha \leq \alpha_{13}$	D<u>H</u>WMES	$\psi = \frac{\alpha}{F_{pre}R}$ $\zeta = \zeta_{base}$
$\alpha_{13} < \alpha \leq_{14}$	DW<u>H</u>MES	$\psi = \frac{1}{F_{post}R}\left[\alpha - \alpha_{13} + F_{post}A_0 T_{wait} + \frac{1}{2} F_{post}(R - L_{dailyavg}N_{avg})T_{wait}^2\right]$ $\zeta = \zeta_1$
$\alpha_{14} < \alpha \leq \alpha_{15}$	DWM<u>H</u>ES	$T_{halt} = \frac{1}{F_{post}A_{max}}[\alpha - \alpha_{14} + F_{post}A_{max}T_{max}]$
$\alpha_{15} < \alpha \leq \alpha_{16}$	DWME<u>H</u>S	$T_{halt} = \frac{1}{\frac{\delta_B}{\delta} F_{post}A_{max}}\left[\alpha - \alpha_{15} + \frac{\delta_B}{\delta} F_{post}A_{max} T_{exh}\right]$
$\alpha > \alpha_{16}$	DWMES<u>H</u>	$T_{halt} = \frac{1}{\frac{\delta_B}{\delta} FA_{max}}\left[\alpha - \alpha_{16} + \frac{\delta_B}{\delta} FA_{max} T_{SEAD}\right]$
$\alpha \leq \alpha_{16b}$	D<u>H</u>WEMS	$\psi = \frac{\alpha}{F_{pre}R}$ $\zeta = \zeta_{base}$
$\alpha_{16b} < \alpha \leq \alpha_{16c}$	DW<u>H</u>EMS	$\psi = \frac{1}{F_{post}R}\left[\alpha - \alpha_{16b} + F_{post}A_0 T_{wait} + \frac{1}{2} F_{post}(R - L_{dailyavg}N_{avg})T_{wait}^2\right]$ $\zeta = \zeta_1$
$\alpha_{16c} < \alpha \leq \alpha_{16d}$	DWE<u>H</u>MS	$\psi = \frac{1}{\frac{\delta_B}{\delta} F_{post}R}\left[\alpha - \alpha_{16c} + \frac{\delta_B}{\delta} F_{post}A_0 T_{exh} + \frac{1}{2}\frac{\delta_B}{\delta} F_{post}(R - L_{dailyavg}N_{avg})T_{exh}^2\right]$ $\zeta = \zeta_1$
$\alpha_{16d} < \alpha \leq \alpha_{16e}$	DWEM<u>H</u>S	$T_{halt} = \frac{1}{\frac{\delta_B}{\delta} F_{post}A_{max}}\left[\alpha - \alpha_{16d} + \frac{\delta_B}{\delta} F_{post}A_{max} T_{max}\right]$
$\alpha > \alpha_{16e}$	DWEMS<u>H</u>	$T_{halt} = \frac{1}{\frac{\delta_B}{\delta} FA_{max}}\left[\alpha - \alpha_{16e} + \frac{\delta_B}{\delta} FA_{max} T_{SEAD}\right]$ $\zeta = \frac{A_0 - Losses}{R}$
$\alpha \leq \alpha_{16f}$	D<u>H</u>WESM	$\psi = \frac{\alpha}{F_{pre}R}$ $\zeta = \zeta_{base}$
$\alpha_{16f} < \alpha \leq \alpha_{16g}$	DW<u>H</u>ESM	$\psi = \frac{1}{F_{post}R}\left[\alpha - \alpha_{16f} + F_{post}A_0 T_{wait} + \frac{1}{2} F_{post}(R - L_{dailyavg}N_{avg})T_{wait}^2\right]$ $\zeta = \zeta_1$

Table 6.2 (continued)

Case	Ordering	Value of Threshold (Shooter Days Achieved)
$\alpha_{16g} < \alpha \le \alpha_{16h}$	DWEHSM	$\psi = \frac{1}{\frac{\delta_B}{\delta} F_{post} R}\left[\alpha - \alpha_{16g} + \frac{\delta_B}{\delta} F_{post} A_0 T_{exh} + \frac{1}{2}\frac{\delta_B}{\delta} F_{post}(R - L_{dailyavg} N_{avg}) T_{exh}^2\right]$ $\zeta = \zeta_1$
$\alpha_{16h} < \alpha \le \alpha_{16i}$	DWESHM	$\psi = \frac{1}{\frac{\delta_B}{\delta} FR}\left[\alpha - \alpha_{16h} + \frac{\delta_B}{\delta} F(A_0 - Losses) T_{SEAD} + \frac{1}{2}\frac{\delta_B}{\delta} FRT_{SEAD}^2\right]$ $\zeta = \frac{A_0 - Losses}{R}$ $\zeta = \zeta_2$
$\alpha > \alpha_{16i}$	DWESMH	$T_{halt} = \frac{1}{\frac{\delta_B}{\delta} FA_{max}}\left[\alpha - \alpha_{16i} + \frac{\delta_B}{\delta} FA_{max} T_{max}\right]$ $\zeta = \zeta_2$
$\alpha \le \alpha_{17}$	DHMWSE	$\psi = \frac{\alpha}{F_{pre} R}$ $\zeta = \zeta_{base}$
$\alpha_{17} < \alpha \le \alpha_{18}$	DMHWSE	$T_{halt} = \frac{\alpha}{F_{pre} A_{max}}[\alpha - \alpha_{17} + F_{pre} A_{max} T_{max}]$
$\alpha_{18} < \alpha \le \alpha_{19}$	DMWHSE	$T_{halt} = \frac{1}{F_{post} A_{max}}[\alpha - \alpha_{18} + F_{post} A_{max} T_{wait}]$ $\zeta = \zeta_1$
$\alpha_{19} < \alpha \le \alpha_{20}$	DMWSHE	$T_{halt} = \frac{1}{FA_{max}}[\alpha - \alpha_{19} + FA_{max} T_{SEAD}]$
$\alpha > \alpha_{20}$	DMWSEH	$T_{halt} = \frac{1}{\frac{\delta_B}{\delta} FA_{max}}\left[\alpha - \alpha 20 + \frac{\delta_B}{\delta} FA_{max} T_{exh}\right]$
$\alpha \le \alpha_{21}$	DHMWES	$\psi = \frac{\alpha}{F_{pre} R}$ $\zeta = \zeta_{base}$
$\alpha_{21} < \alpha \le \alpha_{22}$	DMHWES	$T_{halt} = \frac{1}{F_{pre} A_{max}}[\alpha - \alpha_{21} + F_{pre} A_{max} T_{max}]$
$\alpha_{22} < \alpha \le \alpha_{23}$	DMWHES	$T_{halt} = \frac{1}{F_{post} A_{max}}[\alpha - \alpha_{22} + F_{post} A_{max} T_{wait}]$
$\alpha_{23} < \alpha \le \alpha_{24}$	DMWEHS	$T_{halt} = \frac{1}{\frac{\delta_B}{\delta} F_{post} A_{max}}\left[\alpha - \alpha_{23} + \frac{\delta_B}{\delta} F_{post} A_{max} T_{exh}\right]$
$\alpha > \alpha_{24}$	DMWESH	$T_{halt} = \frac{1}{\frac{\delta_B}{\delta} FA_{max}}\left[\alpha - \alpha_{24} + \frac{\delta_B}{\delta} FA_{max} T_{SEAD}\right]$
$\alpha \le \alpha_{25}$	MDHWSE	$T_{halt} = \frac{\alpha}{F_{pre} A_{max}}$

Table 6.2 (continued)

Case	Ordering	Value of Threshold (Shooter Days Achieved)
$\alpha_{25} < \alpha \le \alpha_{26}$	MDWHSE	$T_{halt} = \frac{1}{F_{post}A_{max}}[\alpha - \alpha_{25} + F_{post}A_{max}T_{wait}]$
$\alpha_{26} < \alpha \le \alpha_{27}$	MDWSHE	$T_{halt} = \frac{1}{FA_{max}}[\alpha - \alpha_{26} + FA_{max}T_{SEAD}]$
$\alpha > \alpha_{27}$	MDWSEH	$T_{halt} = \frac{1}{\frac{\delta_B}{\delta}FA_{max}}\left[\alpha - \alpha_{27} + \frac{\delta_B}{\delta}FA_{max}T_{exh}\right]$
$\alpha \le \alpha_{28}$	MDHWES	$T_{halt} = \frac{\alpha}{F_{pre}A_{max}}$
$\alpha_{28} < \alpha \le \alpha_{29}$	MDWHES	$T_{halt} = \frac{1}{F_{post}A_{max}}[\alpha - \alpha_{28} + F_{post}A_{max}T_{wait}]$
$\alpha_{29} < \alpha \le \alpha_{30}$	MDWEHS	$T_{halt} = \frac{1}{\frac{\delta_B}{\delta}F_{post}A_{max}}\left[\alpha - \alpha_{29} + \frac{\delta_B}{\delta}F_{post}A_{max}T_{exh}\right]$
$\alpha > \alpha_{30}$	MDWESH	$T_{halt} = \frac{1}{\frac{\delta_B}{\delta}FA_{max}}\left[\alpha - \alpha_{30} + \frac{\delta_B}{\delta}FA_{max}T_{SEAD}\right]$

[a]The abbreviations are D for D-Day, W for T_{wait}, S for T_{SEAD}, M for T_{max}, and E for T_{exh}.

[b]Item underscored indicates where halt occurs with respect to the various thresholds. Thus, a notation such as M H S means that halt occurs between T_{max} and T_{SEAD}.

[c]Formulas assume that the exhaustion time must not be less than the wait time. If it is, then the problem can be solved approximately by setting δ to δ_B and using infinite T_{exh}.

or, for cases in which the halt time exceeds the time at which the theater capacity is reached, the explicit formula for T_{halt}. The value of ζ also depends on case:

$$\begin{aligned} \zeta &= \zeta_2 = \frac{A_0 - \text{Losses}}{R} \quad \text{if } T_{halt} \ge T_{SEAD} \\ \zeta &= \zeta_1 = \frac{A_0}{R - L_{dailylosses}} \quad \text{if } T_{wait} \le T_{halt} < T_{SEAD} \\ \zeta &= \zeta_{base} = \frac{A_0}{R} \quad \text{if } T_{halt} < T_{wait}. \end{aligned} \tag{6.4}$$

The value of ζ is indicated explicitly in the third column when it includes the Losses term. In other cases, it is simply A_0/R.

Solutions for the Slowing Effect of the Leading-Edge Strategy

The solutions for the leading-edge strategy involve a number of mathematical subtleties caused by the exhaustion of weapons.

In contrast to the case of the in-depth strategy, the relevant functions have sharp discontinuities. These can be confusing and care is needed to evaluate some of the variables at the "proper side" of the discontinuities. Furthermore, the ability of the interdiction force to slow the attacker is not a monotonic function of time. Instead, it can rise, drop, and then rise again, depending on the order of events. This is illustrated in Figure 6.2, which shows the slowing effect, Δ (t), versus time for the various cases. The critical thresholds are indicated in the figure; some of them occur at discontinuities (not mere kinks), so it becomes necessary to distinguish between values at the different ends of the discontinuous jumps.

Because of these and other complexities, the solutions are provided in Appendix E.

6.3 REFLECTING COMMAND AND CONTROL AND OTHER EFFECTS, SUCH AS THOSE OF TERRAIN AND MANEUVER TACTICS

The models described in this monograph are not intended to represent the entities of command and control systems, the details of ground-force maneuver, terrain, or other aspects of combat. However, all of these are important in a given war and they should be accounted for one way or another in exploratory analysis, even if highly aggregated. We suggest the following methods, which are a great deal better than nothing. It is appropriate here to note the caution that to omit an effect altogether is implicitly to assume that the effect is zero.

Command-Control Gain-Competence Time

Blue's interdiction effectiveness would likely be much smaller than assumed in standard DoD studies if, as of D-Day, Blue's command and control processes had not yet been spun up or tuned. This could occur if, for example:

- The sensors and command-control systems available are too few to deal effectively with large numbers of fast-moving targets and shooters
- The individuals working the systems are not familiar with them, the command's procedures, or regional details
- The individuals have not worked with each other previously
- The command's initial command-control procedures are inefficient.

None of these possibilities is merely hypothetical.[3] To the contrary, they represent the normal situation when a command is hastily convened, deployed, and employed without extensive preparation beforehand. In today's Southwest Asia, the United States enjoys the benefits of a mature theater, mature command system, mature operational planning, and forward presence. That cannot be assumed for crises some years in the future.

In the EXHALT model, we highlight this problem by assuming that per-day shooter effectiveness (a combination of sortie rate and kills per sortie—or shot, in the case of missiles) starts much lower than the normal planning factors and improves over a period that we call the gain-competence time, starting at either strategic or tactical warning. As shown elsewhere (Davis, Bigelow, and McEver, 1999), this effect can readily preclude an *early* halt if the initial competence level is not high or if the gain-competence time is large.

---

[3]Although usually ignored, such effects were discussed and even estimated in the mid-1990s DoD Deep Attack Weapons Mix Study (DAWMS). An empirical base for such estimates is sorely needed.

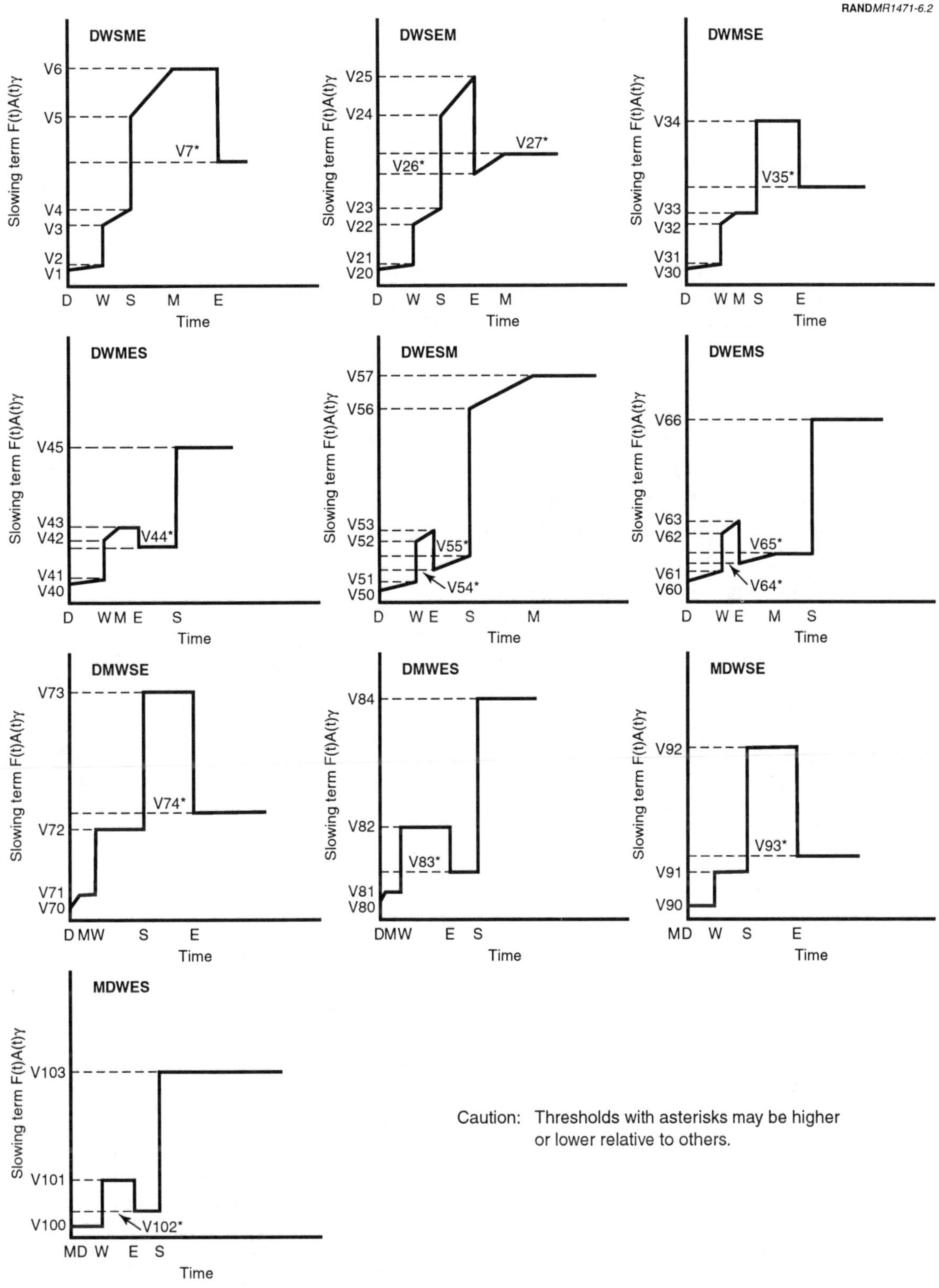

Figure 6.2—Slowing Effect Versus Time for Several Cases of Leading-Edge Attack

Such considerations suggest a priority on rapid, adaptive joint command and control, as emphasized by General Larry Welch of the Institute for Defense Analyses, various Defense Boards (Defense Science Board, 1998), and ourselves (e.g., Davis, Bigelow, and McEver, 1999).

Problems with Early C4ISR

Another command and control problem that is highlighted parametrically in EXHALT is the potential inability to use key sensors effectively early in the conflict. In the future, enemy forces may have long-range surface-to-air missiles (SAMs) that would endanger high-cross-section sensor platforms such as the Joint Surveillance [and] Target Attack Radar System (J-STARS) or unstealthy unmanned aerial vehicles (UAVs). Until those SAMs were suppressed, targeting would be severely hampered. Corrective measures could include satellite systems (e.g., a future version of the Discoverer II program that was canceled by Congress in 2000); stealthy, long-endurance, high-altitude aircraft or UAVs; or special ground units. Today, these are unnecessary, but they could be limiting factors in the future—even if the United States could deliver weapons safely, either from stealthy platforms at close range or from less stealthy platforms from standoff range.

Reflecting Early C2 and ISR Problems

In using the model described in this monograph, which we have implemented as the EXHALT-CF program, users can represent the potential problems with early command-control and early intelligence, surveillance, and reconnaissance (ISR), by "tricking the model"; i.e., by merely reinterpreting what they mean by T_{wait}, T_{SEAD}, F_{pre}, and F_{post}. Mathematically, the model is indifferent to what these parameters mean physically. Table 6.3 suggests an approach.

Effects of C2, ISR, Terrain, and Maneuver Tactics on Shooter Effectiveness

As discussed elsewhere (see Davis, Bigelow, and McEver, 2000a, and Defense Science Board, 1998), the per-sortie or per-shot effectiveness of shooters can vary a great deal—*even by orders of magnitude*—depending on details of terrain, maneuver tactics (notably the spacing between AFVs and the fraction of the time during which armored targets are on the road and visible), the time between the last targeting information provided to the weapon and the moment of impact, and the weapon's footprint. The desert environment in Kuwait and Saudi Arabia greatly mitigates these issues, but even there they can be substantial. In particular, some weapons lose much of their effectiveness when the attacker disperses, or when the "time from last weapon update" (a sensitive function of C4ISR, including processes) is large. Others do not. The United States should plan to have an appropriate mix of area and one-on-one weapons, which mitigates the problem and constrains the enemy's tactics.

If users of this monograph's model wish to reflect some of these effects explicitly, albeit approximately, rough scaling formulas for doing so are provided in Davis, Bigelow, and McEver (2000a). These modify the value of per-sortie or per-shot effectiveness depending on the circumstances. More refined assessments require detailed

Table 6.3

A MECHANISM FOR REPRESENTING TIME DELAYS IN ACHIEVING GOOD C^2 AND ISR

Parameters	Usual Interpretation	Revised Interpretation to Represent Limitations of C^2 and ISR Early in Conflict
T_{wait}, F_{pre}, F_{post}	Time when vulnerable shooters are first committed; fraction of shooters employed before and after that time	Time when C^2 and ISR are sufficiently good to permit employment *and* air defenses are suppressed enough to use a portion of vulnerable shooters; fraction of shooters that can then be employed before and after that time
T_{SEAD}, F	Time when all shooters can be committed; fraction of shooters employed after that against moving armored targets	Time when C^2 and ISR are fully effective *and* air defenses are fully suppressed; fraction of shooters employed at that point against moving armored targets

NOTE: Some readers may prefer to use the acronym C^4ISR to cover all of command, control, communications, computing, intelligence, surveillance, and reconnaissance. If so, they can reinterpret the material in this table accordingly.

modeling of particular weapon systems in the particular environment.[4] Users should be cautious in assuming that the effects can be reflected by merely adjusting normal planning factors by, say, 25 or 50 percent, as is commonly done in sensitivity analysis that is not adequately supported by an empirical base.

Finally, we note that in unpublished companion work we have used the EXHALT simulation to represent some of these effects, notably the weapons and weapons-mix effects highlighted in the Ochmanek study (see previous footnote).

---

[4]Much of our work on such matters draws on the extensive research of our colleagues Randall Steeb, John Matsumura, and Tom Herbert. For an interesting summary of that research see Matsumura, Steeb, Gordon, Glenn, Herbert, and Steinberg (2000). Some of that work is reflected also in Defense Science Board (1998) and a variety of publications for the U.S. Army. Our colleague David Ochmanek also led a recent study on interdiction for the Office of the Secretary of Defense and Joint Staff in which some of these issues were explored in considerable depth—drawing on both high-resolution modeling at RAND and a range of data and insights from the operational community.

7. DEALING WITH RISK AND UNCERTAINTY

7.1 PURPOSE OF CHAPTER

Prior chapters have described underlying theory and a set of increasingly complex models. This chapter shifts to discussion of risk and uncertainty and how to use the models to analyze risk using the methods of exploratory analysis (Davis, 2001a; Davis and Hillestad, forthcoming). We use the implementation of EXHALT-CF in Analytica. We illustrate output displays and experimental designs for exploring uncertainty with both parametric and probabilistic methods. Chapter 8 discusses results of some related analysis.

7.2 RISK AND UNCERTAINTY FOR THE EARLY-HALT PROBLEM

Reviewing the Significance of Early-Halt Capability

Ensuring an *early*-halt is much more difficult than having capabilities to defeat an adversary in a long war. Strategically, however, it is a good challenge on which to focus because (1) ensuring an early halt is often important (Kuwait, Seoul), (2) the capabilities to accomplish it would provide strong deterrence, and (3) the challenge is a forcing function for DoD's transform efforts (Davis, 2001b).

Among the strategic reasons for an early halt is the desire to avoid the economic and military costs of a lengthy war with a counteroffensive followed by occupation and pacification of large territories.[1] A second reason is that as the length of crisis and conflict increase, so also is it likely that coalitional stresses will develop. Coalitional instability is a particular concern in the Persian Gulf[2] and will become more so if adversaries there develop more accurate missiles and mass-destruction weapons. Finally, having the capability to ensure an early halt would provide the best deterrent, since it would make it more difficult for Saddam or a successor to underestimate risks. Both history and psychological modeling tell us that would-be aggressors who believe they will achieve a quick initial victory can find many ways to rationalize why they could maintain the fruits of that victory. In particular, such aggressors can convince themselves that their opponents would not be willing to pay the price of a lengthy war because of casualty aversion.[3] Again, then, we come back to the potential significance of mass-destruction weapons. It can reasonably be argued that an aggressor would reason that his mass-destruction weapons would be a credible de-

[1]NATO's decision in the early 1960s to embrace a forward defense of Germany was due in part to strategic and economic concerns. Later, conventional wisdom came to be that the forward defense was a political imperative resulting from the lack of depth in West Germany, but this is belied by the fact that NATO had originally planned for much deeper defense lines (Brzezinski, 1986). Robert McNamara discussed the economic issue in his reflections in office (McNamara, 1968).

[2]These concerns played an important role in the 1990–1991 Gulf War, as discussed by President Bush and General Scowcroft (Bush and Scowcroft, 1998).

[3]For a prescient early discussion, see Hosmer (1987).

terrent against a counteroffensive and, particularly, against invasion of his own nation.[4]

If capabilities for an early halt are important, then it follows that the requirement should apply for as broad and demanding a range of circumstances as it seems reasonable to consider. That is, we want capabilities that would make an early halt highly probable. *The measure of risk, then, is how probable it is that the United States would be able to accomplish an early halt* (e.g., to halt an invasion within, say, 100 km). How much insurance against risk is enough depends on economic and political considerations that are outside the scope of this monograph.

Source of Risk (Factors Reducing the Probability of an Early Halt)

Assessing the risk is not as simple as, say, varying the size of the postulated threat. Indeed, the size of the threat is typically less important than other factors. In particular, conflict could begin with an attack on U.S. Achilles' heels.[5] One obvious Achilles' heel is the U.S. dependence on regional bases; hence the current concern about future *anti-access strategies.* For example, Iraq might threaten its neighbors with mass-destruction weapons, coercing them into denying access to U.S. military forces early in a crisis.

There are many other concerns. These include the potential—in a future post-sanctions environment—of short-warning attacks, of attacks made under the umbrella of more sophisticated surface-to-air missiles, and of synergies between short-warning attacks and possession of mass-destruction weapons. A sudden grab of Kuwait might not be easy to reverse if regional states were threatened by Iraq's threatened use of mass-destruction weapons against their cities.

It follows that we are less interested in assessing capability in canonical scenarios such as have traditionally been used by the Department of Defense for force sizing, than in a diversity of more challenging cases.

The Upside of Uncertainty

Paradoxically, it is also appropriate to look at cases much *less* challenging than canonical scenarios. U.S. forces might be called upon for counter-maneuver operations other than stopping a classic large-scale invasion. They might be used to support an opposition army if one materialized. Or they might be used to deter maneuver of

---

[4]For discussion of such matters with respect to Saddam Hussein and his decisions in 1990–1991, and for more general discussion of deterrence, see National Research Council (1997). Appendix J summarizes Davis' prior work on psychological modeling on opponents. See also Watman, Wilkening , Arquilla, and Nichiporuk (1995).

[5]Much current discussion refers to adversaries using "asymmetric strategies." Actually, it is normal for commanders to seek to engage asymmetrically. A given commander wishes to attack his enemy's weak points and to avoid exposing his own weak points. American history includes the image of patriots avoiding pitched battle with British regulars, and instead firing from cover and then fleeing. Even in the Gulf War of 1990–1991, Saddam *attempted* to fight asymmetrically by avoiding air combat (and even sending his aircraft to the safety of Iran), while entertaining the notion that U.S. forces and the American public would be unable to stomach a down-in-the-mud ground war.

ground forces or to compel their redeployment. In such cases, the object of U.S. concern might be a relatively few divisions with only moderate morale and competence. It is therefore of interest to avoid the usual error of looking only at high-end depictions of threat and to assess potential capability against lesser threats as well.

To put the matter differently, uncertainty creates not only risks but also *upside opportunities*—what U.S. forces could accomplish with a certain amount of luck. The intention here is not to understate risk or prudent force requirements, but rather to recognize that uncertainties work in both directions. If one ignores the upside, the result may be to make strategic errors by underestimating capability for deterrence, compellence, or quick victory; or to make operational errors by not planning sufficiently to exploit good breaks if they should arise (e.g., a sudden collapse of opposition).

It follows that we need a rich conception of risk and uncertainty.

Types of Risk

The concept of risk is multifaceted and subtle. We have a considerable literature on risk assessment,[6] but no simple formulas. For our purposes, it seems important to focus on two issues:

> The *operational risk* (i.e., the risk of mission failure) at the time of a future conflict as a function of scenario details.
>
> The *strategic risk* (i.e., the risk that future operational risks will be high because of adverse changes in circumstance to which the United States is unable to adapt).

In addressing operational risk, [7] we can ask, for example, with what probability (or, at least, with what degree of confidence, even if not estimated precisely) would the United States be able to achieve an early halt if Iraq attempted to reinvade Kuwait today? What if warning were short and access delayed? What if the United States no longer had permanently stationed forces on the ground?

Turning now to strategic risk, the question is with what probability will the United States be able to achieve and maintain capabilities for an early halt even though the threat and many other circumstances may change substantially over time. Perhaps Iraq will rebuild its army; perhaps it will improve its air defenses; perhaps it will develop the capability to attack forward bases with chemical and biological weapons; perhaps regional states will distance themselves increasingly from the United States and become reluctant to provide assured access in times of crisis. Responses are possible to most such developments, but adaptations are always uncertain because of political factors[8] and, more important for planning purposes, may not be possible if

---

[6]See Morgan and Henrion (1998), Davis and Hillestad (forthcoming); and, for risk assessment as an iterative process with diverse communities and stakeholders, National Research Council (1996).

[7]Some useful discussion of risk issues in force planning were made in a recent study by National Defense University (McKenzie, 2000; Flournoy, 2001). We adopt a rather different approach here.

[8]History provides both examples and counterexamples of countries adapting strategically. On the one hand, the United States increased the size of its conventional forces and improved their capabilities a great deal when, in the early 1960s, the conclusion was reached that nuclear deterrence was no longer suf-

the necessary groundwork has not been laid—not just in research and development, but also, perhaps, in limited procurements and long-lead-time regional planning. Reducing strategic risks, then, relates to *hedges*.

The distinction between these two classes of risk is blurred, but the distinction is important nonetheless. *Running strategic risks increases the likelihood of higher than currently anticipated operational risks at the time of a future conflict.*

With this qualitative background, let us now consider how we might deal analytically with the two kinds of risks.

7.3 STRUCTURING UNCERTAINTY ANALYSIS: THE CONCEPT OF A SCENARIO SPACE (OR ASSUMPTIONS SPACE)

We shall measure risk by modeling the halt campaign and observing how easy or difficult it is to achieve early halts (e.g., at distances less than 100 km).[9] We shall consider a very large "scenario space" (or what might be called an "assumptions space")—interpreting "scenario" to mean not just the name of conflict, as in "Iraq invades again," but the many other details such as threat size, warning time, time of access, and so on. Much of the discussion will be in Red/Blue terms.

To clarify the concept of analyzing results in a scenario space, suppose that our problem had only two variables X and Y, which could have values between X_{min} to X_{max} and from Y_{min} to Y_{max}. The scenario space would then be as shown at the left in Figure 7.1. To explore the scenario space means to explore how outcomes vary as X and Y vary within the shaded area (right side of Figure 7.1). For the problem we shall be discussing, however, there will be many more dimensions.

The generic dimensions of scenario space can be characterized as follows, with the understanding that each of the items below is a broad dimension with many components:[10]

> ***Political-military circumstances*** (e.g., who is fighting whom; who is allied with whom; how much strategic warning applies; . . .)
>
> ***Strategies and tactics*** (e.g., for Red, number of attack axes, number of columns per axis, dispersion of vehicles, possible use of weapons of mass destruction; for

---

ficient and that the Soviet military threat to Europe was a problem. Similarly, the United States developed what has become U.S. Central Command when, in the late 1970s and early 1980s, it concluded that vital interests in the Persian Gulf were insufficiently protected (against both regional threats such as Iraq and from Iranian incursions into the region). These were classic strategic adaptations. On the other hand, the United States was insufficiently prepared for World War II and the Korean War—despite warnings. Similarly, the British ten-year rule was extended too long and Britain was poorly prepared for the war that began in 1939–1940.

[9]This criterion is conservative because the model measures where the nose of advancing columns could be halted. If halted at such a point, the attacker would likely require a day or more to move in substantial forces, occupy the objective, and protect its forces by dispersal or intermingling.

[10]For development of these ideas, see Davis (1993, Chapters 1, 2, and 5). Early versions emerged in the mid-1980s development of the RAND Strategy Assessment System (RSAS) sponsored by Andrew Marshall, the Director of Net Assessment in the Office of the Secretary of Defense.

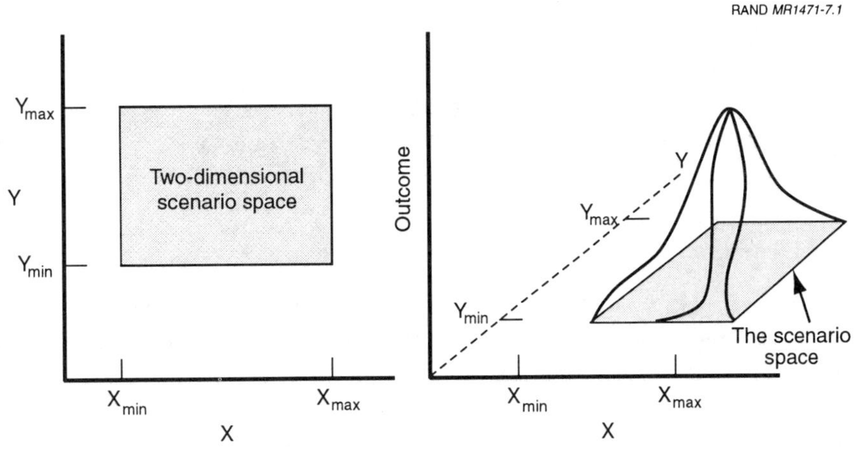

Figure 7.1—Two-Dimensional Scenario Space and Outcome Within It

Blue, choice of in-depth or leading-edge strategy, employment versus time of shooters to anti-armor missions, potential preemption because Red crosses a red line"

Forces (e.g., size and number of attacking divisions; number of initial shooters and subsequent deployment rates; availability of ground forces for early insertion)

Force effectiveness (e.g., Red's movement rate; kills per sortie or shot; time for Blue to suppress air defenses; capability of early Blue ground forces)

Environmental factors (e.g., weather, terrain, Blue's base capacity)

Other model assumptions (e.g., Red's break points; delays resulting from initial strikes; effects of plausible deception on warning time).

Most studies ignore the majority of uncertainties in these variables by accepting the legitimacy of standard planning scenarios and planning assumptions. That, however, is indefensible when the uncertainties are as large as they are (often factors of two or more). A small set of planning scenarios can be quite useful, but such a set should be constructed *after* extensive uncertainty analysis and designed to motivate the range of capabilities needed for a diversity of challenges. That is, the planning scenarios should not be "best estimates" but rather cleverly constructed challenges to help force development of appropriate capabilities. To do that clever construction requires an understanding of the full scenario space. This monograph and the EXHALT models make broad exploratory analysis under uncertainty feasible and systematic.

7.4 ENABLING SCENARIO-SPACE ANALYSIS WITH A MULTIRESOLUTION MODEL

It is desirable to simplify the model for our scenario-space analysis of uncertainty. We next describe the motivation for simplification and how to accomplish it, and then lay out an analysis. The enabler of the simplifications needed is further use of multiresolution, multiperspective modeling (MRMPM) principles.

MRMPM Depiction

Constructing a scenario space for analysis requires defining the key variables and their plausible ranges of values. Given a suitable model, we can explore how conflict outcome would vary within the scenario space (assumptions space) and, in the process, identify the factors that matter most. EXHALT-CF is suitable for this purpose. Moreover, because it is a multiresolution, multiperspective model, we can explore the consequences of uncertainty by considering only a relatively small number of high-level (aggregate-level) variables and then, if we wish to see more detail, zoom in to higher resolution.

Figure 7.2 illustrates this for one variable, AFVs to kill (denoted ξ in the mathematics). We can input ξ directly, rather than inputting separately number of threat divisions, number of AFVs per division, number of AFVs killed in an initial strike (if any), and break point. We can treat all of those inputs as inputs if we wish the higher level of resolution.

Figure 7.3 gives a second example. As discussed in Chapter 3, we can separately explore a wide range of scenarios varying C-Day, the time that access is granted, and so on, so as to better appreciate what is plausible and possible for the number of D-Day shooters (A_0). We can then use A_0 as the input.

These two examples, then, illustrate MRMPM design. Unfortunately, it is not always quite so straightforward.

RAND*MR1471-7.2*

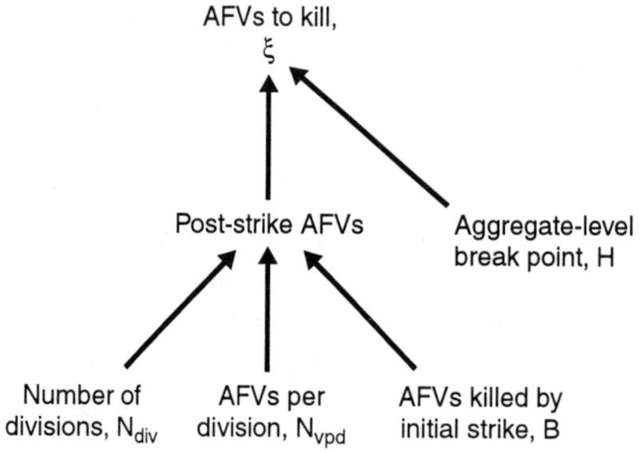

Figure 7.2—Inputting AFVs to Kill, Rather Than More Detailed Variables

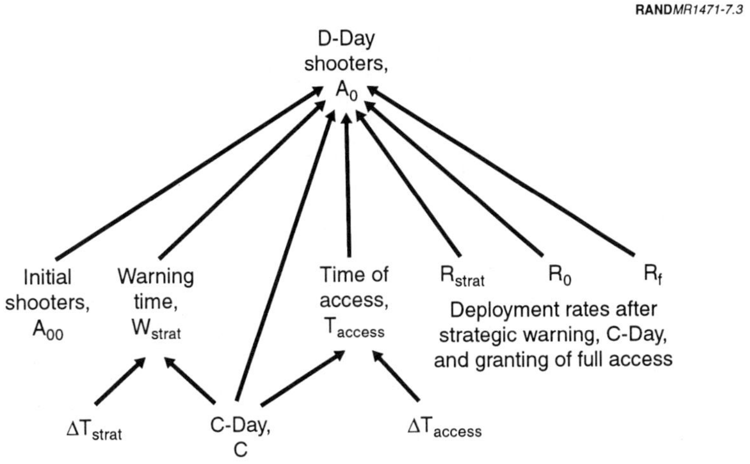

Figure 7.3—Inputting D-Day Shooters (A_0) Rather Than More Detailed Variables

The Composite Model and Simplifications

Moving to a view of the halt problem as treated in this monograph, Figure 7.4 diagrams the variables and relationships of the model, but abbreviates some of the depictions and omits the leading-edge strategy. The diagram indicates that the problem breaks into a number of fairly well-defined components, but that their separation is imperfect: The dashed lines indicate relationships among variables in different portions of the problem. If all the lines were equally dark, the diagram would merely look cluttered—with little evident structure. *This is the nature of typical models, whether force-on-force models in defense work, or policy models in many other domains, except for rule-of-thumb models.* As models evolve and gain in sophistication, the level of detail and number of interactions among components tend to increase—especially when a premium is put on verisimilitude rather than analytical flexibility.

Reasons for Simplification. If the only issue were computation, the complications suggested by the clutter in Figure 7.4 would not be particularly troublesome. The model of Chapter 6 describes the necessary computations and computer speeds are fast and increasing. Thus, we could just make the calculations. In fact, however, there are many other reasons for seeking a simplification (Davis and Bigelow, 1998). To *understand* and to have the basis for believing an analysis, one typically needs to modularize the problem and work through issues module by module. If everything depends heavily on everything, then cause-effect is difficult to understand. Moreover, to comprehend the whole, the problem must be reducible to a relatively small number of abstractions: People cannot handle a large number of variables simultaneously, much less explain cause-effect relationships and implications convincingly to others. To be sure, if the model were perfect and if everyone were satisfied with "Well, the best option is C—it's not clear why, but that's what the model says," then the simplification would be unnecessary. That, however, is almost never the case in policy analysis. The model is almost never perfect and decisionmakers

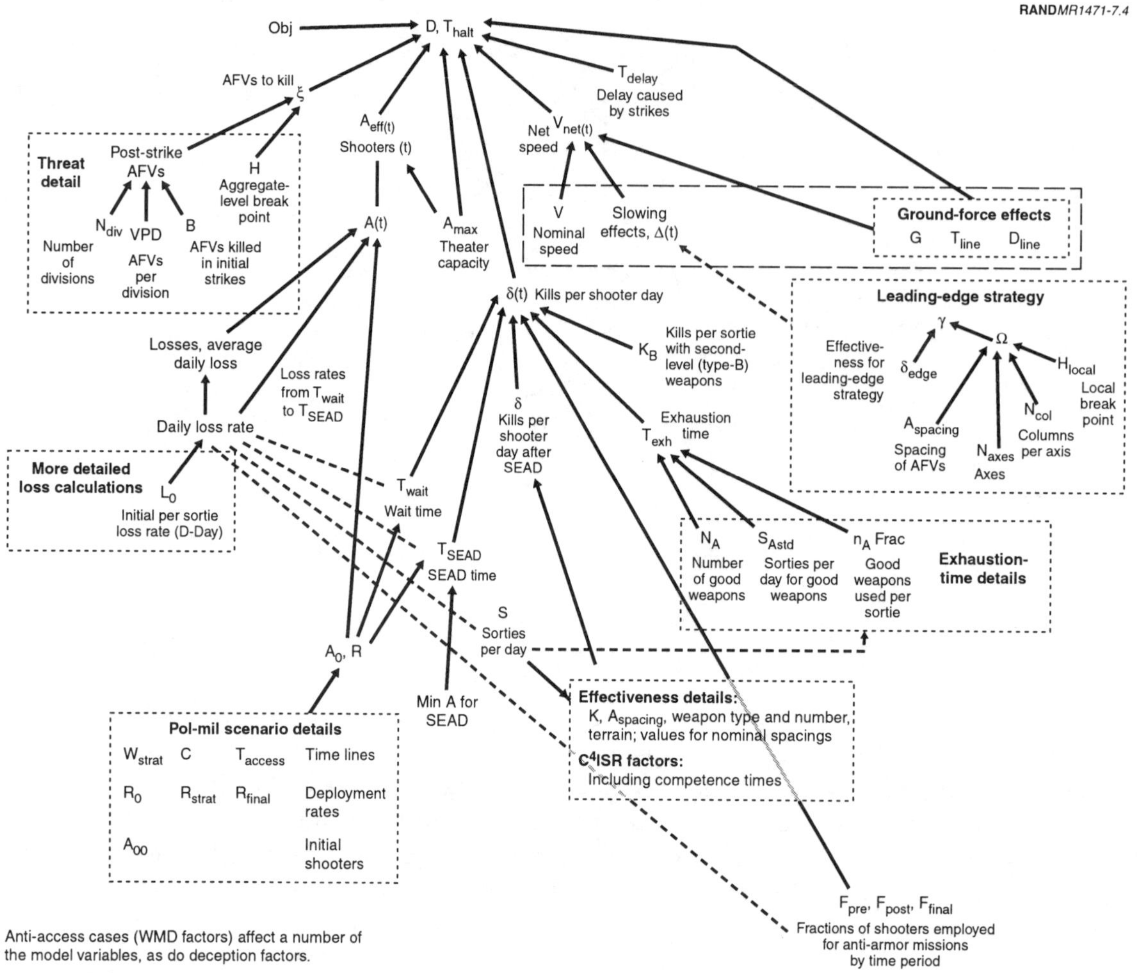

Figure 7.4—A Schematic View of the Model

therefore need to understand the underlying logic supporting the recommended decision.

The last reason we mention here is technical. The benefits of a multiresolution modeling system are greatest when one understands well how to calibrate a given parameter to results of modeling at the next level of detail. Ideally, choosing the value of an aggregate parameter as an input (e.g., the number of D-Day shooters) is akin to running a more detailed model over a representative set of detailed scenarios and taking an average. Similarly, the range of values one chooses to consider for the aggregate parameter should be informed by the variation of results generated from the more detailed model (if it is sufficiently credible). Such "zooming" to study a part of the problem in more detail (e.g., what is the reasonable range of values for D-Day shooters?) is most practical when the next level of detail is itself confined to a module of the larger problem, as in Figures 7.2 and 7.3. Thus, an ideal multiresolution design is hierarchical, without cross-branch interactions of the sort that clutter Figure 7.4.

The Role of Approximations. The principal difficulty is that the interrelationships are real: they will not go away with sophisticated mathematics or programming. This said, an important underlying MRMPM principle—beyond that of seeing virtue in MRMPM designs—is recognizing that many of the interrelationships can be broken by using respectable approximations. Such simplification does not come naturally in simulation modeling—where embellishment is often considered a virtue—but it has a long tradition in theoretical work and analysis. The trick is to find the approximations.

Figure 7.4 suggests with dashed lines where, based on sensitivity analysis or physical reasoning, we believe that simplifications can be made. The criterion here is not whether the items simplified are "important" in the abstract, but rather whether they are important quantitatively *when measured in terms of effect on the final model outcome* (Davis and Bigelow, 1998).

Similarly, the calculations shown in the dashed boxes are optional. In some cases, one wants to give the issues they treat visibility or because one has data at that level of detail. For other purposes, they provide unnecessary resolution—especially for broad exploratory analysis. Thus, they can be omitted with inputs made at the next higher nodes. The details can be added back as needed for specific purposes. For example, inputting D-Day shooters directly is a good approach for initial exploration, but if one wants to see explicitly the effects of delayed warning, delayed decisions, delayed access, and so on, then the module at the bottom center can be activated—without activating details in the other parts of the problem.[11]

Figure 7.5 demonstrates how the problem collapses if we omit most of the optional detail and introduce approximations that allow us to drop the dashed relationships. For the sake of illustration, we have retained some of the detail in describing exhaustion time—the time at which the best of the precision weapons have been used up, forcing Blue to use less effective weapons. Exhaustion time could be inputted directly, but in our experience treating exhaustion time as an exogenous variable is rather unnatural. It also tends to cause mathematical problems because it is difficult to ensure that the values chosen are consistent with the other inputs. Thus, we calculate exhaustion time explicitly. However, to limit degrees of freedom, we can hold sortie rate and number of weapons per sortie constant in our initial analysis. This does not reduce generality, because we know that the effect of doubling N_A is the same as the effect of halving n_A or S_A (unless inuts are made at a deeper level where S also affects loss rates and kills per sortie).

The inputs in Figure 7.5 can be treated as independent in deterministic exploratory analysis. However, they are correlated when one thinks about the relative likelihood of cases. In particular, a "large threat" is likely to have a large ground force *and* more troublesome air defenses. Further, a clever "asymmetric strategy" involving strategic deception would deny Blue the opportunity to make early strikes while Red's force is

[11]Students of complex adaptive systems will recognize many examples of analogous issues in natural systems—including the human body, which was described by Nobel laureate Herbert Simon as a *nearly* decomposable system. Many examples exist also in economics and other disciplines. Some of the deeper issues involved are discussed in the literature on semiotics (Meystel, 1995).

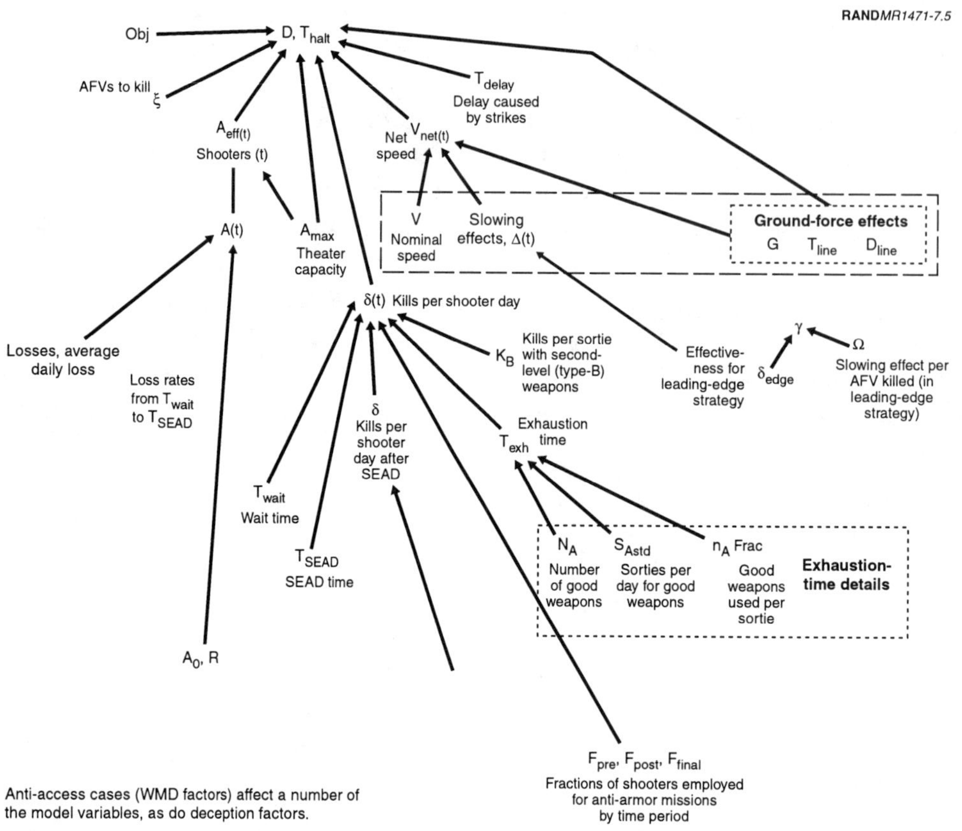

Figure 7.5—A Modularized View of the Overall Model, Based on Some Approximations Reducing Interactions

massing *and* to deploy large numbers of shooters early *and* to deploy ground forces in advance of the invasion. Further, such a strategy might surprise Blue enough so that initial command-control and C4ISR would be poorer than it could be logically. It follows that we can treat the variables as independent mathematically, but we must consider correlations when assessing the significance of cases. To put the matter differently, the conditions of a war are not randomly chosen; indeed, it is the *job* of a commander to find the corners of the problem where his side has maximal advantage.

7.5 ILLUSTRATIVE SCENARIO SPACES AND EXPERIMENTAL PLANS

Having refined our model, let us now proceed with illustrative scenario-space analysis. We shall consider both parametric and probabilistic versions of exploratory analysis (Davis et al., 2001; Davis and Hillestad, forthcoming).

Parametric Exploration

In parametric exploration, we assign alternative discrete values to the various uncertain parameters. We then consider results for all the various combinations of values.[12]

Table 7.1 shows an illustrative experimental plan developed using EXHALT-CF and the scenario-space concept discussed above, but with unclassified numbers. In this example, we have minimized treatment of the political-military circumstances component of scenario space. It is represented simply by assuming an invasion occurs with an objective some 600 km from the border, and by assuming that warnings make plausible the insertion of ground forces at a defense line. In contrast, there is greater detail in the specification of the problem with respect to forces, strategy, and force effectiveness. In a different application using the same model, we might have numerous variables characterizing the pre-war factors (e.g., strategic warning time, the time at which access is granted, and so on, as discussed in Chapter 3). Or we might deal with the leading-edge strategy, in which case we would need inputs characterizing the attacker's dispersion, number of axes, and so on. The point is that the experimental plan is merely an explicit method for covering the ground for the analysis at hand. In our experience, using the scenario-space discipline invariably sensitizes analysts to the need to include variables they would otherwise have treated as constant.

As an aside, it is sometimes arbitrary whether one treats a given input variable as in one rather than in another dimension of scenario space.

The scenario space for the experimental design of Table 7.1 is defined by the sets of input values considered—it is the region of the n-dimensional hyperspace interior to the extreme values in column 3 for the various parameters.

Given such an experimental design, one can use EXHALT-CF to accomplish the parametric exploration. The number of cases involved is about 11,000 for the design of Table 7.1. To run the roughly 11,000 cases takes about 30 seconds on a personal computer,[13] after which what appears on the computer's screen is Figure 7.6. The various "rotation boxes" at the top indicate that one can see results for other values of the parameters by merely rotating through the menus (by clicking on the arrows). Response is instantaneous, which is important for exploratory analysis: If response is within one's "cognitive cycle," then one can explore the outcome space efficiently. Note that this is hardly what people ordinarily think of when referring to sensitivity analysis: One is seeing the effects of 12 different parameters being

[12]A subset of the cases could be used, based on principles for pruning discussed in texts on experimental design. However, for the problems of interest here, the brute-force approach is convenient.

[13]Run times depend on details such as the model itself, the memory allocated to Analytica (not relevant with Windows), whether other applications are running simultaneously, the version of the model used, and, most important, the number of cases. Figure 7.5 ran in about 30 seconds on a Macintosh 400 MHz system with 256 MB RAM plus virtual memory.

Table 7.1

ILLUSTRATIVE EXPERIMENTAL PLAN FOR ASSESSING RISK AND UNCERTAINTY IN A PERSIAN GULF HALT CAMPAIGN

Scenario-Space Dimension	Input Variable	Values to Be Used in Experiments	Comments
Political-military circumstances	Obj	600 km	Red's maximum objective. Need not be varied.
Political-military circumstances	T_{line}, Time defense line is established	2 days	Blue's time to reach defense line.
Political-military circumstances	T_{delay}, Delay imposed by early strike on assembling forces	0, 2 days	Treated as a pol-mil variable, because it would be enabled by a red line concept.
Strategy and tactics	Ground-force use	Yes and no	Calculations are done with and without Blue having the capability and willingness to use ground forces if circumstances permit.
Strategy and tactics	D_{line}, Depth of defense line (km)	80 km	Blue's choice of defense line.
Strategy and tactics	T_{wait}, Wait time	1, 3 days	Time when Blue begins to use nonstealthy platforms for anti-armor attacks. Reflects tradeoffs between mission and losses.
Force effectiveness	F_{pre}, Initial anti-armor fraction of relevant shooters	0	Fraction of Blue's forces that are stealthy or otherwise almost invulnerable to air defenses, *and* that would be ready for immediate anti-armor use on D-Day.
Strategy and tactics	F_{post}, Anti-armor fraction of relevant shooters from T_{wait} until T_{SEAD}	0.25	Reflects Blue's judgments about vulnerability and importance of early employment. Depends also on quality of C^4ISR.
Strategy and tactics	F, Anti-armor fraction of relevant shooters after T_{SEAD}	1	Blue's post-SEAD anti-armor fraction, which should approach 1 if A(t) counts only those aircraft that can be used against armor. Other aircraft would continue indefinitely to maintain air-defense suppression.
Forces	ξ, AFVs to kill for halt	1000, 2000, 4000	Red. Covers gamut from small current threat to plausible future threat. Reflects size of threat and break point, which would be considered under "Other model assumptions" if explicit.
Forces	A_0, D-Day shooters	0, 100, 300	Blue's D-Day shooters resulting from forward presence, use of strategic warning, and full-scale deployment.
Forces	R, Deployment rate	12, 24 equiv. shooters/day	Blue's average buildup rate, including naval aviation.
Forces	N_A, Number of good weapons	2000; 100,000	Number of Blue's top-of-line precision weapons.
Forces	G, Capability of ground forces at defense line	1000	Number of AFVs that Blue's ground forces could deal with if in place in time.

Table 7.1 (continued)

Scenario-Space Dimension	Input Variable	Values to Be Used in Experiments	Comments
Force effectiveness	V, Movement rate	40, 70 km/day	Red's average rate of advance after any initial delay from strikes, and before slowing caused by a leading-edge strategy.
Force effectiveness	T_{SEAD}, SEAD time	1, 3, 6 days	Time for Blue to suppress air defenses.[a]
Force effectiveness	Min A_0, for fast SEAD	24	Minimum number of shooters before SEAD can begin.
Force effectiveness	S_{std}, Standard sortie rate	2	Blue's standard sortie rate. Held constant.[b] Used only to calculate T_{exh}.[b]
Force effectiveness	Eff_n_A Good (type-A) weapons per sortie	6	Blue's standard weapon load times average fraction of load used. Depends on C^4ISR and other factors. Held constant.[b]
Force effectiveness	δ, Kills per shooter day with type-A weapons	2, 4, 8	Reflects combination of kills per sortie/shot and sorties/shots per day.
Force effectiveness	δ_B, Kills per shooter day with type-B weapons	1	Effectiveness after top-quality weapons are exhausted. Held constant.[b]
Force effectiveness	$L_{dailyavg}$, Daily losses from T_{wait} to T_{SEAD}	2	Reflects qualities of both Red and Blue forces, as well as C^4ISR and tactics. Not varied because effect is assumed modest and number of cases is already large.
Environmental factors	A_{max}, Theater capacity	200, 1000	Blue's theater capacity. Lower limit determined by naval carriers and long-range bombers.
Other model assumptions	None at this level of detail		Several variables could be treated in this category. For example, V is not really a matter simply of doctrine and capability, but also a matter of luck and fog of war. So also T_{delay}. At the next level of modeling detail, the break points would be good examples of model assumptions to vary. At this level, that is accomplished by varying the number of AFVs to be killed, ξ.

[a]Nominal value. Model may adjust the value for consistency with other parameters.

[b]Can be held constant because effects of variation are same as for other parameters, which are varied.

changed simultaneously.[14] In contrast, traditional sensitivity plots deal with one to three parameters—the others being held constant.[15]

[14]We have emphasized the visual approach, but one can also analyze the data generated by the experiments with statistical methods. There are advantages and disadvantages to doing so.

[15]RAND has been refining exploratory analysis methods since the mid-1980s. The first major success was achieved by using the theater model JICM and the highly parameterized but complex RSAS model. The best source for up-to-date information on JICM and related analyses are colleagues Daniel Fox and Carl Jones in RAND's Washington office.

RANDMR1471-7.6

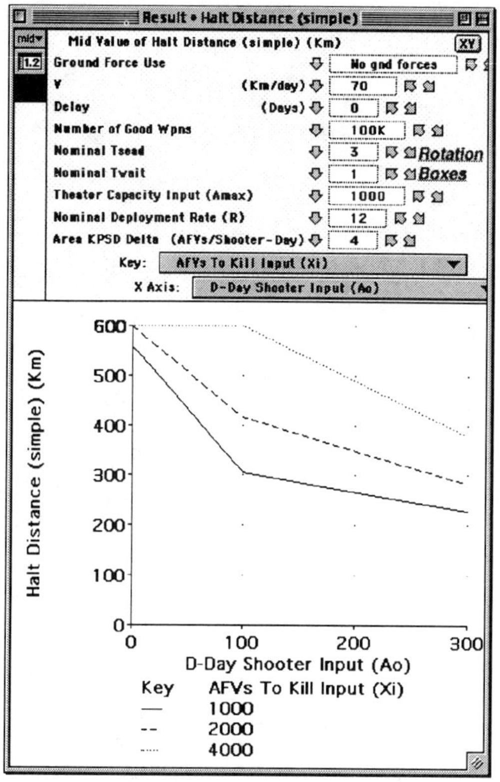

Figure 7.6 —Illustrative EXHALT-CF Display of Parametric Exploration: Simultaneous Variation of 12 Parameters

Displaying Results of Parametric Exploration

The printed page is a notoriously poor way to convey the sense of an interactive model such as EXHALT-CF. Perhaps the reader will take on faith our assertion that a great many insights can be gained by a single analyst in an hour working at his computer, interactively changing the various parameters. This, in our experience, is far more effective than working with hard copy. Nonetheless, it is necessary to display results and to demonstrate the basis of insights to others. A number of possibilities exist or are emerging.

Juxtaposing Line Plots Taken Directly from EXALT-CF. The most straightforward approach when using a program such as EXHALT-CF is to juxtapose figures. Figure 7.7 illustrates this. In a single page one can summarize exploratory analysis across the values of four parameters.

The x axis of the top-left display and the family of curves in that same display provide for two. Moving to the right panel varies a third, and moving to the lower panels varies a fourth. In this example, the parameters are D-Day shooters, nominal kills per shooter day, SEAD time, and attacker speed. By adding a similar page, one could

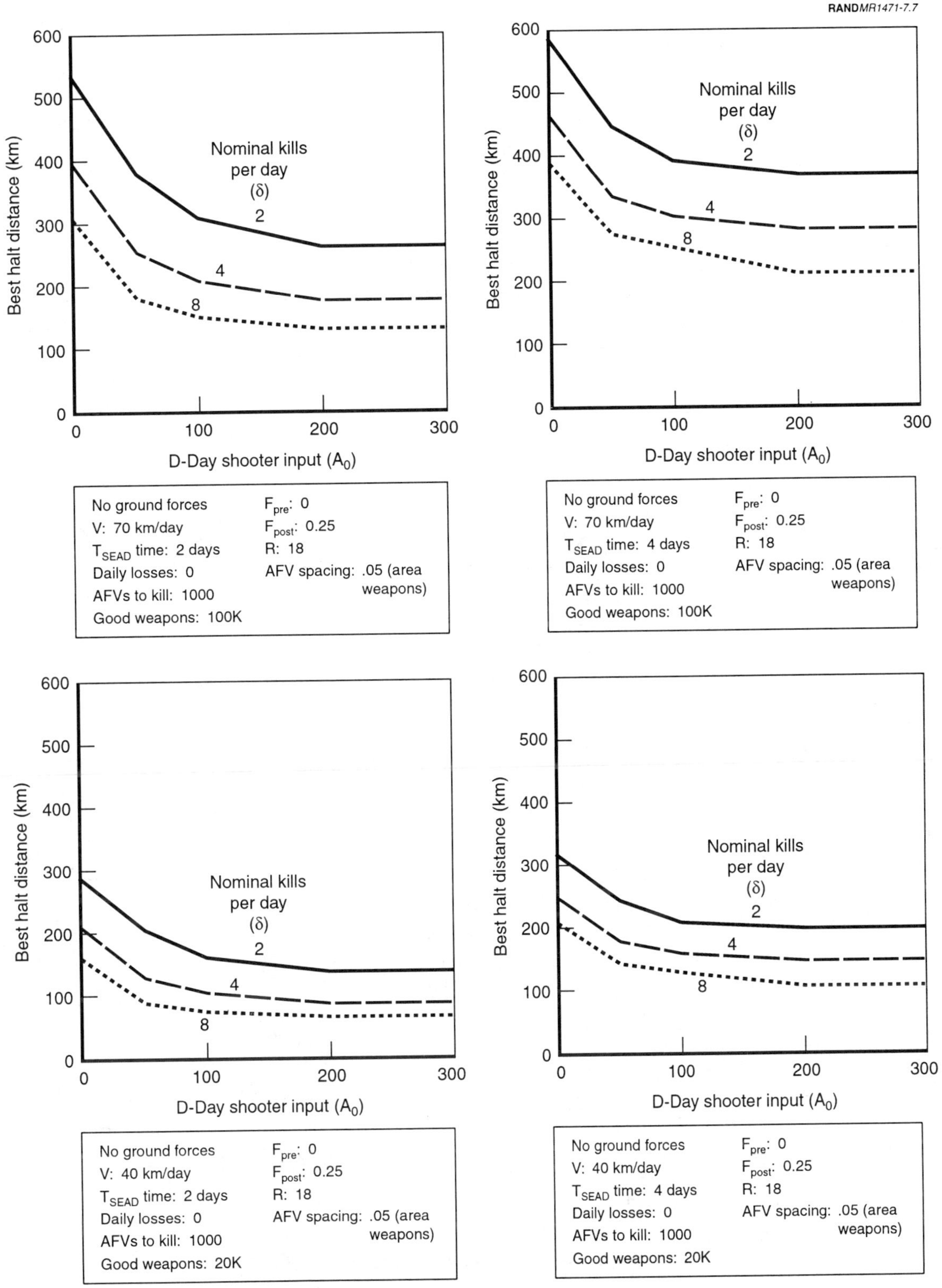

Figure 7.7—Summarizing Exploration of Four Parameters in Analytica

add a fifth parameter; by adding yet another pair of pages, one could add a sixth. It is relatively easy to construct such displays.

Nomograms. An old technique for showing results across a large parameter space is nomograms, which were until recent years a standard tool of engineers engaged in tradeoff calculations. Figure 7.8 illustrates the nomogram methodology with work from a 1997 study (Davis et al., unpublished). It shows outcomes as a function of four parameters, but for linear problems the same format would show results for five parameters. The arrow shows how to use a nomogram such as this. One starts at the bottom left (at a deployment rate of 18 along the y axis), moves horizontally until reaching the line corresponding to the α value of interest (2000 shooter days in the example), moves vertically to the top left panel and to the line corresponding to 50 D-Day shooters (λ), then rightward to the curve in the right top panel corresponding to the same deployment rate as before (this is necessary for the particular nonlinear problem being modeled), and down to the appropriate line for speed V (40

RANDMR1471-7.8

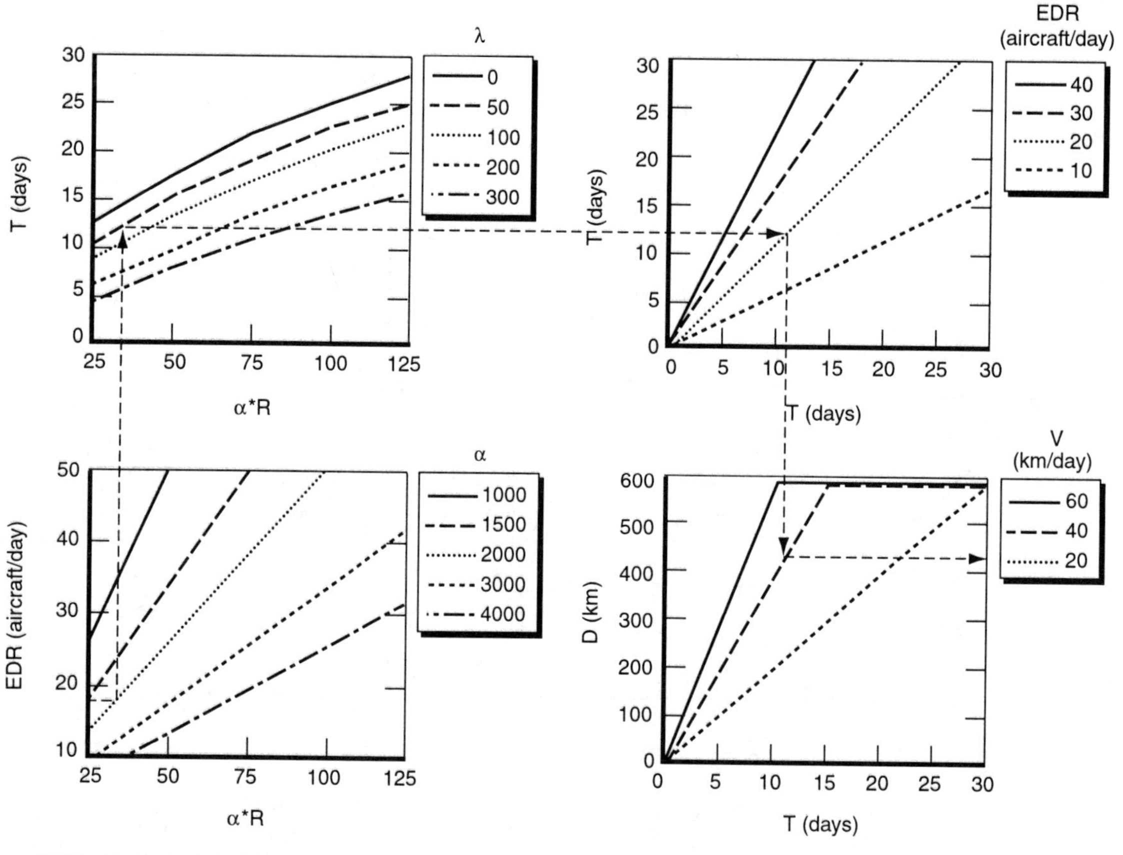

EDR = Equivalent deployment rate.

Figure 7.8—An Illustrative Nomogram with Compounding Uncertainty

km/day). Finally, one moves to the right (or left) horizontally to read the result: a halt distance of 430 km.

Using such a nomogram is essentially to use what colleague Glenn Kent refers to facetiously as an old-fashioned analog computer. One might think that it is just an inferior way to calculate the results of a case. However, by indicating with shading the credible range of parameter values for a particular context, as in Figure 7.9, one can generate an overall assessment of uncertainty. This is exploratory analysis, not normal sensitivity analysis. One can extend nomograms to involve multiple sheets of paper, in which case a larger number of parameters can be treated. Unfortunately, ways to construct them—especially with desktop computers of the sort that analysts ordinarily use—apparently do not currently exist. Instead, one must resort either to hand graphing or engage in some relatively treacherous cut, paste, and align operations with spreadsheet graphics.[16]

RAND *MR1471-7.9*

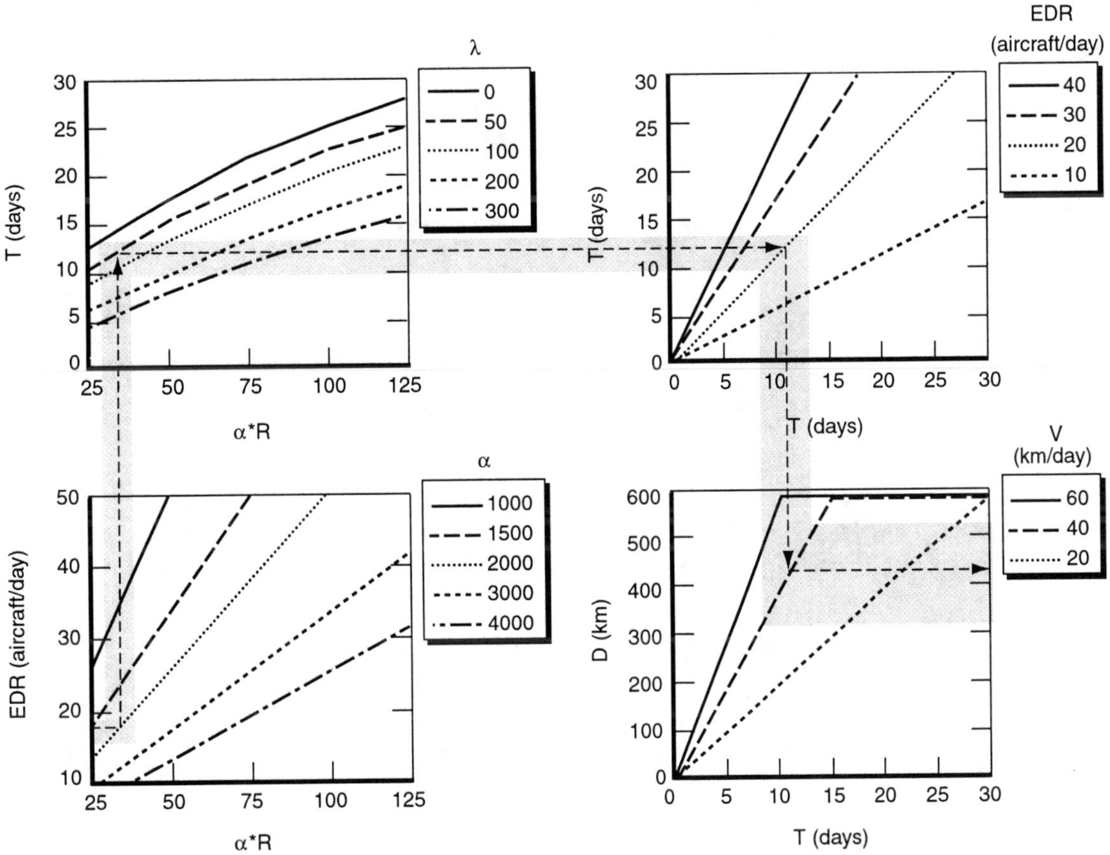

EDR = Equivalent deployment rate.

Figure 7.9—Exploratory Analysis with a Nomogram

[16]To make things worse, spreadsheet graphics are notorious for not printing correctly when copied into a word processing program and then used as input for commercial publications.

Color-Coded Three-Dimensional Displays. RAND has made considerable use of a tool, Data View, developed by colleagues Steven Bankes and James Gillogly in the early 1990s. It has been used in some of our earlier work and in many other RAND studies. Data View is available to users of RAND's theater-level campaign model, JICM. Figure 7.10 illustrates this (albeit, in gray scale rather than color), using a graphic from an earlier study based on a much more primitive halt model (Davis and Carrillo, 1997). In these Data-View displays, each square represents one run of the model. The x, y, and z axes show independent parameters. The outcome is read not along one of the axes, but as the color or gray scale of a square, which is coded to correspond to a range of halt distances (Figure 7.11). A black result is very bad, whereas a white square indicates a very good result (an early halt).

Taken together, the four panels of Figure 7.10 summarize parametric exploratory analysis more than five parameters (three within a panel—the panel's x, y, and z axes, one for a row of two panels, and one for a column of two panels). With four such pages, one can cover results for seven parameters.

There is a buy-in price to understand the displays, but—once the price is paid—results can be perused and assimilated rapidly. We shall not discuss such displays further in this monograph. We include them merely to indicate that rigorous coverage of results across a scenario space can be presented economically.

RANDMR1471-7.10

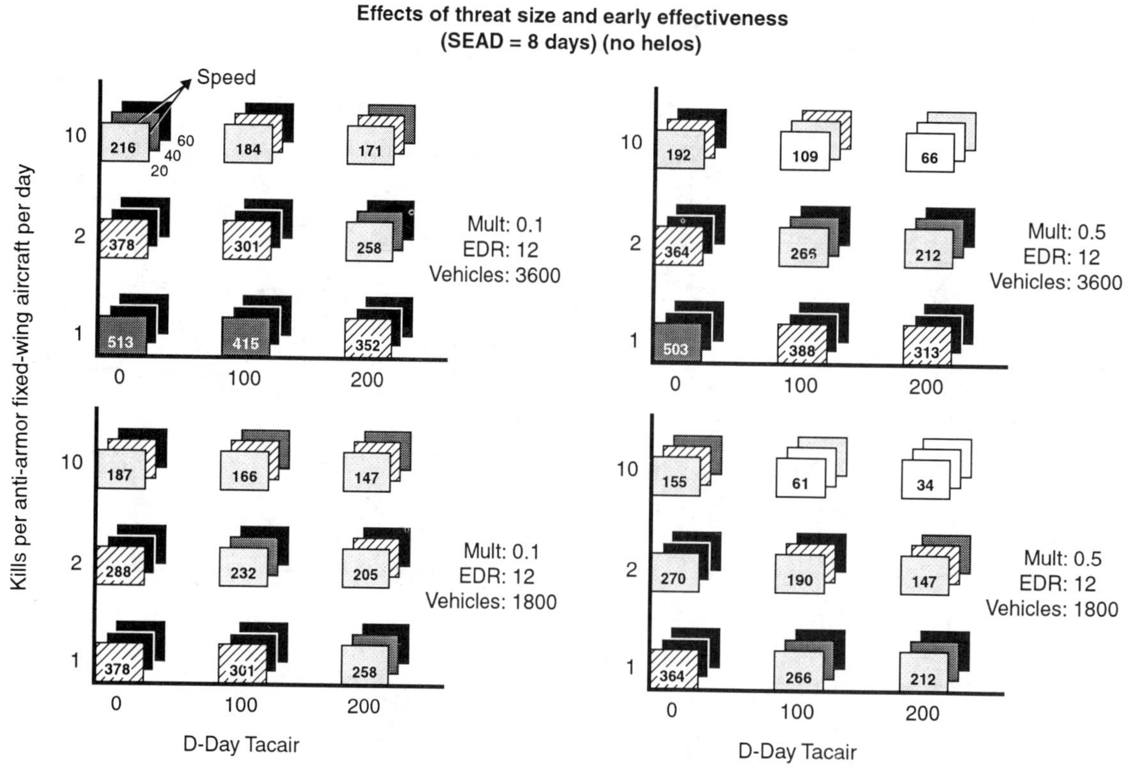

Mult.: fraction of shooters used before SEAD time; EDR: equivalent deployment rate; Vehicles: AFVs to be killed for halt.

Figure 7.10—A Data-View Display Showing Effects of Three Parameters

RAND MR1471-7.11

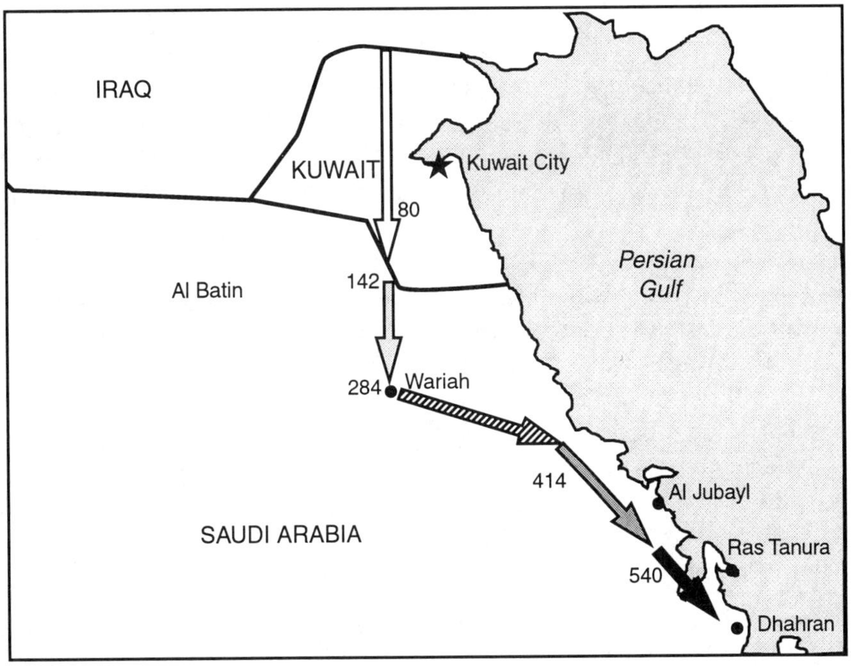

Figure 7.11—Illustrative Coding for "Color" (Gray Scale) of Data-View Displays

A more advanced graphics system named CARs is under commercial development by Bankes.[17] CARs can generate displays closely similar to Figure 7.10, but also quite a number of other types. As part of the research for this monograph, we developed a variant of EXHALT-CF coded in C, embedded it in CARs, and used that interactively. Although CARs was not yet mature enough for our application, it will have substantial power. It incorporates many of the features that are regarded as particularly important for exploratory analysis (Davis and Hillestad, forthcoming).

Stochastic Features and Probabilistic Exploration

The Mechanics of Probabilistic Calculations. The analysis underlying Figure 7.6 was deterministic, although the values of the parameters were highly uncertain. The underlying image in such work is that when an event occurs, it will be described by a deterministic model; the only problem is that we don't know the values of that model's parameters for the future event. An alternative is to say that even on the eve of the event, there would remain major uncertainties because of hidden factors that may change routinely. Planning factors, even when updated, are only approximations at best, and are sometimes merely educated guesses. What will *really* happen remains a matter of chance. To reflect this type of problem, which we refer to as stochastic variation, we can represent any or all of the input parameters by probability distribu-

[17]See www.evolvinglogic.com for information.

tions. Let us first show how to do this and then, in the next subsection, post caveats related to the problem of correlated parameters.

Table 7.2 illustrates the approach with an experimental design equivalent to the previous one, except that we treat Blue's deployment rate, effectiveness per shooter day, and time to suppress air defenses (SEAD time) as stochastic. Because we are doing so, it makes no sense to vary the nominal values of those parameters as much as previously: Instead, the discrete values we maintain in the design should represent reasonable planning-factor values. Thus, in Table 7.2, for example, we use a nominal value of 18 for Blue's deployment rate, but use a triangular probability distribution between about half and twice that. In considering nominal effectiveness (kills per shooter day, δ), however, we test with values of both two and four for the medians of lognormal distributions with geometric standard deviations of two. The result is that if the nominal value of kills per shooter day (KPSD) (δ) is four, the actual number used in the calculations is given by the distribution in Figure 7.12: Depending on the luck of the draw, Blue's actual effectiveness varies enormously.[18] Figure 7.13 shows the equivalent information in the form of a cumulative probability distribution. The median value is about four, but a wide range of values is possible.

Again we emphasize that these calculations are merely illustrative—presented to illustrate the methodology. At the same time, we note that actual uncertainties are indeed quite large. Sensor-fuzed weapons, of which an F-16 can carry six, *each* carry large numbers of bomblets capable of causing mobility kills to armored vehicles. The high end of lethality per weapon is, then, very high. The low end, however, which might correspond to the attacker being in reasonably dispersed formation (e.g., 50 or even 100 m per AFV), C^4ISR being less than perfect, and pilots being highly cautious because of the occasional SAM threat that might pop up despite SEAD, might be assessed as unlikely to be less than half the planning-factor value, which already assumes such difficulties.

Figure 7.14 illustrates an output of analysis using the assumptions of the experimental plan in Table 7.2. The SEAD time, kills per sortie, and deployment rate have been varied stochastically, but with nominal values as indicated in the figure. The result is a cumulative probability distribution for halt distance.

Correlations and Other Subtleties in the Use of Probabilistic Variables. Probabilistic exploration has an allure. It is relatively easy—given the appropriate software—calculations can be very fast, and the results are expressed in terms that make them sound mathematically solid ("probability" of a given halt distance occurring). In fact, however, the methodology has both strengths and weaknesses and should be used with caution.

On the positive side, consider Figure 7.13 again. Even by varying only three variables stochastically (holding all the other inputs constant), one sees that the range of possible outcomes is quite large. This should be humbling to anyone who takes

[18]The choice of probability functions is not entirely arbitrary, but we shall not discuss the choices further in this monograph. See, for example, discussions in Morgan and Henrion (1990) and Davis and Hillestad (forthcoming).

Table 7.2

EXPERIMENTAL PLAN INCLUDING STOCHASTIC VARIATION OF A FEW VARIABLES

Scenario-Space Dimension	Input Variable	Values to Be Used in Experiments	Comments
Political-military circumstances	Obj	600 km	Red's maximum objective. Need not be varied.
Political-military circumstances	T_{line}, Time defense line is established	2 days	Blue's time to reach defense line.
Political-military circumstances	T_{delay}, Delay imposed by early strike on assembling forces	0, 2 days	Treated as a pol-mil variable, because it would be enabled by a red line concept.
Strategy and tactics	D_{line} , Depth of defense line (km)	80 km	Blue's choice of defense line.
Strategy and tactics	T_{wait}, Wait time	1, 3 days	Time when Blue begins to use non-stealthy platforms for anti-armor attacks. Reflects tradeoffs between mission and losses.
Force effectiveness	F_{pre}, Initial anti-armor fraction of relevant shooters	0	Fraction of Blue's forces that are stealthy or otherwise almost invulnerable to air defenses, *and* that would be ready for immediate anti-armor use on D-Day (for missiles, depends on C^4ISR).
Strategy and tactics	F_{post}, Anti-armor fraction of relevant shooters from T_{wait} until T_{SEAD}	0.25	Reflects Blue's judgments about vulnerability and importance of early employment. Depends also on quality of C^4ISR.
Strategy and tactics	F, Anti-armor fraction of relevant shooters after T_{SEAD}	1	
Forces	ξ, AFVs to kill for halt	1000, 2000, 4000	Red. Covers gamut from small current threat to plausible future threat. Reflects size of threat and break point.
Forces	A_0, D-Day shooters	0, 100, 300	Blue's D-Day shooters resulting from forward presence, use of strategic warning, and full-scale deployment.
Forces	R, Deployment rate	18 equiv. shooters per day Triangular (1/2 nominal, nominal, 2 nominal)	Blue's average buildup rate, including naval aviation.
Forces	N_A, Number of good weapons	2000; 100,000	Number of Blue's top-of-line precision weapons.
Forces	G, Capability of ground forces at defense line	1000	Number of AFVs that Blue's ground forces could deal with if in place in time.

Table 7.2 (continued)

Scenario-Space Dimension	Input Variable	Values to Be Used in Experiments	Comments
Force effectiveness	V, Movement rate	40, 70, 100 km/day	Red's average rate of advance after any initial delay from strikes, and before slowing caused by a leading-edge strategy
Force effectiveness	T_{SEAD} , SEAD time	1, 3 days Triangular (0.5, nominal, 8)	Time for Blue to suppress air defenses.[a]
Force effectiveness	S_{std}, Standard sortie rate	2	Blue's standard sortie rate. Held constant. Used only to calculate T_{exh}.
Force effectiveness	Eff_n_A Good (type-A) weapons per sortie	6	Blue's standard weapon load times average fraction of load used. Depends on C^4ISR and other factors. Held constant.
Force effectiveness	δ, Kills per shooter day with type-A weapons	2, 4 Log normal (nominal, 3), where 3 is the geometric standard deviation	Reflects combination of kills per sortie/shot and sorties/shots per day.
Force effectiveness	δ_B, Kills per shooter day with type-B weapons	1	Effectiveness after top-quality weapons are exhausted. Held constant.
Force effectiveness	$L_{dailyavg}$, Daily losses from T_{wait} to T_{SEAD}	0	Reflects qualities of both Red and Blue forces, as well as C^4ISR and tactics. Not varied in this example because effect is small and number of cases is already large.
Environmental factors	A_{max}, Theater capacity	200, 1000	Blue's theater capacity. Lower limit determined by carriers and long-range bombers.
Other model assumptions			

[a]Nominal value. Model may adjust the value for consistency with other parameters.

planning factors seriously. It is like saying that even if we have the very best values for all the planning factors that could reasonably be obtained by hard work, the inherent residual uncertainty is substantial.

To be sure, we might have obtained that conclusion by comparing deterministic results with different values of the three parameters. However, in such an approach there is a tendency to take more seriously than one should the extremes in which all of the parameters being varied take on their extreme values. How likely is it that the SEAD time will be twice as long as expected *and* that the deployment rate is 50 percent lower than expected *and* the kills per shooter day half as large as expected? Perhaps we should consider being "lucky" on two of the parameters and unlucky on another. The probabilistic calculations take all of these possibilities into account and generate a net assessment of the consequences of the input assumptions, including uncertainty.

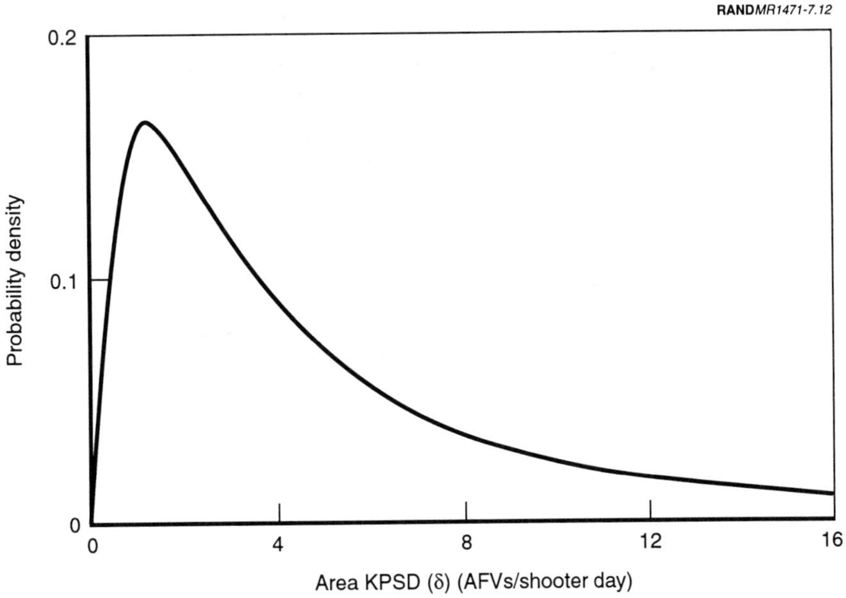

Figure 7.12—Illustrative Probability Density Assumed for Kills per Shooter Day (if mean value is 4)

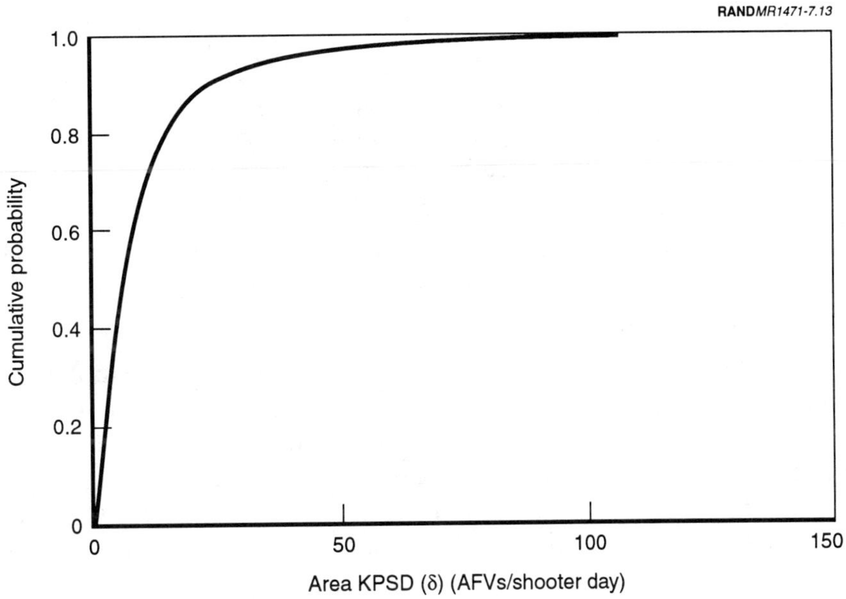

Figure 7.13—Illustrative Cumulative Probability Density Assumed for Kills per Shooter Day (if mean value is 4)

RANDMR1471-7.14

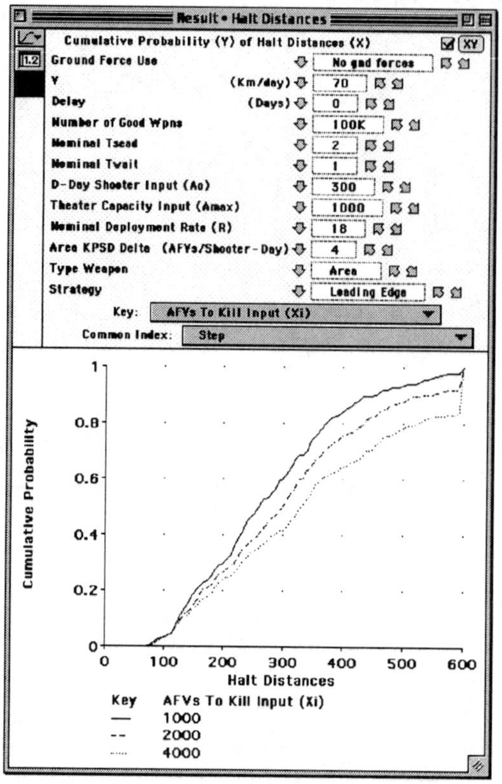

Figure 7.14—Cumulative Probability of Halt Distance for Illustrative Calculation Treating Some Variables as Stochastic

Problems using the probabilistic approach are several. First, overdoing the stochastic feature (with too many of the important inputs treated probabilistically) buries the "cause" of the variation of results.

Also, it is easy to interpret the "probabilities" generated by the methodology too literally, forgetting that some uncertainties are undoubtedly not included and that some of the variables that are included are correlated.[19] In particular, some of the important inputs may not be strategically independent. For example, a clever adversary might be able to reduce Blue's warning time (and thus reduce D-Day shooters) *and* move at a faster-than-expected pace once invasion begins *and* delay completion of SEAD by holding some air defense batteries in reserve and hiding them from overhead surveillance.

Mathematical techniques exist for correlating uncertainties, but the effort tends to become unwieldy and opaque rather quickly. For analytical purposes, then, it is usually preferable to deal with such matters by establishing "cases." This is a traditional

[19]The variables treated stochastically in Figure 7.14 (R, δ, and T_{SEAD}) might reasonably be expected to be independent. Even this is not certain, however. For example, if Blue deployed late after minimal warning, command and control might be poor, affecting all three parameters.

procedure and is sometimes characterized by distinctions between, say, a high threat and a low threat. A "high" threat may be not only large, but also more capable and likely deceptive. Table 7.3 illustrates use of this approach. For the sake of the concocted example, several scenario features are worse in case A than in case B. Stochastic variation exists in both cases, but the nominal planning factors around which variations are computed are different. For example, we see that SEAD time is assumed to be random, following a triangular probability distribution, but that the most probable value for SEAD time is one day in case A and three days in case B.

Even with such embellishments, interpretation of probabilistic exploration should be approached cautiously. As mentioned above, some uncertainties are likely not to be included (the models, after all, are imperfect), some uncertainties may not be realistically estimated, and so on. Nonetheless, we find probabilistic exploration to be a useful adjunct to parametric exploration.

7.6 INTERFACE MODELS FOR DEALING WITH CROSS-CUTTING FACTORS SUCH AS C^4ISR IN EXPLORATORY ANALYSIS

A difficult issue facing U.S. planners is how to represent the effects of high-leverage support systems, often abbreviated in a clump called C^4ISR, even though it is usually better to separate the contributions of command-control, surveillance and reconnaissance, and so on. One temptation in analysis is to associate the C^4ISR with a single effect, which understates the potential value of the capability. On the other hand, the temptation also exists to ignore the adversary's ability to change procedures and make substitutions to compensate for degradations caused by Blue's C^4ISR-enhanced capabilities.

A mechanism for better highlighting the *potential* effect of C^4ISR or other cross-cutting factors is to use *interface models*. These translate "meta variables" into parameter values of the underlying model and, in doing so, account for correlations that would be extremely difficult to account for mathematically in other ways. We illustrate this in Table 7.4, which shows meta variables of WMD threat level, deception level, and Blue's C^4ISR quality. In the first column, then, we list a number of EXHALT-CF input variables. Each cell of the table's interior, then, can indicate how one of the meta variables affects the model's basic input parameters. We have shown the effects built into the baseline version of EXHALT-CF, but have indicated with question marks a number of effects that one might choose to represent in a given analysis.

In baseline EXHALT-CF, then, if one wishes to use the meta variable of Red WMD, the effect is to multiply Blue's theater capacity by a factor of 0.25 or 0.5 if the WMD threat is characterized as high. Blue's kills per shooter day are reduced by a factor of 50 percent if the WMD threat is either medium or high. In an actual analysis with detailed regional information regarding bases, in-place infrastructure, and so on, realistic numbers could be established for these items.

Although not included in the baseline version of EXHALT-CF, one could easily modify the model so that in cases of Red deception, the range of values considered for A_0 would be reduced and lowered. Similarly, one might take the view that with

Table 7.3

USING STRATEGIC CASES TO CORRELATE ASSUMPTIONS

Scenario-Space Dimension	Input Variable	Value Used by Case A	Value Used by Case B	Comments
Political-military circumstances	Obj	600 km		Red's maximum objective. Need not be varied.
Political-military circumstances	T_{line}, Time defense line is established	2 days		Blue's time to reach defense line.
Political-military circumstances	T_{delay}, Delay imposed by early strike on assembling forces	0 days	2 days	Treated as a pol-mil variable, because it would be enabled by a red line concept.
Strategy and tactics	D_{line}, Depth of defense line (km)	80 km		Blue's choice of defense line.
Strategy and tactics	T_{wait}, Wait time	1 day	3 days	Time when Blue begins to use nonstealthy platforms for anti-armor attacks. Reflects tradeoffs between mission and losses.
Force effectiveness	F_{pre}, Initial anti-armor fraction of relevant shooters	0		Fraction of Blue's forces that are stealthy or otherwise almost invulnerable to air defenses, *and* that would be ready for immediate anti-armor use on D-Day (for missiles, depends on C^4ISR).
Strategy and tactics	F_{post}, Anti-armor fraction of relevant shooters from T_{wait} until T_{SEAD}	0.25		Reflects Blue's judgments about vulnerability and importance of early employment. Depends also on quality of C^4ISR.
Strategy and tactics	F, Anti-armor fraction of relevant shooters after T_{SEAD}	1		
Forces	ξ, AFVs to kill for halt	1000, 2000, 4000		Red. Covers gamut from small current threat to plausible future threat. Reflects size of threat and break point.
Forces	A_0, D-Day shooters	0, 100, 300		Blue's D-Day shooters resulting from forward presence, use of strategic warning, and full-scale deployment.
Forces	R, Deployment rate	Triangular (1/2 nominal, nominal, 2 nominal) 18	18	Blue's average buildup rate, including naval aviation.
Forces	N_A, Number of good weapons	100,000		Number of Blue's top-of-line precision weapons.
Forces	G, Capability of ground forces at defense line	700		Number of AFVs that Blue's ground forces could deal with if in place in time.
Force effectiveness	V, Movement rate	40, 70 km/day		Red's average rate of advance after any initial delay from strikes, and before slowing caused by a leading-edge strategy.

Table 7.3 (continued)

Scenario-Space Dimension	Input Variable	Value Used by Case A	Value Used by Case B	Comments
Force effectiveness	T_{SEAD}, SEAD time	Triangular (0.5, nominal, 8) with nominal value by case 1	3	Time for Blue to suppress air defenses.[a]
Force effectiveness	S_{std}, Standard sortie rate	2		Blue's standard sortie rate. Held constant. Used only to calculate T_{exh}.
Force effectiveness	Eff_n_A Good (type-A) weapons per sortie	6		Blue's standard weapon load times average fraction of load used. Depends on C^4ISR and other factors. Held constant.
Force effectiveness	δ, Kills per shooter day with type-A weapons	Log normal (nominal, 3), where 3 is the geometric standard deviation and nominal value is by case 2	4	Reflects combination of kills per sortie/shot and sorties/shots per day.
Force effectiveness	δ_B, Kills per shooter day with type-B weapons	1		Effectiveness after top-quality weapons are exhausted. Held constant.
Force effectiveness	$L_{dailyavg}$, Daily losses from T_{wait} to T_{SEAD}	0		Reflects qualities of both Red and Blue forces, as well as C^4ISR and tactics. Not varied in this example, since effect is small and number of cases is already large.
Environmental factors	A_{max}, Theater capacity	200, 1000		Blue's theater capacity. Lower limit determined by carriers and long-range bombers.
Other model assumptions				

[a]Nominal value. Model may adjust the value for consistency with other parameters.

Table 7.4

INTERFACE MODEL

	WMD (Multiplication)			Deception (Addition)			Blue's C^4ISR Quality		
	Low	Med	High	Low	Med	High	Low	Med	High
R				?	?	?			
δ, δ_B		.5	.5	?	?	?	?	?	?
A_0		?	?	?	?	?			
A_{max}			.25, .5						
T_{line}		?	?	?	?	?	?	?	?
T_{wait}				?	?	?	?	?	?
T_{SEAD}				?	?	?	?	?	
ΔT_{access}		?	?	0	2	4			
ΔT_{Strat}				0	1	2			

little warning (the result of deception), Blue's command and control would not be able to support immediate D-Day operations effectively. As a result, although air strikes might be conducted against prime stationary targets such as assembly areas, bridges, or other choke points, the United States might be unwilling to risk pilots in anti-armor operations until SEAD operations were substantially complete, and those operations might take somewhat longer than had warning existed. And so on.

The point here is that one should think of EXHALT and EXHALT-CF as tools for war gaming, not as answer machines. Even in studies about procurement issues, a great deal of attention should be paid to development of cases and what we refer to here as explicit interface models. One virtue of the EXHALT family is that assumptions can be expressed and described clearly, rather than buried deep in model databases that only professional programmers are willing to look at.

Table 7.5 illustrates how an analyst could specify enhancements to the interface model with respect to the cross-cutting variables of WMD threat and deception, which are central to the problem of anti-access strategies. A medium level of deception, for example, would be treated as increasing the time at which ground forces could reach the defense line by five days. A more complex specification would include more interactions between WMD and deception, but even this example includes some: Where WMD effects are specified in terms such as "Max of 12," the WMD and deception effects interact.

Using Interface Models for Gaming

Using interface models is also a way to allow for some explicit gaming.

Analytical models are typically inappropriate for representing explicit measure-countermeasure phenomena or for permitting interactive games such as are possible with some simulation models, such as JICM. This is unfortunate, since many of the important phenomena in warfare occur as competitions ("games") at the tactical or operational level. To represent such issues while using EXHALT-CF, more work needs to be done off line. For example, if in a particular run of the model one is assuming that Red disperses his forces more than in the baseline case, one may want to assume that Blue moves to point weapons rather than area weapons. Similarly, if one wants to postulate a "surprise attack" providing Blue very little usable warning, then one may want to limit the size of the attack as well: The act of preparing large numbers of divisions for attack provides strong strategic warning.

The Red countermeasure of holding a portion of its air defense batteries in hiding to prolong the period Blue requires to complete the SEAD attack can be reflected by increasing the assumed SEAD time and—because Blue would likely realize what Red was up to—allowing Blue to commit more of his forces to anti-armor missions prior to completion of SEAD. That is, the parameter F_{post} might be increased. Blue would suffer more losses, but that might be necessary.

Although some of the competition can be reflected in work with an analytical model such as EXHALT-CF, those interested in pursuing game issues in more depth should

Table 7.5

ILLUSTRATIVE SPECIFICATION OF INTERFACE-MODEL EFFECTS

Scenario-Space Dimension	Input Variable	Values to Be Used in Experiments	WMD Threat			Deception		
			Low	Med	High	Low	Med	High
Political-military circumstances	Obj	600 km						
Political-military circumstances	T_{line}, Time defense line is established	2 days			Un-likely	+0	+5	+7
Political-military circumstances	T_{delay}, Delay imposed by early strike on assembling forces	0, 2 days						
Strategy and tactics	D_{line}, Depth of defense line (km)	80 km			NA			
Strategy and tactics	T_{wait}, Wait time	1, 3 days				+0	+1	+3
Force effectiveness	F_{pre}, Initial anti-armor fraction of relevant shooters	0						
Strategy and tactics	F_{post}, Anti-armor fraction of relevant shooters from T_{wait} until T_{SEAD}	0.25						
Strategy and tactics	F, Anti-armor fraction of relevant shooters after T_{SEAD}	1						
Forces	ξ, AFVs to kill for halt	1000, 2000, 4000				–0	–0	–1500
Forces	A_0, D-Day shooters	0, 100, 300						Max of 150
Forces	R, Deployment rate	18 eq. shooters/day Triangular (1/2 nominal, nominal, 2 nominal)		Max of 12	Max of 9	–0	–3	–6
Forces	N_A, Number of good weapons	2000; 100,000						
Forces	G, Capability of ground forces at defense line	700, 1200			NA			
Force effectiveness	V, Movement rate	40, 70, 100 km/day						
Force effectiveness	T_{SEAD}, SEAD time	1, 3 days				+0	+1	+2
Force effectiveness	S_{std}, Standard sortie rate	2			X 0.5			

Table 7.5 (continued)

Scenario-Space Dimension	Input Variable	Values to Be Used in Experiments	WMD Threat			Deception		
			Low	Med	High	Low	Med	High
Force effectiveness	Eff_n_A Good (type-A) weapons per sortie	6						
Force effectiveness	δ, Kills per shooter day with type-A weapons	2, 4 Log normal (nominal, 3), where 3 is the geometric standard deviation				X 1	X 0.75	X 0.5
Force effectiveness	δ_B, Kills per shooter day with type-B weapons	1			X 0.5			
Force effectiveness	$L_{dailyavg}$, Daily losses from T_{wait} to T_{SEAD}	0, 10						
Environmental factors	A_{max}, Theater capacity	200, 1000		Max of 500	Max of 200			
Other model assumptions								

turn to other tools such as man-machine war games. Further, it will often be necessary to use models (or game boards) with a richer depiction of terrain, individual systems, and tactical-level decisions.

8. ILLUSTRATIVE ANALYSIS TOWARD ADAPTIVE STRATEGY

8.1 INTRODUCTION

In earlier chapters, we have derived and documented a model for exploratory analysis of the halt problem and related counter-maneuver challenges. In this final chapter, we illustrate analysis using the model—starting with a discussion of the "mission-system approach" and following with discussion of how a number of the key variables affect outcomes. At the end of the chapter, we sketch conclusions on how the U.S. Air Force can adapt to foreseeable difficulties in maintaining a high-confidence counter-maneuver capability in the Persian Gulf over the years ahead.

8.2 TAKING A MISSION-SYSTEM PERSPECTIVE

Basic Concepts

Exploratory analysis is most useful when it is directed by a system perspective. Otherwise, it may not convey much of a story. Taking a system perspective is neither a new idea nor controversial, but the system's boundaries are often drawn too narrowly. Discussions of the interdiction mission may treat a number of potentially crucial factors superficially, if at all. These include:

- Access problems (resulting from lack of permission or a decision to avoid use of forward bases within range of missiles with mass-destruction weapons)
- Deception affecting usable warning time
- Command and control (including all the elements of C^4ISR)
- Synergies between interdiction and ground forces
- Affecting the attacker with something less than very high levels of attrition, such as by causing delays or collapse of units that have less than superb cohesion and morale.

If ensuring capabilities for an early halt is a key mission and if one takes the view that the proper measure of capabilities is a sober assessment of what could *actually* be accomplished operationally, then the job may be very different from what is often depicted. This is not so much the case today in the Persian Gulf—when U.S. forces are forward deployed, at high readiness for conflict, and faced with a severely degraded and constrained Iraqi military. It is very much of interest, however, for the longer term—especially if sanctions are lifted, Iraq's military is strengthened, U.S. presence is somewhat reduced, and readiness for war is not so high as it is today.

Figure 8.1 indicates schematically how U.S. forces might be expected to build over time in response to warning and the start of war. It also shows (the lower, dashed line) that "full-system competence" for making good use of the forces available might lag—perhaps because of lags in the stabilization and preparation of joint command groups (a function partly of high-level decisions), obtaining all of the surveillance

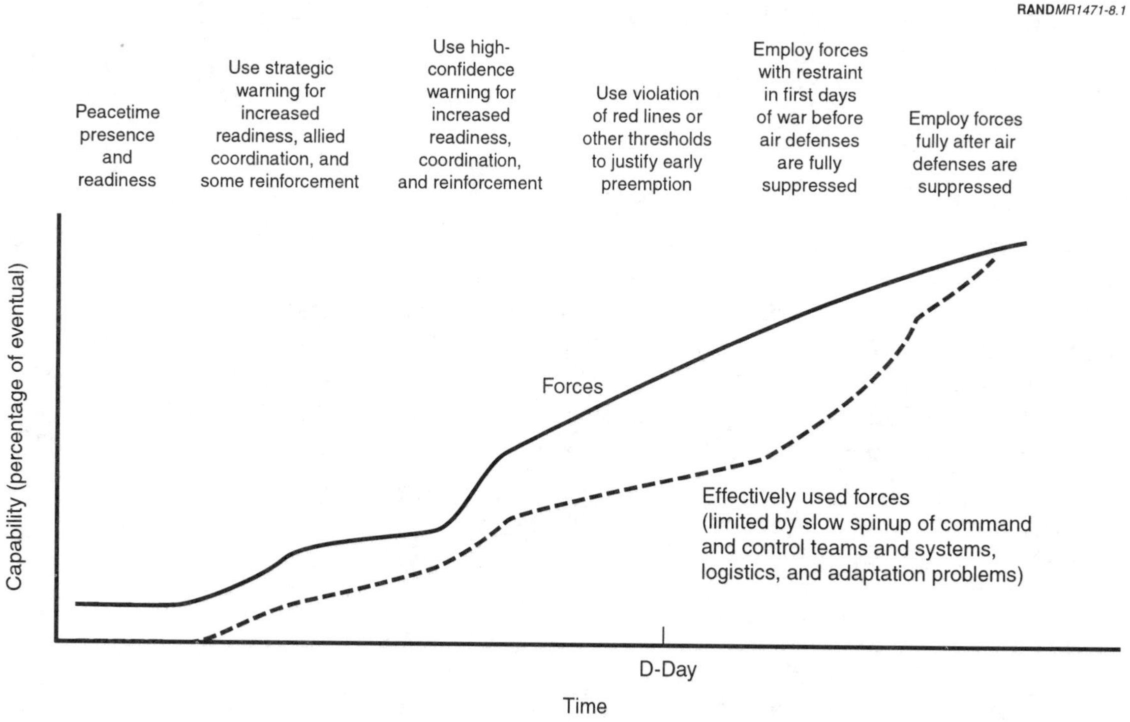

Figure 8.1—Schematic Baseline of System Capabilities Versus Time

and reconnaissance systems needed, preparing for large-scale operations rather than much smaller ones, and dealing with formidable logistics problems if unexpected adaptations were necessary. Full-system competence would likely build slowly and might not reach a high level until after D-Day.

Some might dispute this image, but the empirical record is sobering. Even with heroic efforts, U.S. deployment and preparation of forces for war in Desert Shield were substantially worse than was expected from force planning studies. Despite the fact that deployment did not begin for a week after invasion, it proceeded slower than planning factors anticipated. More serious were the delays in stabilizing the command, adapting the war plan, and changing the deployment flows. Had Saddam Hussein continued his invasion into Saudi Arabia, many problems would have been evident that instead remained below the surface. They were discussed extensively, however, in lessons-learned activities at the time.

The situation might be better today, but senior officers who served in the Bosnian and Kosovo conflicts also reported difficulties. Some, like General John Jumper (USAF), concluded that standing command groups were necessary. The 9th Air Force, under Lt General Charles Wald, has recently established such an organization.[1]

---

[1]The combined air-operations center (CAOC) emphasizes not only standing capability at high readiness, but also extensive interactions with regional allies. For discussion of related Blue Flag exercises, see http://www.hurlburt.af.mil/commando/archives/000310/000310-002.html.

The goal should be similar to that sketched in Figure 8.2, where full-system competence is achieved quickly and deployed forces can be used efficiently from the outset of war. This goal is not a mere "nice to have," because overall *mission-system capability* depends on it.

An Example of Mission-System Analysis

An early analytical discussion of the mission-system view can be found in Defense Science Board (1998) and Davis, Bigelow, and McEver (1999). We review some of the findings to provide a top-down view of the problem before discussing effects of individual variables in more detail.

Drawing from the earlier work, Figure 8.3 illustrates how major component capabilities for the halt mission can be aggregated from detailed factors from the results of hundreds or thousands of cases tested by a model. The three components highlighted are early forces in place (essentially D-Day shooters), ability to fly early (i.e., ability to conduct anti-armor missions from early in the war), and early C^4ISR effectiveness. Light is good; dark is bad. Figure 8.3 shows "fuzzy logic" aggregations of underlying factors to generate natural-language characterizations of the three components. For example (next to bottom row), if the number of forward-deployed forces is inadequate, tactical warning time (D-day – C-Day) is two days, and strategic warning time is eight days or more, then the component "early forces in place" can be judged to be fair. These combining rules for the analysis of Davis, Bigelow, and

Need to measure and improve rate of gaining "full system competence," as well as deployment rate

RANDMR1471-8.2

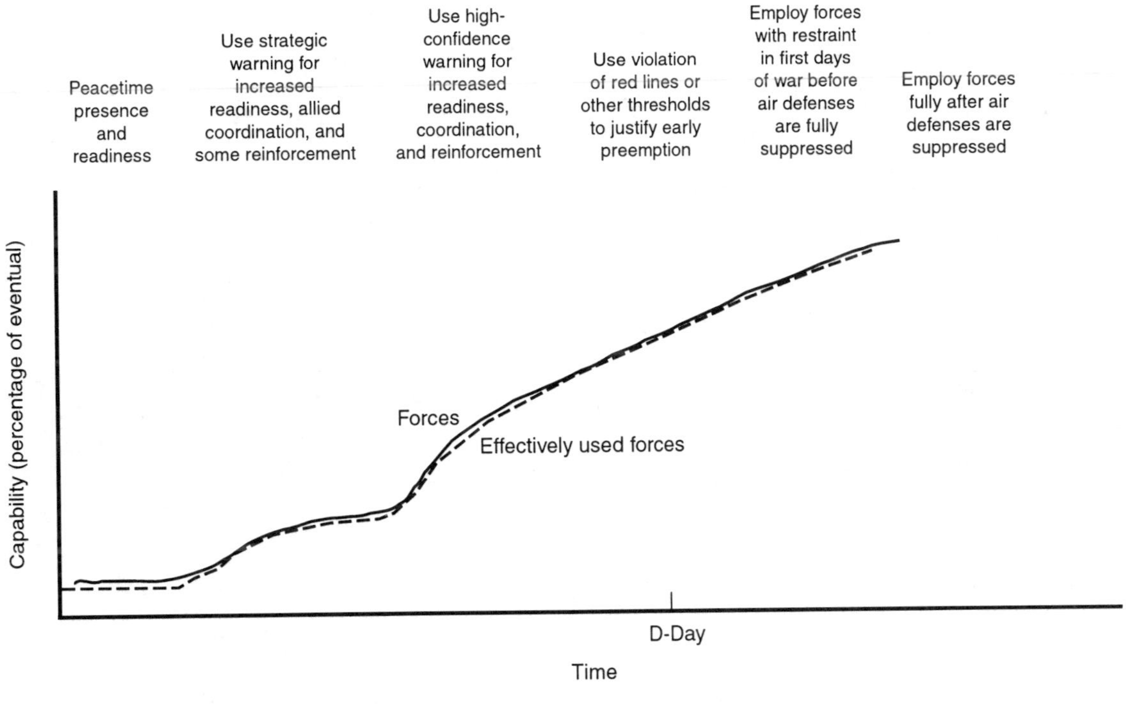

Figure 8.2—Schematic of Improved Capabilities Versus Time

RANDMR1471-8.3

Early forces in place

Forward-deployed forces	Tactical warning time	Strategic warning time	Result: Forces in place
Adequate	2 days	2 days	Good
Adequate	2 days	8 days	Good
Adequate	8 days	8 days	Good
Inadequate	2 days	2 days	Bad
Inadequate	2 days	8 days	Fair
Inadequate	8 days	8 days	Good

Ability to fly early

SEAD time	Use of stealth	Result: Ability to fly early
2 days	Full	Good
2 days	Some	Good
6 days	Full	Good
6 days	Some	Bad

Early C4ISR effectiveness

Competence time from warning	Strategic warning time	Early C4ISR assets	Result: Early C4ISR effectiveness
4 days	2 days	Not survivable	Fair
4 days	2 days	Survivable	Fair
4 days	8 days	Not survivable	Good
4 days	8 days	Survivable	Very good
10 days	2 days	Not survivable	Bad
10 days	2 days	Survivable	Bad
10 days	8 days	Not survivable	Fair
10 days	8 days	Survivable	Fair

Figure 8.3—Aggregating Lower-Level Variables into Mission-Capability Components

McEver (1999) were not arbitrary, but rather the result of extensive exploratory analysis. The purpose of the figure was to reduce complexity to simple conceptual chunks. The ability to fly early, in this limited analysis, depended on the ability to operate anti-armor missions before SEAD was complete. In this case, the combining rule was an "or" condition. That is, if SEAD is accomplished quickly, *or* if anti-armor platforms are stealthy or can be used anyway (e.g., as with long-range standoff missiles), then Blue shooters have the ability to fly early. Early C4ISR effectiveness is shown as a function of competence time from warning (i.e., how long it takes the real-world command and control team to be fully effective and efficient), the duration of the strategic warning causing such preparations to begin, and the quality of the C4ISR assets that are available early (are they survivable or not). Although the competence-time factor may seem abstract, it could be measured in exercises and refined through improvements in doctrine, readiness standards, and distributed operations during strategic warning.

Figure 8.4 now shows how these components can be combined in a mission-system assessment. The top part of the figure assumes a small threat; the lower part assumes a large one (but with a less stringent objective of 300 km). In each of the two blocks, the format is as follows: each column corresponds to a set of analytical cases. For

RANDMR1471-8.4

Small Red Force (500 AFVs to kill, 100 km Objective)

Forces in place	G	G	F	B	F	B	G	F	B	G	F	B	G	G	F	F	G	B	B	F	B	G	F	B
Ability to fly early	G	B	G	G	B	B	G	G	G	B	G	G	B	G	B	G	B	B	G	B	B	B	B	B
Early C^4ISR effectiveness	VG	VG	VG	VG	VG	VG	G	G	G	F	F	F	G	B	G	B	F	G	B	F	F	B	B	B
Result: Red distance (km)	47	47	116	116	116	116	144	161	172	176	192	199	201	257	284	285	286	297	312	326	339	424	451	453

<100 | 100–200 | >200

Large Red Force (4000 AFVs to kill, 300 km Objective)

Forces in place	G	F	B	G	G	G	F	F	B	F	B	B	G	G	F	F	B	B	G	F	B	G	F	B
Ability to fly early	G	G	G	G	B	G	B	G	B	G	G	G	B	B	B	B	B	B	G	G	G	B	B	B
Early C^4ISR effectiveness	VG	VG	VG	G	VG	F	VG	G	VG	F	G	F	G	F	G	F	G	F	B	B	B	B	B	B
Result: Red distance (km)	114	164	199	280	290	336	342	347	363	389	402	435	501	521	534	557	558	573	591	614	644	711	725	739

<300 | 300–500 | >500

VG Very good | G Good | F Fair | B Bad | VB Very bad

NOTE: Each column is a case; result of case is in lowest row. Light outcomes are good; dark outcomes are bad. Numbers in bottom row are halt distances.

Figure 8.4—A Mission-System View Summarizing Outcomes from Exploratory Analysis

example, the first column shows results for cases in which forces in place is good, ability to fly early is good, and early C^4ISR effectiveness is very good. In such cases, the average halt distance from simulation was 47 km—a very good result. Thus, the first three rows are inputs; the last row gives corresponding outputs.

Upon looking at all the various cases in Figure 8.4, one sees graphically the main point: that the *mission-system capability is poor unless all of the critical component capabilities are achieved.*[2]

[2]The mission-system view described here is analogous to the concept of mission-capability packages discussed in Alberts, Garstka, and Stein (1999).

A Requirements Diagram

Figure 8.5 is a visual summary from the same earlier analysis, but one expressed in terms of a requirements surface. The figure assumes a small Red threat (500 AFVs to be killed) and uses an average shooter effectiveness, which is the product of the average number of Blue shooters during the halt campaign and the number of kills per shooter day. To achieve an early halt—i.e., one at less than 100 km—Blue's shooter effectiveness and SEAD time must be below the three-dimensional surface. Equivalently, consider a particular Red movement rate. That corresponds to a horizontal plane through the figure and Blue's requirement is then for lethality and wait time to be inside the corresponding two-dimensional curve (into the paper). For example, if Red's speed is 20 km/day (the lowest slice shown), then if Blue's SEAD time is 0, his lethality can be as little as 100 kills per day, as indicated by the leftmost •. Moving along the curve in the plane corresponding to 20 km/day (coming toward the reader and to the right), Blue could also achieve an early halt with a wait time of four days and a shooter effectiveness of 500 kills per day (see the rightmost •). The reader may have trouble seeing this: Such displays are visually interesting and economical, but they are difficult to read and take some getting used to. Thus, except for this example, we have not used such displays in this monograph. Nonetheless, using this example to reinforce the point of this section, note that the equal effectiveness curves for a given Red speed are strongly curved, rather than straight lines. This is a visual indication that while Blue can trade off shooter effectiveness and SEAD time to some extent, that extent is very limited: If SEAD time is too long or if shooter effectiveness is too little, Blue fails.

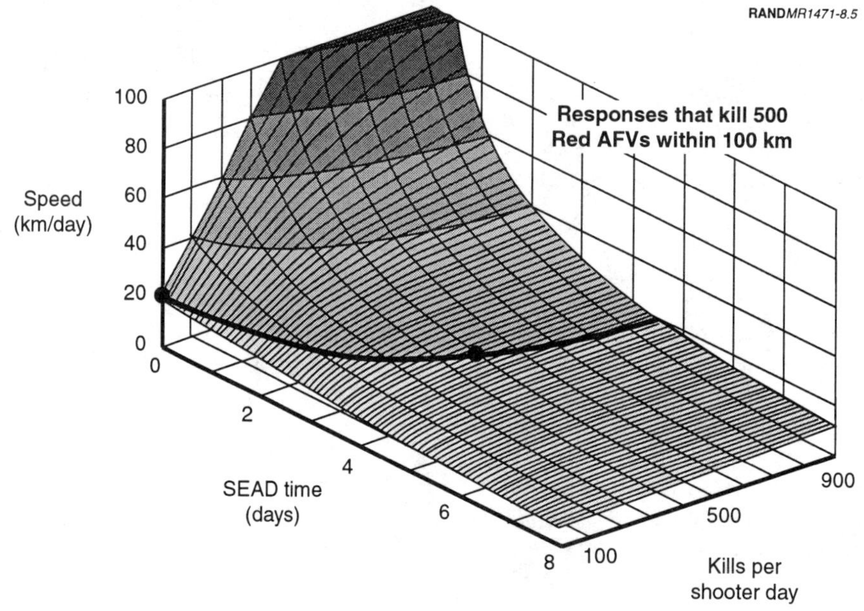

Figure 8.5—A Three-Dimensional "Requirements Envelope" for Achieving an Early Halt

Summary on Mission-System View

With this prefacing discussion, we have attempted to develop a high-level perspective before discussing exploratory analysis on the effects of individual elements of the problem.

8.3 SELECTED OBSERVATIONS FROM ANALYSIS

We now illustrate the analysis of individual effects and their interactions. Such analysis can sharpen and quantify the issues, although it must be supported with high-resolution work to be credible. Since the purpose here is illustration, we will show examples of output graphics to make various points. We do not present complete exploratory analyses because the results would be tedious. Nonetheless, the conclusions we draw are based on broader exploration. At the end of the chapter, we illustrate relatively comprehensive summaries of exploratory analysis.

Preventing a Quick Takeover

The system perspective requires us to note that a critical element of success is preventing a sudden takeover (coup de main), such as could be accomplished by a surprise attack spearheaded by special forces and units that had been "exercising" on the border. In the absence of effective resistance, a sudden attack could largely accomplish a takeover within a day if the distances are short, as they are from Iraq to Kuwait City. This scenario mirrors what happened in 1990 and there are numerous historical precedents for coups de main (although time scales for them have shortened).[3] Halt models such as that in this monograph are irrelevant for analyzing such events.

To prevent such sudden collapses would likely require the defender to have significant forces on high-readiness alert and to maintain vigilant surveillance in the skies and over shipping. U.S. air forces could assist in such matters, but many of the key elements would depend on the defender itself.

Movement Rates

Figure 8.6 describes the strong role of the attacker's baseline movement rate V. The upper panels of Figure 8.6 shows how difficult it is for Blue—even in favorable cases—to achieve an early halt (less than 100 km or so) if speeds are fairly high (70 and 100 km/day). Most of the assumptions for these figures have been set optimistically for Blue, as indicated in the rotation boxes. The threat is small (only 1000 AFVs to kill), Blue has essentially unlimited weapons (20,000), SEAD time is reasonably short (two days), theater capacity is not a problem (1000 shooters), and deployment

[3]On August 2, 1990, the Iraqi attack began at 1 am. Victory was claimed by Baghdad radio by 11 am and forces secured Kuwait City by 7 pm. The emir had fled in the morning. Iraq's invasion was led by three Republican Guard divisions and a special operations force that made heliborne and amphibious assaults (DoD, 1992, p. 3; Hiro, 1992, Ch. 2). Other relatively quick and painless takeovers have included the Soviet-British invasion of neutral Iran in 1941 (Stewart, 1988) and the Soviet invasion of Afghanistan in 1979.

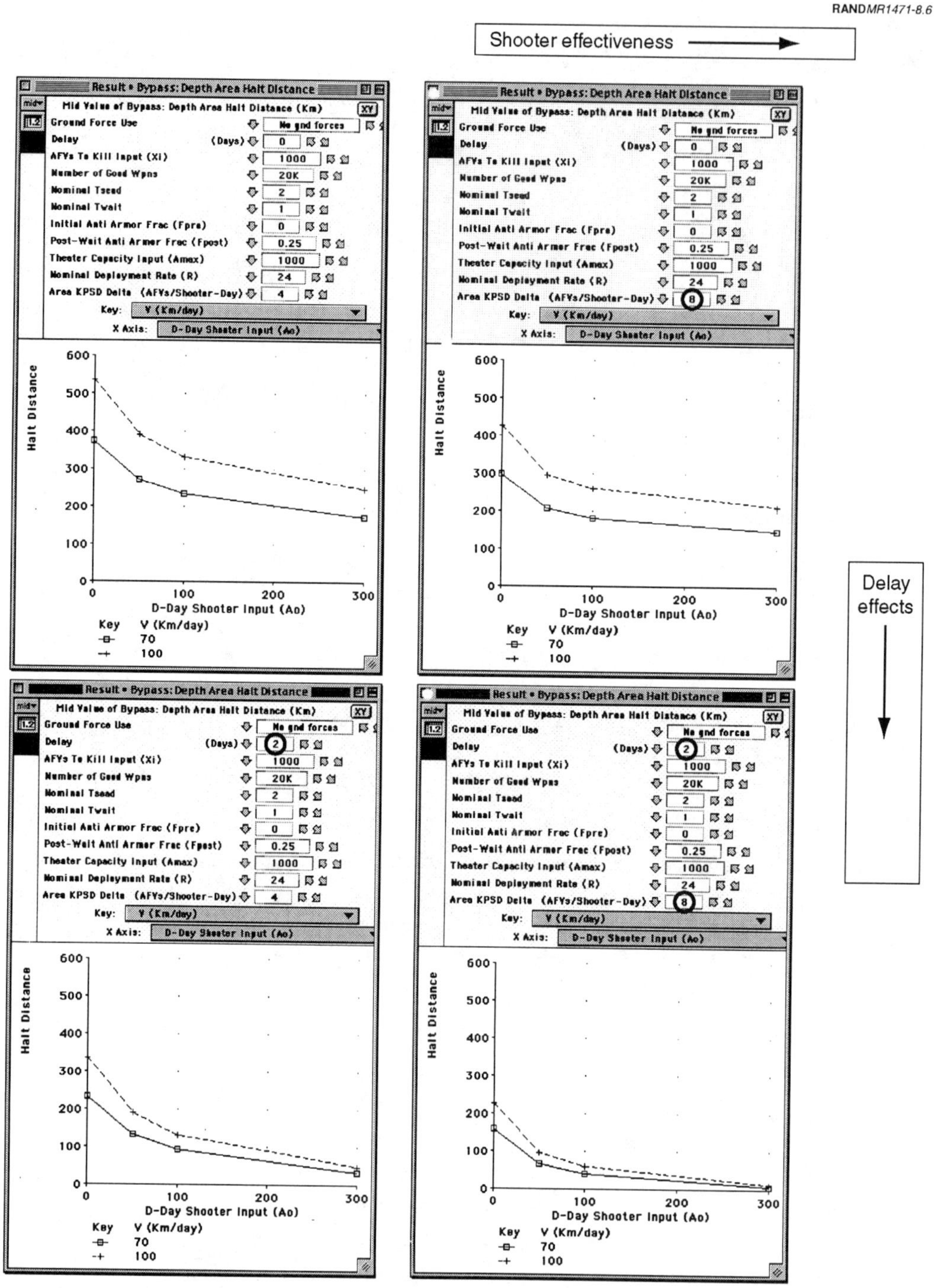

NOTES: Calculations assume in-depth strategy; all shooters used against armor after SEAD (i.e., F = 1); no air defense; area weapons; a delay in SEAD if D-Day shooters are less than 24; and 50-meter separation between AFVs (the nominal spacing assumed in characterizing shooter effectiveness). All other parameters of the model are explicit in the figures.

Figure 8.6—Effects on Halt Distance of Attacker's Movement Rate, Delays Caused by Initial Strikes, and Weapon-System Lethality

rate is quite fast (24 shooters per day). In addition (see note at bottom), the attacker is only modestly dispersed, with 50 m between AFVs. Finally, we show explicitly the effects of increasing kills per shooter day from four to eight (right panel versus left panel).

As points of calibration, the distance to Kuwait City is less than 100 km, the distance to the Kuwaiti border is roughly 140 km, the distance to northern Saudi Arabia is roughly 140–410 km, and the distance to Dhahran is roughly 600 km.

The lower panels remind us, however, that the story could change if Red could be delayed—perhaps by Blue's attacking Red as soon as Red's forces crossed a red line, as discussed earlier. The results show the effect of two days' worth of delay.

The key point is that *doing something about Red's movement rate is essential for the early halt.*

Later we show how the leading-edge strategy can reduce average speed in many cases (but not in others). This strategy and other tactics could plausibly reduce Red's average rate of advance—if Blue was prepared in advance and employed effectively. Tactics include in-place regular ground forces trained for delay operations (rather than stand-up-and-die operations), barriers defended with fires, and special operations forces to disrupt Red's movement and force him to move more deliberately.

Because slowing Red's advance rate is both critical and plausible, we show outcomes for lower speeds in many of the following examples.

D-Day Shooters

Figure 8.6 also indicates the need for sufficient D-Day shooters, an abstraction that accounts for the effects of permanent presence, warning times, reinforcement rates, and pre-D-Day-access permissions. As suggested in Figure 8.6 (but for otherwise quite favorable assumptions), halt distances are typically large unless the number of D-Day shooters is substantial—at least 100 and preferably many more. [4] Unfortunately, the standard databases adopted in studies often result in hundreds of D-Day shooters, thereby obscuring this problem. To be sure, if deployment rates are high enough, A_0 is less important, but achieving such rates would be extremely hard.

Fortunately, having some D-Day shooters is plausible, although not easy. Consider that 50 long-range bombers flying from the United States, an Air Force fighter wing of fighters for anti-armor missions, and a carrier battle group's wing might amount to 150 or more equivalent shooters. That number might double or triple with larger loads, advanced munitions, much improved C^4ISR, and regional basing of bombers. It is reasonable to think in terms of 0–300 equivalent shooters on D-Day. *The higher figures, however, assume clear strategic warning, which would require a change in de facto national crisis doctrine.*

[4]The calculations shown in this chapter include the adjustment of SEAD time when D-Day shooters are below a minimum threshold (taken here as 24, merely as an example). In such cases, SEAD operations cannot begin until a threshold level of shooters has been deployed (a proxy for the time to deploy sufficient SEAD aircraft to begin missions). See discussion in Chapter 6.

Shooter effectiveness versus load size needs to be studied empirically and in high-resolution simulation

Regional basing for long-range bombers could, in principle, increase sortie rates and numbers of equivalent shooters—if crew ratios were sufficient and the bases' infrastructure were adequately developed and tailored for those bombers (a nontrivial matter). Small smart bombs and other methods of increasing loads, for both fighters and bombers, would increase kills per shooter day, but not in a straightforward way because of targeting and survivability issues that need to be elucidated by realistic experimentation and the development of realistically detailed simulations. By and large, we would expect the kills per weapon carried to drop significantly as the size of an aircraft's load increases. That would probably be less true for aircraft that could loiter survivably.

Protracted SEAD, Delays in C^4ISR, and Staged Operations

Continuing in the spirit of a system perspective, suppose that the United States *does* have sufficient D-Day shooters. Results are still poor if they cannot be used early because of delays in SEAD operations *and* the absence of anti-armor shooters that can be used before air defenses are suppressed. The same result would occur if shooters could not be engaged effectively because of delays in establishing good C^4ISR. Indeed, we can use SEAD time as a proxy for whatever causes forces to stage (i.e., to delay employing shooters against the moving armored vehicles). Figure 8.7 illustrates the effects of staging by assuming 100 and 300 D-Day shooters (left and right panels) and plotting results as a function of the kills per shooter day and SEAD time. Only when the SEAD time is quite short (lowest curve, one day) are results good—and then only when the kills per shooter day are reasonably high. The sensitivity to SEAD time depends on the other variables. As a point of departure, average kills per anti-armor sortie were only about 0.25 in the Gulf War, but reportedly approached 1 for the best systems (F-15Es using Mavericks). The United States should be able to do much better with more advanced weapons, such as sensor-fuzed weapons (Ochmanek et al., 1998). With two kills per sortie and two sorties per day, the result would be a value of 4 for the kills per equivalent-shooter day.[5]

Shooter Effectiveness

Halt distance is shortened by having good weapons (i.e., effective shooters). Figure 8.7 also shows the dependence of outcome on kills per shooter day for otherwise favorable assumptions (300 D-Day aircraft, rapid deployment rate, etc.). Achieving four or more kills per shooter day is necessary for an early halt. Remember that this corresponds to the product of kills per sortie and sorties per day. For more difficult cases, much higher effectiveness would be needed.

---

[5]The peculiar shapes of the top-most curves in Figure 8.7 result because the shooter effectiveness is high enough for the halt to be accomplished prior to completion of SEAD by the fraction F_{post} of shooters able to operate in the period.

RANDMR1471-8.7

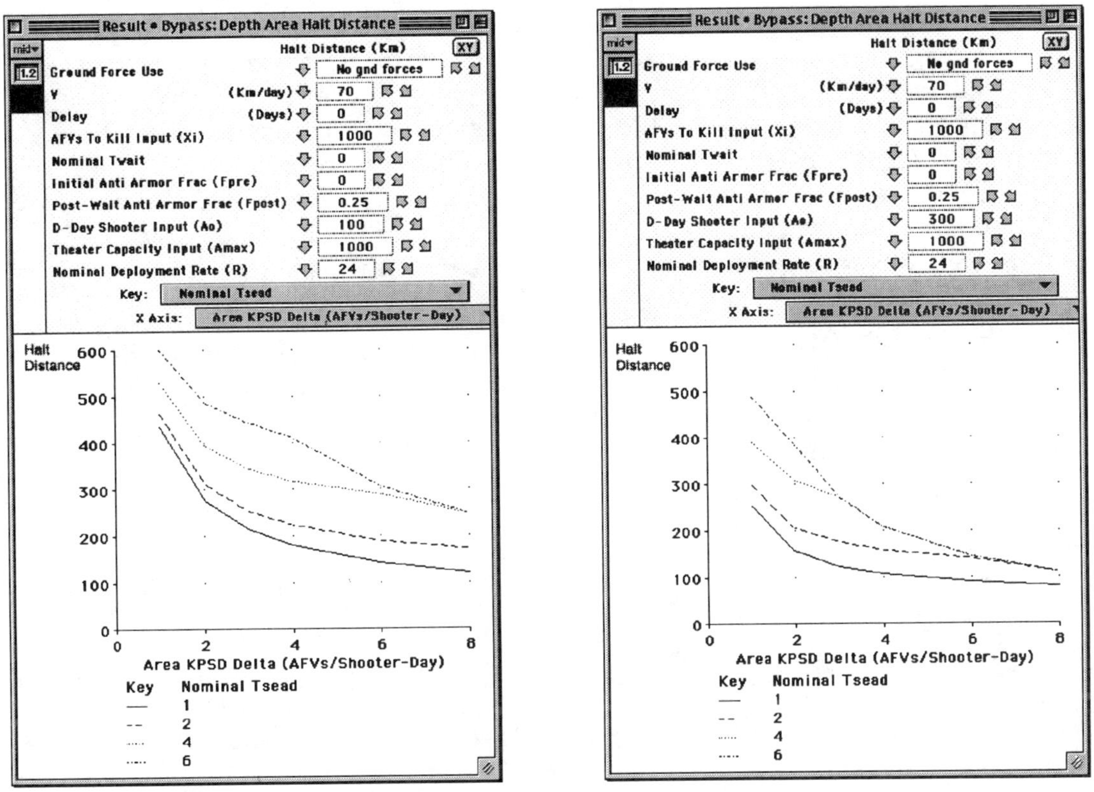

Figure 8.7—SEAD Time as a Limiting Factor

Number of Top-Quality Munitions

Traditionally, the Air Force has been reluctant to buy huge quantities of precision weapons—despite the cost effectiveness suggested by analysis. There are several reasons, some organizational and some rational. Organizationally, the "stove pipe" nature of many budgets makes it difficult to shift money from one account to another. Another problem is that buying more weapons must compete with buying new fighter aircraft or improved C^4ISR. In addition, Air Force leaders are very much aware that the next generation of weapons (e.g., the Low Cost Autonomous Attack System, LOCAAS) will always be even better and that purchases of today's best weapons (sensor-fuzed weapons) may come at the expense of delayed buys of those even-better weapons. Thus, the buys are much smaller than they might be. That will likely continue to be the case until and unless a big war appears imminent. The result, of course, is that the United States runs certain risks.

It is of interest, then, to measure the consequences. Figure 8.8 illustrates results for an otherwise very good case. The invader is moving slower than in the baseline (an average of 40 km/day instead of 70 km/day, perhaps because of air and missile strikes or a leading-edge strategy), theater capacity is not a problem, and the kills per shooter day approach eight. Results in the left panel are for a large threat (3500 AFVs to be killed). A relatively early halt is possible if the number of D-Day shooters approaches 300 (lower curve) and plenty of weapons are available. However, the upper curve shows the effect of having only 2000 of the top-quality weapons, with effectiveness dropping to two kills per shooter day thereafter (which is already significantly higher than in Desert Storm).

This effect, however, depends on other factors. In this case, the most important factor is probably the size of the threat itself. As shown in the right panel, the effect largely goes away for small threats.

Losses to Air Defenses

Although our models include attrition from air defenses, that attrition has negligible direct effects on outcomes of analysis (not shown here). The principal effects are

RANDMR1471-8.8

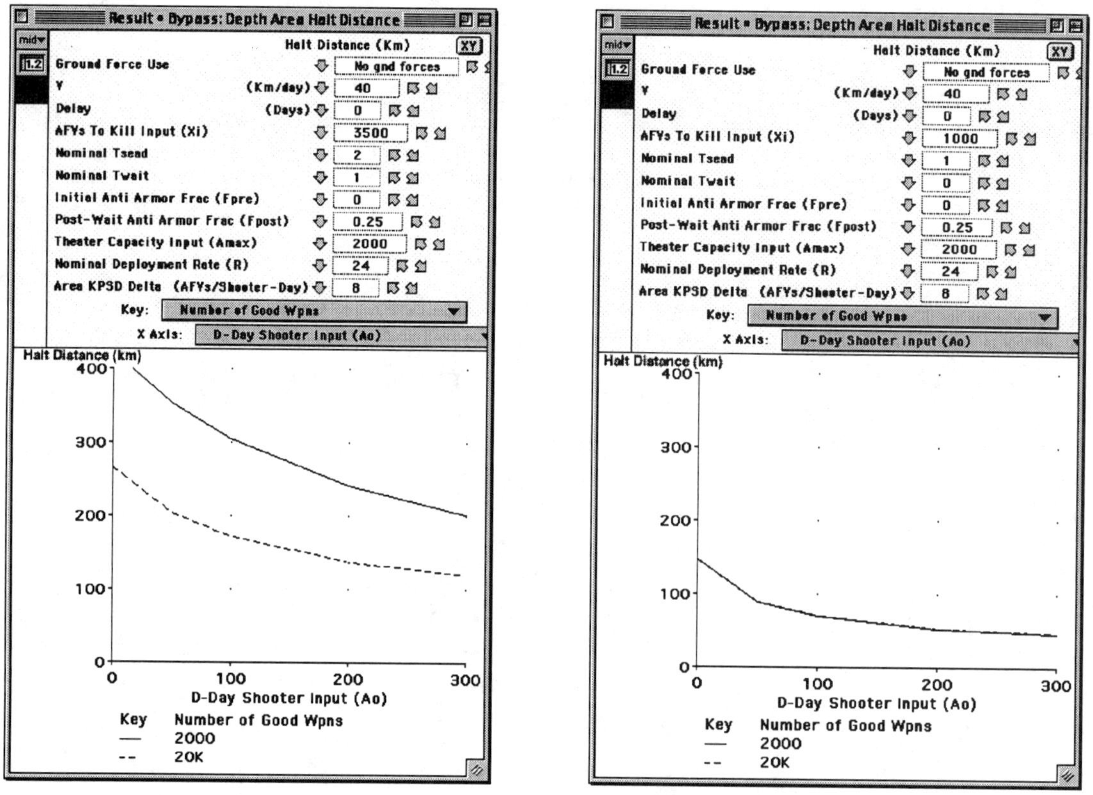

NOTES: Other assumptions are as in preceding figures, except that less-capable (type-B) point weapons are used when good weapons are exhausted. Type B weapons are assumed to achieve two kills per shooter day.

Figure 8.8—Effect of Insufficient Top-Quality Weapons

indirect. To the extent that U.S. forces attempt to avoid losses altogether, the effect is to force operations into phasing, which delays anti-armor attacks. This effect can be catastrophic for accomplishing an *early* halt. The response, of course, is to ensure somehow the ability to employ at least a significant portion of the available force against armor even before air defenses are found and destroyed. That would result in at least some losses, although there is no empirical basis for believing that even detailed models with equally detailed data on SAMs can accurately calculate the loss rate. Thus, the model assumes a simple exponential decay. We do not show graphs for this effect, because no insights emerge that are not otherwise obvious. We shall discuss the effects of phasing later.

Deployment Rates

Deployment rates are not usually as pivotal in determining outcomes in the current analysis for reasons discussed in Chapter 3 *except* that (1) results are sensitive to the number of D-Day shooters, which depends implicitly on deployment rates during the warning period; and (2) deployment rate is critical if the number of D-Day shooters is small (Figure 8.9). Unfortunately, it is difficult to increase deployment rates enough to compensate for a small number of D-Day shooters. Such considerations suggest that it is the *initial deployment rates that matter most, not the average rate of sustained deployment*. Faster is always better, but the highest leverage is up front. Conversely, high rates after a long delay do not compensate for low rates early. This can be seen in the explorations of Figure 8.9 in that the several curves in each panel, which correspond to different assumed deployment rates, are not very different except for small values of D-Day shooter. As shown in the lower panels, however, good results can be obtained with few D-Day shooters if Red can be delayed, deployment rates are high, and shooter effectiveness (kills per shooter day) is high.

Anti-Access Problems and Weapons of Mass Destruction

Another class of problems is that if weapons of mass destruction are used or threatened, U.S. operations could be severely degraded. Figure 8.10 illustrates this. Again, to make the point strongly, we consider an otherwise favorable case: a small threat, short SEAD time, and substantial D-Day shooters (300). However, not all of the potentially available shooters may be usable because—if WMD problems are "medium" or "high"—we assume that aircraft would be diverted to more distant bases with a concomitant reduction of sorties. Also, we assume that base capacity would also be reduced substantially (Chapter 3). Some prior studies have assumed that the overall effect would be a reduction of perhaps 50 percent, corresponding to a sortie reduction rate if shooters were driven to longer ranges,[6] but it could be much larger unless alternative bases had been well prepared (fuel, fuel hydrants, ramp space, etc.) and stocked with munitions. Figure 8.10 assumes a factor-of-four effect on theater capacity in high-WMD cases. The top panels assume a large threat with a movement rate

[6] One effect of greater range is a reduction of sortie rates that can readily be a factor of two (Stillion and Orletsky, 1999, App. B). Other considerations include ramp space, hydrants, fuel storage, weapons storage, and general infrastructure. See O'Malley (2001).

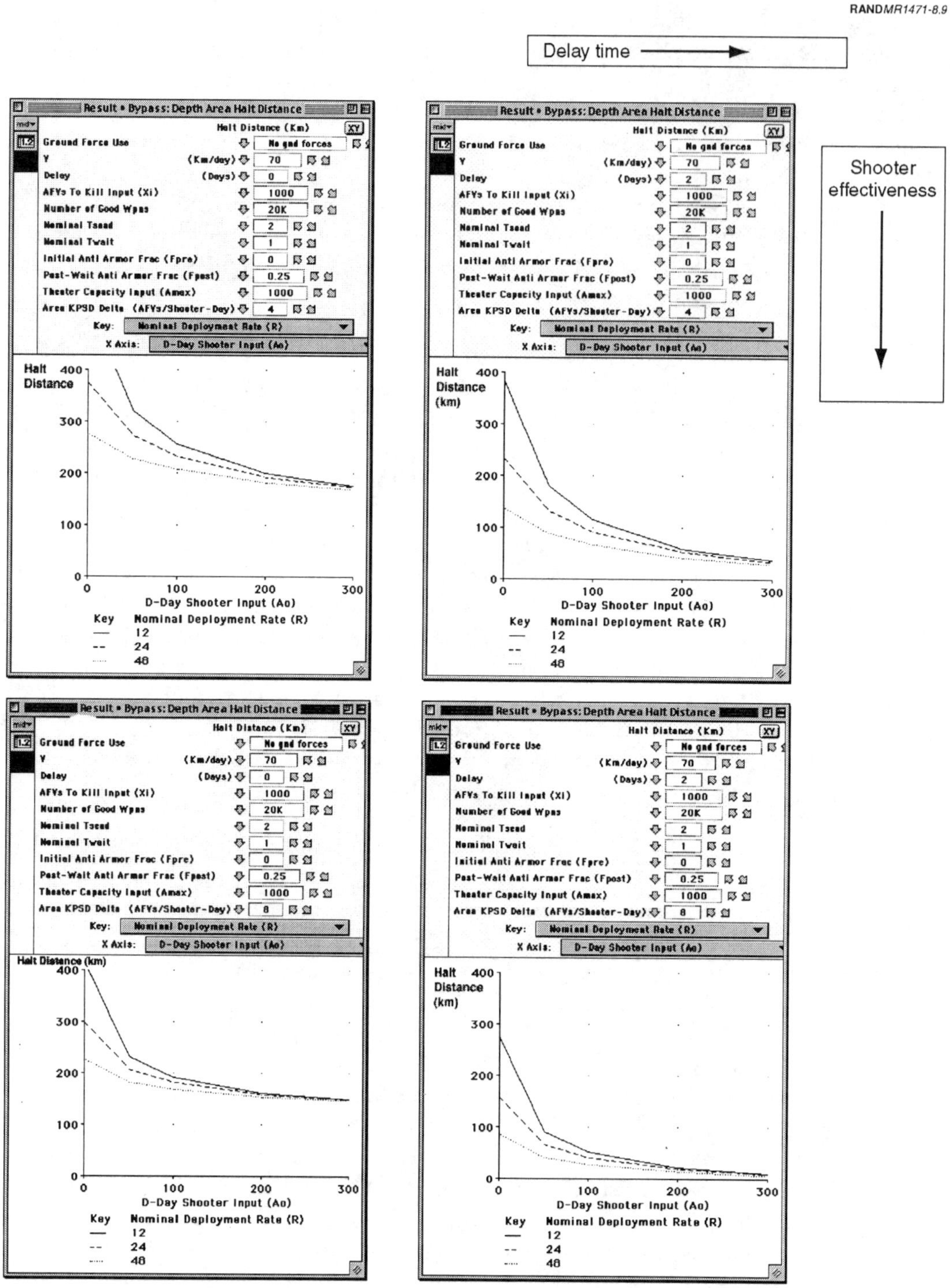

Figure 8.9—Sensitivity to Deployment Rate Is Highest When Number of D-Day Shooters Is Small

RANDMR1471-8.10

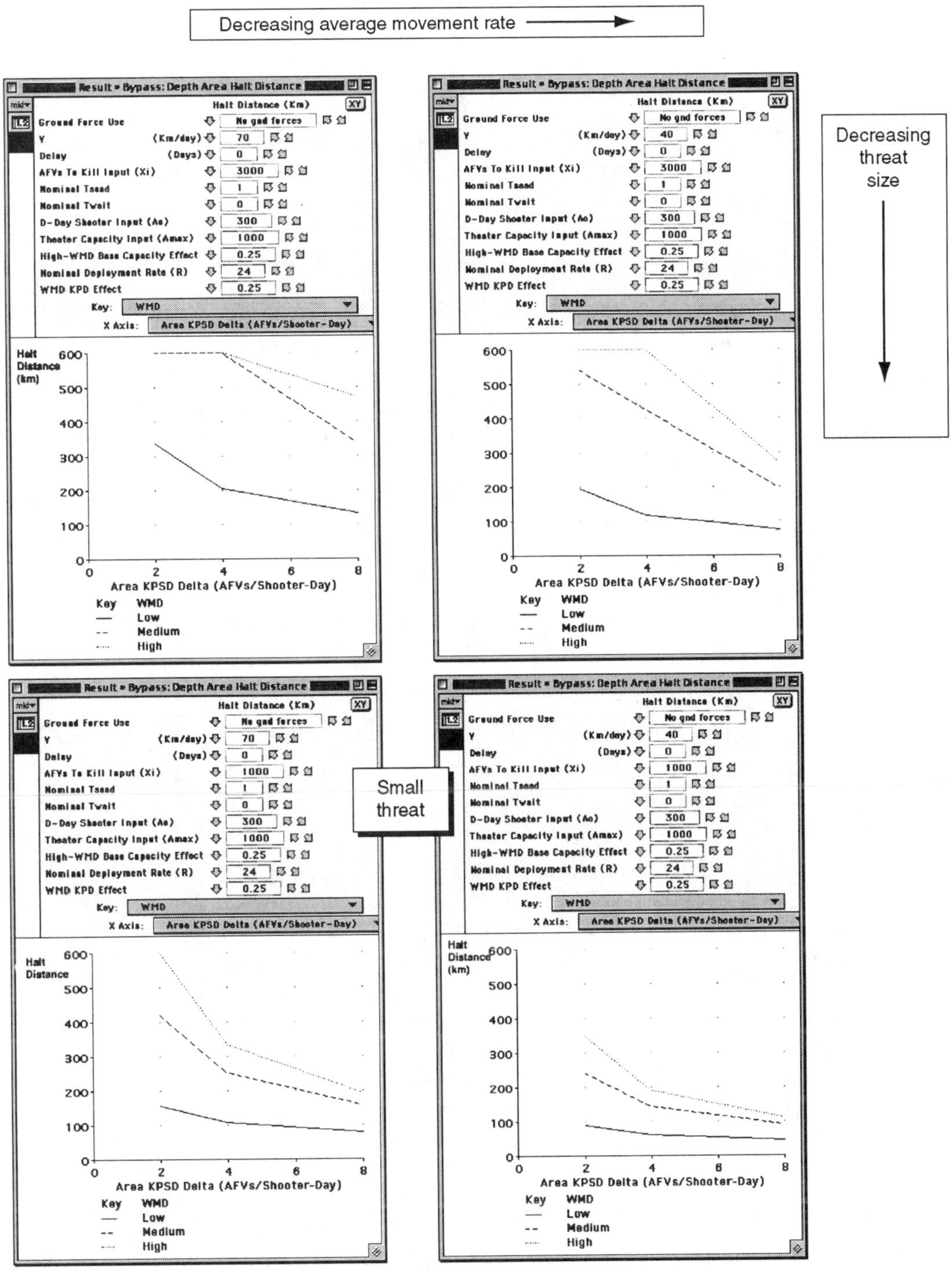

NOTE: Other model assumptions are as in earlier figures.

Figure 8.10—Enemy Missiles and Mass-Destruction Weapons Would Worsen Results of 70 km/day (left) and 40 km/day (right). Note that the scales go to 600-km halt distance. An early halt is obtained only in the bottom right (small threat, slow speed).

Effects of Delayed Access to Regional Bases

One effect of anti-access strategies—even if not backed up by credible mass-destruction threats to bases—might be to reduce the base capacity available for U.S. shooters. This would not affect long-range bombers or naval carriers, and it is unlikely that *all* regional bases would be denied. Thus, we might ask about the effect of capacity constraints in the range of 100 to 1000 (essentially no limit).

Perhaps surprisingly, in most regions of the scenario space, this capacity constraint has relatively little effect on outcomes. Either by visual exploration, statistical analysis, or some thought followed up by visual exploration, one can find where (i.e., with what combinations of other parameters) capacity constraints matter most. Logically, they should matter when the halt depends on mass, rather than per-shooter effectiveness, such as when the threat is large and the per-shooter-day effectiveness is low. The left panels of Figure 8.11 represent corresponding slices through the scenario space. For this slice, theater capacity matters significantly for large threats. The right panels show much smaller effects for small threats. Theater capacity would matter a great deal more, of course, if we ruled out the use of long-range bombers and aircraft carriers. In that case, if capacity were very low, then the problem would be intractable.

Slowing Movement: Effects of Force Employment Strategy

An option discussed in this report, based primarily on earlier work (Ochmanek, Harshberger, Thaler, and Kent, 1998), is the leading-edge strategy. Our work confirms the earlier work, for equivalent assumptions. However, as indicated by earlier exploratory analysis (Davis and Carrillo, 1997), the strategy would only sometimes work in Southwest Asia. In particular, the leading-edge strategy would provide little or no advantage—if the attacker used many columns per axis of advance, if there were an effectiveness penalty for using the leading-edge strategy rather than the in-depth strategy (associated with the smaller attack domain and the need to carefully deconflict sorties and avoid air defenses expecting attacks on the leading edge), *and if* the attacker could maintain high rates of advance (more like 70 than 40 km/day) on a multiaxis attack. What an attacker could reasonably do, however, is arguable (see discussion in Ochmanek et al., 2000). Thus, the issue merits more analysis.

Figure 8.12 shows some parametrics for the leading-edge strategy. In the top panels, we plot results versus the size of the threat and, to sharpen issues, the composite parameter of slowing per AFV killed (Ω in the mathematics). This is the single parameter that characterizes the attacker's susceptibility to the leading-edge strategy. It is inversely proportional to the number of attack axes, the number of columns per axis, and the local halt fraction. It is also proportional to the spacing between AFVs. Thus, to minimize susceptibility to the slowing effect for a given effectiveness of defender weapons, the attacker should bunch up his AFVs, use many axes, and have

RANDMR1471-8.11

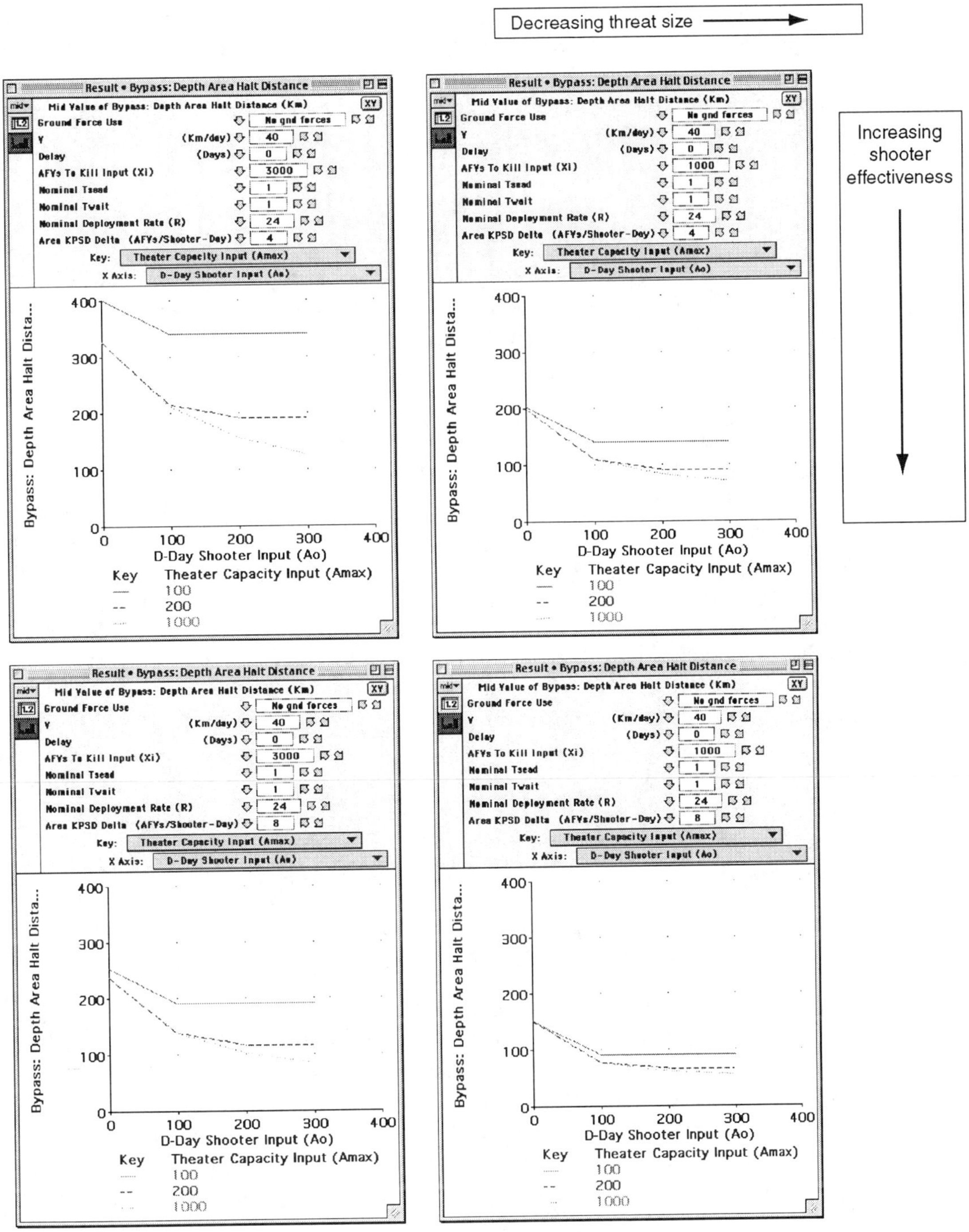

NOTE: Assumptions of other variables are as in previous figures.

Figure 8.11—Illustrative Effect of Theater Capacity

units that persist despite high attrition rates. The lower two curves in each of the panels correspond to plausible configurations vulnerable to the leading-edge attack. For example, in these cases the attacker may have only one axis of advance *or* his units may break at 50 percent rather than 75 percent attrition. The upper two curves represent much more resistant cases, but may be operationally difficult. They might correspond, for example, to three to five axes, each with two columns, *and* a break point of 75 percent. Note that *if the slowing effect is strong* (lower curves)*, halt distance is not very strongly dependent on the size of the threat.*

By increasing the spacing between AFVs (right panels), Red can do better because Blue's area munitions are less effective. However, Red is still slowed—decreasing halt distance. Further, he would likely find it more difficult to command and control his forces. Finally, it would take him longer to maneuver his forces. The optimum strategy for Red is to spread his AFVs sufficiently so that he is indifferent to whether Blue uses area or point munitions.[7] Further dispersion would have no benefit.

The lower two panels of Figure 8.12 plot halt distance against the number of D-Day shooters and the sensitivity to the slowing effect, assuming a large threat (3000 AFVs to be killed). Here we assume a fast base movement rate,[8] but we vary Blue's effectiveness from four to eight kills per shooter day. Several observations emerge. First, if the top curves represent little or no benefit to the slowing effect, then we see that the leading-edge strategy has a very large "potential upside." No one can predict confidently something like Red's break point, but if it is lower than usually assumed, then the slowing effect will also be enhanced. Further, if Red is unable to operate on multiple axes effectively, the slowing effect will be enhanced. Thus, in both force planning and operations planning, the United States might do well to take the leading-edge strategy quite seriously. Unfortunately, it is not proven. For example, it has been speculated that Blue's per shooter-day effectiveness could be reduced with the leading-edge strategy by deconfliction problems and other operational considerations. We are not convinced that this should be so. Indeed, the opposite could be true—especially if vehicles toward the front of the moving columns were bunched, if the number of weapons per shooter were increased (thereby reducing deconfliction problems per weapon delivered), or if deconfliciton were simply not a problem (as, for example, with attacks by either standoff bombers or long-range missiles).

On the negative side, Red could detect imminent attack by aircraft or missiles, forces could disperse off road—significantly reducing vulnerability to sensor-fuzed weapons (but not to large-footprint weapons such as the Brilliant Antiarmor Munition [BAT] used on ATACMS). A future threat operating in the desert could perhaps move primarily off road—at least for relatively short distances and at the expense of more logistical problems. Although logistics vehicles are typically road bound today, they could be given improved off-road capability. On the other hand, such

[7]The optimum spacing depending on weapon characteristics. This game-theoretic issue has been worked out by colleague Glenn Kent.

[8]We are not convinced by the arguments in Ochmanek et al. on this matter. Although movement might slow on some of the secondary rows, ground-force planners include a lot of slack in their time lines. Further, movement would not slow on the main axes.

RANDMR1471-8.12

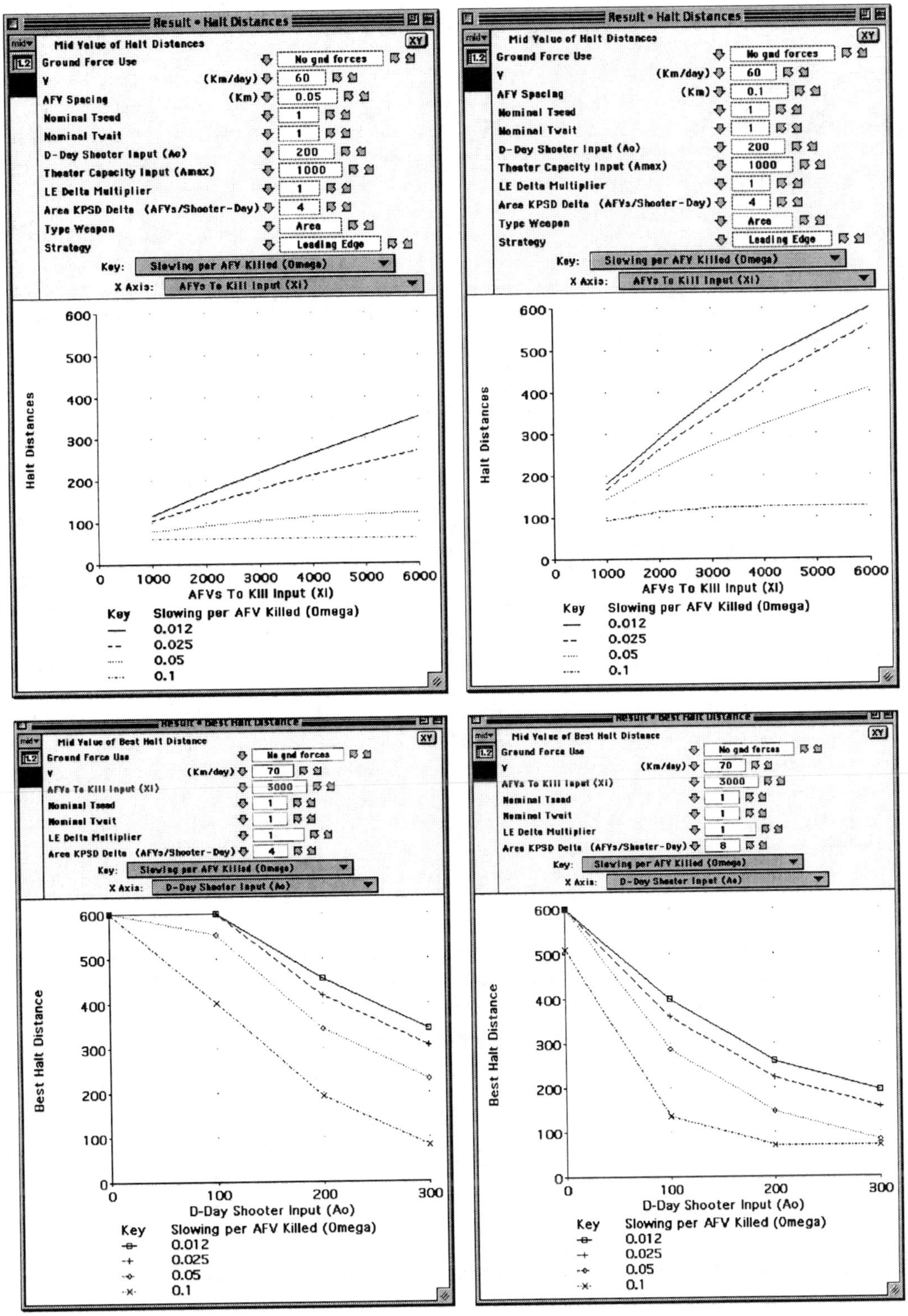

Figure 8.12—Halt Distance for Leading-Edge Strategy

maneuver choices would reduce movement rate substantially. Further, the United States could move to larger-footprint weapons.

Leading-edge strategy merits serious empirical study because of its substantial upside potential.

On balance, then, and in contrast with earlier studies, it appears that *the leading-edge strategy is a very interesting candidate for force employment*—even in the Persian Gulf. It is vulnerable to tactical countermeasures, but it is unclear that mediocre ground forces would be capable of those countermeasures. Further, it is quite possible that the break points of individual maneuver units would be far less than frequently assumed—which would enhance the value of the leading-edge strategy. It follows that this concept of force employment deserves more careful empirical study. We emphasize "empirical" because there are uncertainties both as to what Red could plausibly do and what Blue could plausibly do. Simulations can represent such matters a good deal better if they have a basis in empiricism.

Slowing and Confronting: Immediate Air Strikes and the Potential Use of Early Arriving Ground Forces

One possibility for improving outcomes is the use of early air and missile strikes on assembling invasion forces or on choke points along the invader's march routes to cause a delay. Such early strikes might or might not achieve much attrition, but could have major effects. Such attacks would be most plausible with constraints such as currently exist (no-drive zones) or red line equivalents. With such boundary conditions, it is plausible that the United States would attack the invading force or approach corridors before the invasion itself actually began.

Figure 8.13 illustrates the potential value of having both a two-day delay in the movement of the invasion force *and* a defense line manned by ground forces (local or U.S. forces) capable by themselves of killing a 1000 AFV force (e.g., a two large-division force that could be halted with 50 percent losses). In this illustrative case, we assume a larger threat (2000 AFVs to be killed, corresponding to perhaps four large divisions with a break point of 50 percent), near-immediate SEAD (one day), theater-access problems limiting the number of shooters to 200, and a baseline shooter effectiveness (4). We also assume the leading-edge strategy. In this instance, we find that the ground forces substantially improve prospects for an early halt (in this example, at a defense line 80 km from the enemy border). However, this result is achieved only if the number of D-Day shooters is substantial (200). This could be reduced to 100 if Blue's effectiveness were doubled (not shown), but in that case the ground forces would not be as important.

Based on exploratory analysis not presented here, it becomes evident that only in very special circumstances would it be reasonable to employ small ground forces in this way, but that—in those circumstances (as in Figure 3.13)—they could be critical to outcome.

Improving Anti-Armor Operations Before SEAD Is Complete: The Value of Partial Stealth

Figure 8.14 illustrates the benefit of having increasingly large portions of the shooters able to operate after a minimal wait time (one day), but well before SEAD is complete

RANDMR1471-8.13

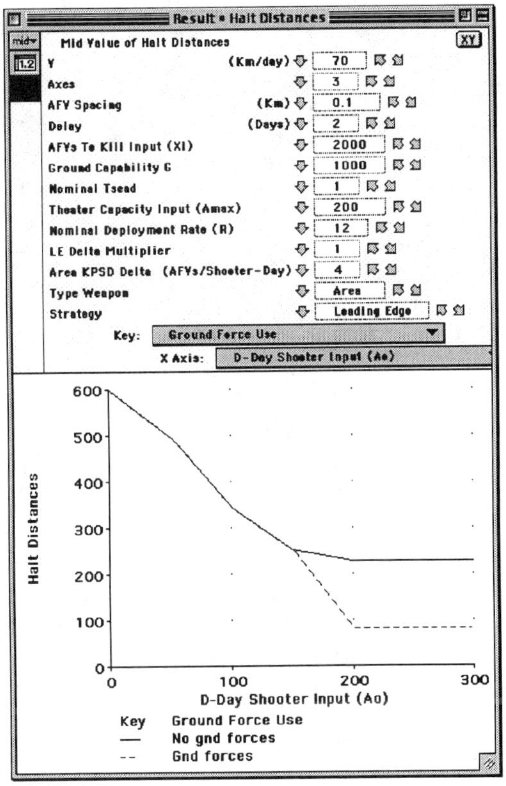

Figure 8.13—Synergy Between Interdiction and Ground Forces

(in the example, after three days). It assumes a large threat (3000 AFVs to kill), a fast movement rate (70 km/day), a modest deployment rate (12 per day), and a moderately good shooter effectiveness (six kills per day). The plot is of halt distance versus
D-Day shooters and the fraction of those shooters that can be employed against armor between days 1 and 4 when SEAD is completed.

These shooters might be stealthy aircraft, aircraft with long-range standoff weapons, relatively long-range missiles such as the Army's ATACMS/BAT, or attack helicopters. They would probably need to be operating in daylight and, in the case of stealthy aircraft, would probably need to be accompanied by survivable fighters to defend against enemy fighters and provide jamming and continuing defense suppression with missiles.[9] Further, the C^4ISR systems would need to be operating. Thus, employing forces against armor early is not a simple matter, nor would it be solved merely by procuring more stealthy bombers. Other measures would also be necessary.

---

[9]Such matters are discussed in more detail by colleague Donald Stevens in other work for the Air Force.

RANDMR1471-8.14

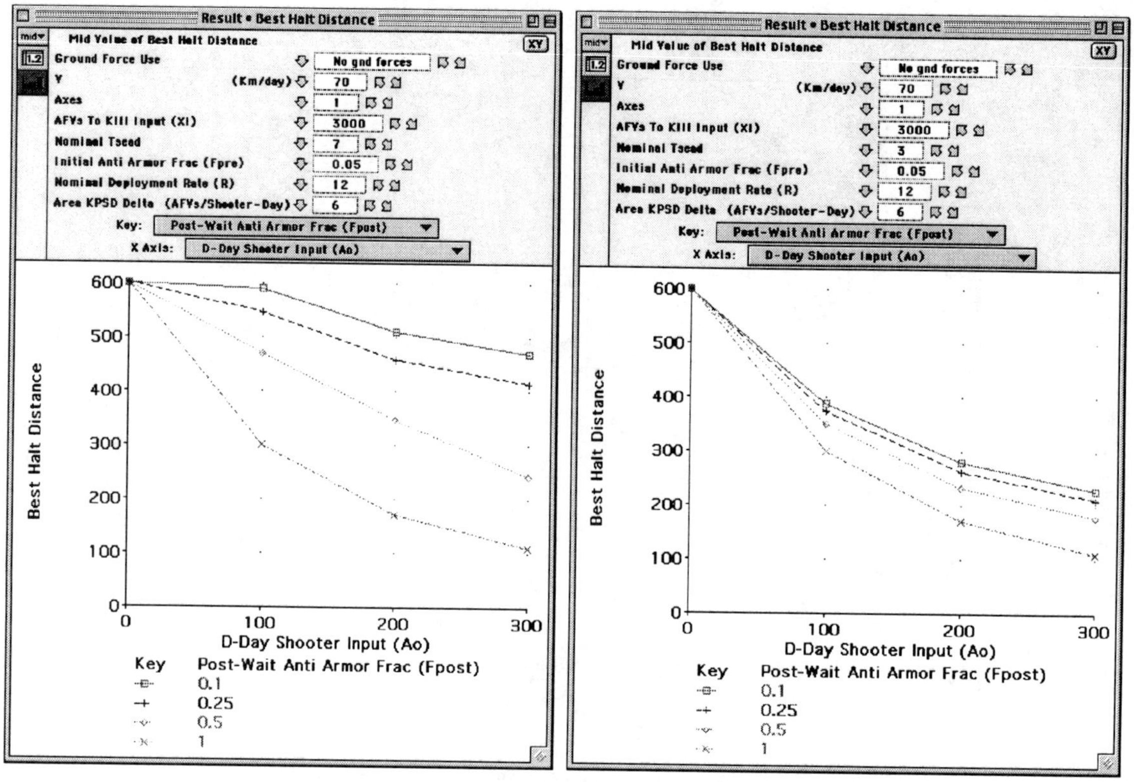

Figure 8.14—Potential Value of Increased Striking Power Before Air Defenses Are Suppressed (stealth or standoff weapons)

With these postulated circumstances, as the curve indicates, the halt distance is substantially reduced when the fraction of shooting power that can be so used is 25 or 50 percent, depending on the number of D-Day shooters. Very early halts would likely require a smaller threat (or, equivalently, threats with lower break points) and short SEAD times. The price of this policy, of course, would likely be significant attrition. That tradeoff can be estimated using EXHALT-CF (not shown here), although such issues demand backup analysis at much higher resolution. Actual losses would be sensitively dependent on details of employment, terrain, countermeasures, and other factors.

Effects of Probabilistic Calculations

Most of this monograph focuses on the development of EXHALT-CF and parametric exploratory analysis, which uses EXHALT deterministically but varies the parameter values. Probabilistic calculations can also be made, as described in Chapter 7. We shall show only an example here to make a particular point. Figure 8.15 compares mean estimates of halt distance for a case of a small threat (1000 AFVs to be killed) moving rapidly (70 km/day), interdicted by Blue with no delay but with a short

RANDMR1471-8.15

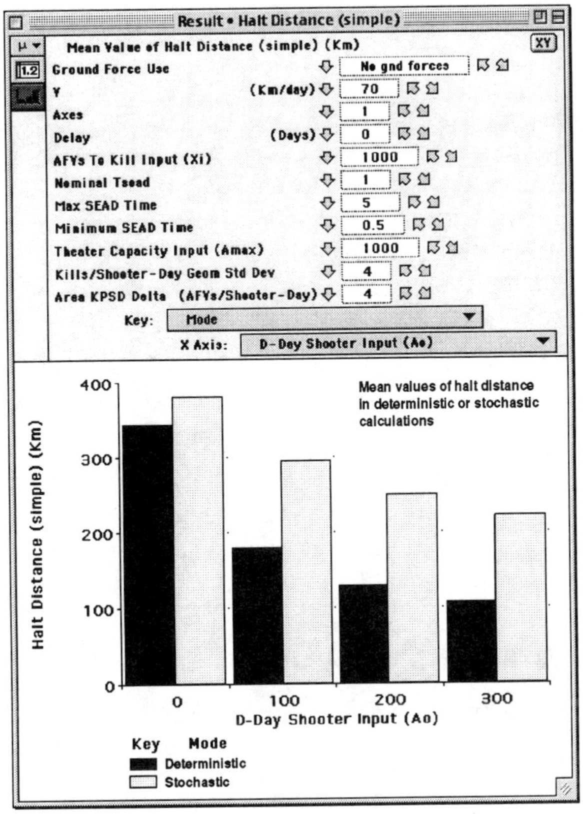

Figure 8.15—Example

nominal SEAD time, fair lethality (four kills per shooter day), and no theater capacity problems. The deterministic results are shown on the left of each bar-graph pair and the results of the stochastic (probabilistic) calculations on the right. In making the probabilistic calculations, we assumed that even if the nominal (most probable) SEAD time was one day, there could be a significant range of values—here assumed to be one to five days. Further, although an effectiveness of four kills per shooter day might be a good planning factor, we assumed that it was merely the median of a log normal distribution with a large geometric standard deviation (4). In this case, at least, the differences in outcome are substantial. Moreover, as so often happens when one takes stochastic variation into account, the stochastic results are worse.[10] One reason this frequently happens is that the nominal planning factors are something like "most probable" values (or modes) of distributions that are skewed in a "bad" direction because it is easier for things to go wrong than for them to go even better than assumed. That is not always the case. In this example, SEAD time has a long unfavorable tail but number of kills per shooter day has a long favorable tail. It

[10]See Lucas (2000) for an interesting survey of concrete instances in which this has occurred. A similar point has also been made over the years by Timothy (Jim) Horrigan.

happens, with this combination of assumptions, that the net result is for the stochastic results to be worse for Blue than the deterministic ones.[11]

8.4 SUMMARY RESULTS OF EXPLORATORY ANALYSIS

We do not present more extensive results in this monograph in part because to do the job well—so that the values chosen are reasonable and the "best estimate" values are in the center—would require sensitive information. Thus, in what follows we summarize high-level parametric exploration over five parameters: size of the threat, threat movement rate, number of D-Day shooters, SEAD time, and kills per shooter day. All of the results assume a deployment rate of 12 shooters per day (recall that this counts only the anti-armor shooters, not aircraft dedicated to missions such as surveillance, reconnaissance, SEAD, and strategic bombing).

Figures 8.16 and 8.17 display the high-level summary in eight panels over two pages. Note that an early halt is achievable only in special instances. Figure 8.18 displays the same information in a different format using bar charts. This allows the information to be reduced to a single page. Even more condensed presentations are possible, but would be more cluttered.

8.5 POSSIBLE ADAPTATIONS TO IMPROVE OUTCOMES

We next identify potential mechanisms for improving mission capability.

It requires no new analysis to identify many nice-to-have capabilities, such as greater numbers of weapons per sortie, more effectiveness per weapon and sortie (strongly dependent on C^4ISR), shorter SEAD times, long-endurance stealthy or otherwise survivable C^4ISR systems such as unmanned vehicles or satellites, large numbers of good weapons, and so on. The value of the methods and tools presented here, however, is that they can support complex tradeoff analysis. Tradeoffs are complex because (1) system capability depends on many system components working effectively, (2) the leverage provided by more of a given capability (e.g., more top-quality weapons) depends on the level of capabilities of the other system components, (3) there are many nonlinearities.

Some of the complex interdependencies can be noted even in the small number of examples provided above. For example, ground forces could be quite useful against relatively small threats—but only if the forces were present early enough and only if interdiction forces could reduce the size of the threat they would have to face, and perhaps slow it as well. Conversely, if ground forces were present, the attacker's movement rate would probably be slowed, which would *greatly* leverage the effectiveness of interdiction forces—if the number of D-Day forces were small or the time to suppress air defenses more than a day or two. Having sufficient high-quality

[11]Because of these issues, analysts should ensure that planning factors used in deterministic calculations are more like means or medians of the distribution functions representing knowledge, rather than the allegedly "most likely" or if-everything-goes-well values. Doing so can significantly mitigate the error caused by using deterministic calculations.

RANDMR1471-8.16

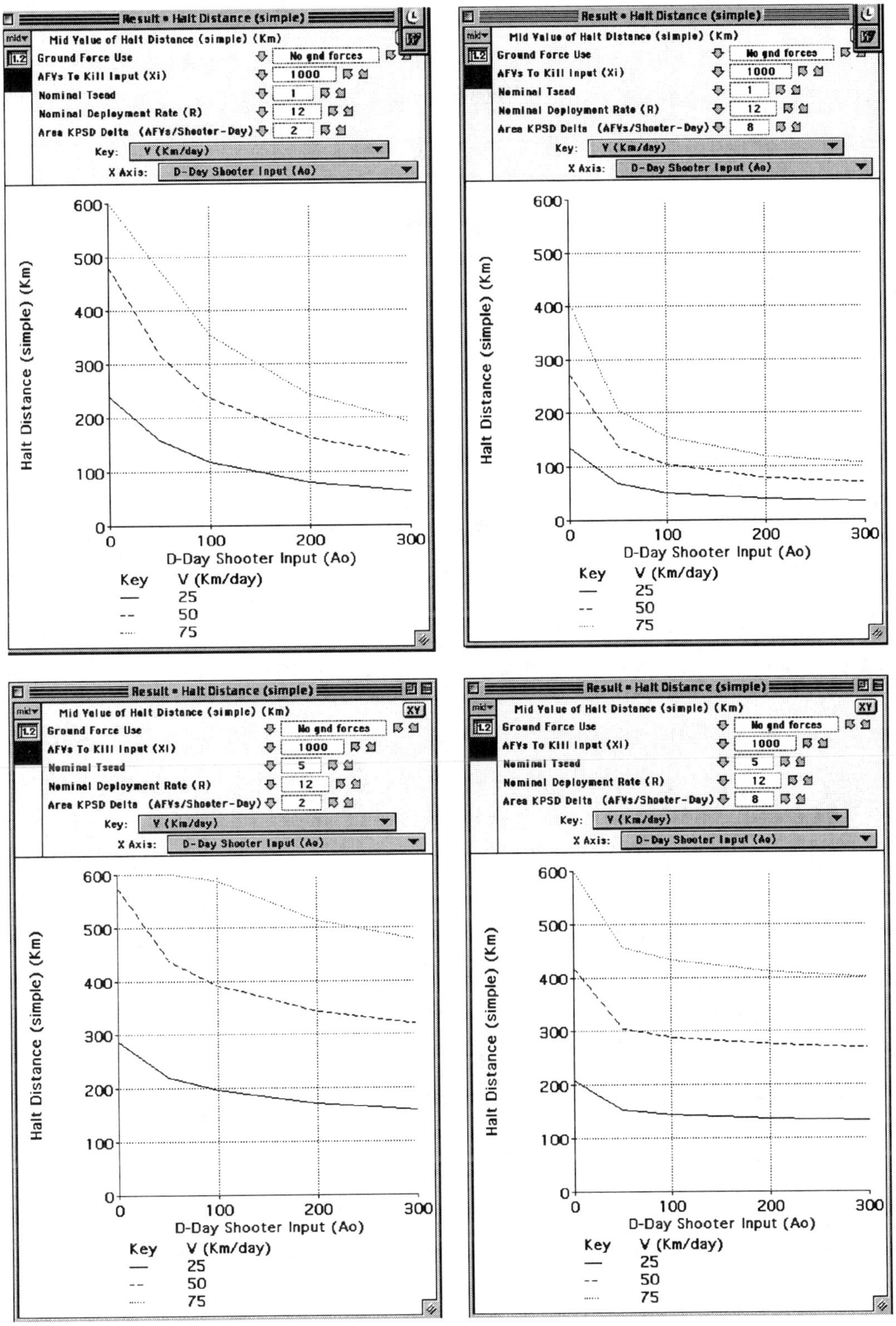

Figure 8.16—High-Level Parametric Summary for Small Threat (1000 AFVs to be killed)

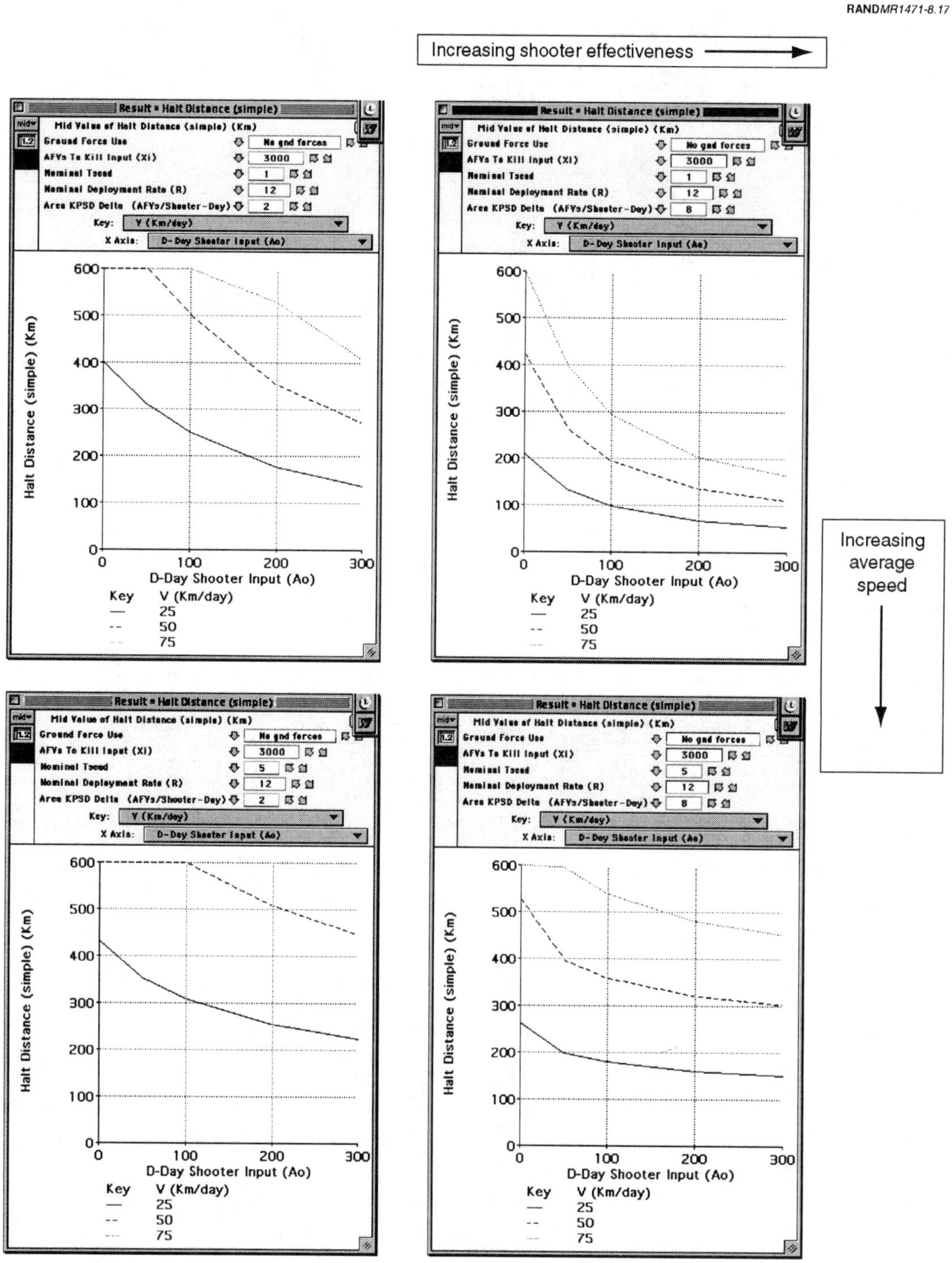

Figure 8.17—High-Level Parametric Summary for Larger Threat (3000 AFVs to be killed)

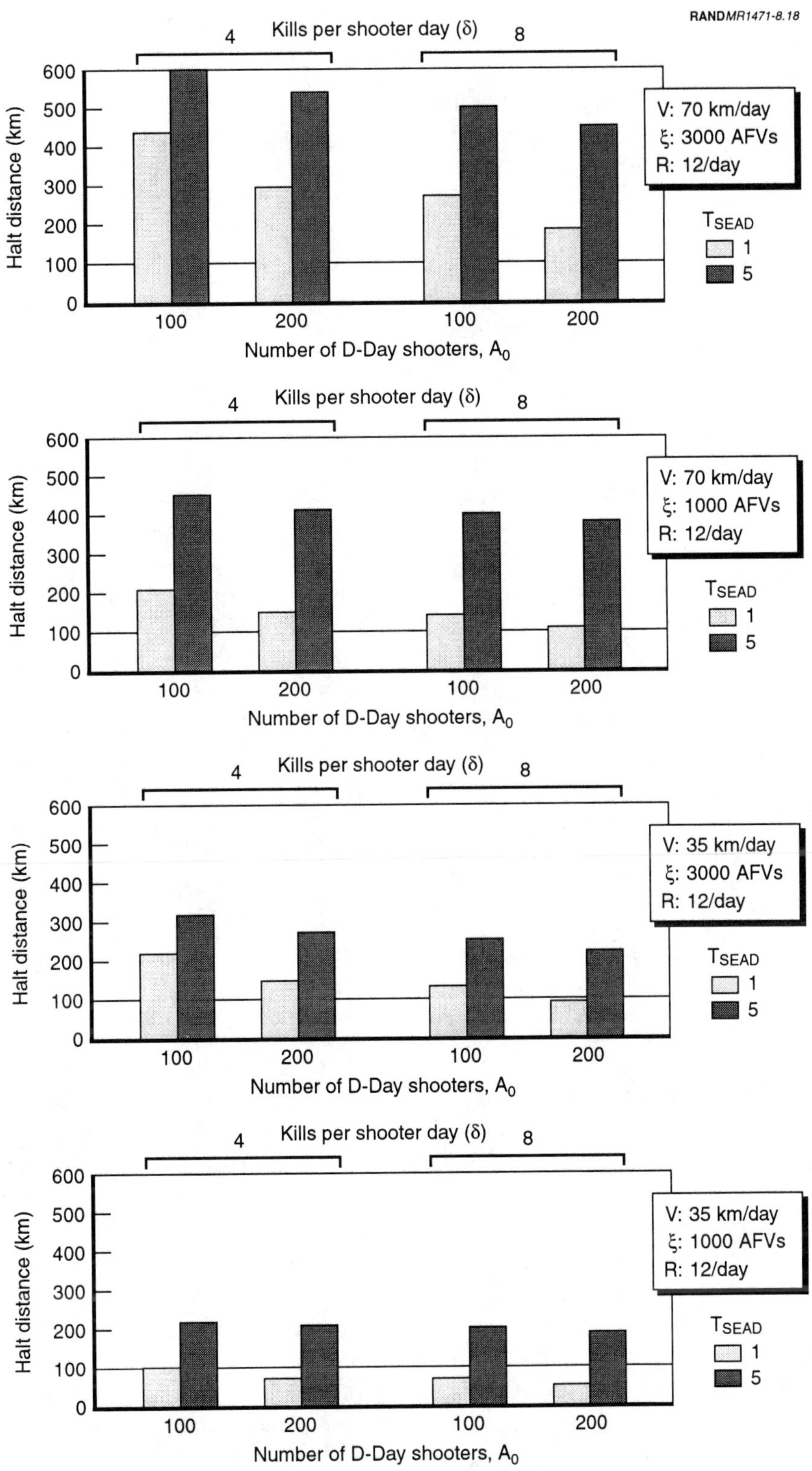

Figure 8.18—Alternative Summary of Exploratory Analysis (bar-chart form)

munitions would be limiting in many scenarios, but only when other system capabilities were good enough to give interdiction a "fighting chance."

Another complex interdependency with considerable significance for adaptive planning involves the size and cohesion of the threat. Many of the capabilities that the United States can bring to bear even in a post-sanctions regime would be sufficient if the size of the threat is not too large (more like today's Iraq than like a restoration of the 1990 Iraqi army). If the threat is quite large, however, as assumed in typical planning scenarios, then many of the adaptations would not be sufficient. For example, a small ground force could do little and quite possibly would not even be employed in a forward-defense position. This said, the biggest question about threat in quantitative analysis may actually be the break point. Excessive conservatism on the matter can be self-defeating. If, for example, analysis focuses on large high-cohesion threats with no logistics problems, and if sanctions are lifted and U.S. presence is reduced, then an early halt might seem analytically to be impossible. That could lead to shifts of strategy, which in turn could undercut regional policies and credibility. In contrast, if U.S. planning allows for the possibility (not the certainty) of early strikes that could cause delays as well as attrition, for the possibility (which might better be termed a probability) that Iraqi invasion forces would be less than the enthusiastic heroes often assumed in analysis, and for the possibility that well-developed interdiction campaigns would have many bonus effects through the shattering of logistics, then what can be accomplished looks very different. When using the model presented here, it is a matter simply of assuming a smaller threat (recall that the threat being measured is the number of armored fighting vehicles that must be killed—which could be a small or large fraction of the whole). For more discussion of how to reflect such issues in effects-based analysis, see Davis, Bigelow, and McEver (2001).

Fortunately, analysis can now begin to look at such a diversity of issues.

Against this background, Table 8.1 summarizes elements of a U.S adaptive strategy (with emphasis on the U.S. Air Force) over time, in response to possible developments by Iraq.

Finally, Table 8.2 lists system problems that may face planners attempting to ensure U.S. halt and other counter-maneuver capabilities. The second column suggests solutions. Ultimately, the United States has a great many ways to adapt to increasing threats in the region if those indeed develop. However, the adaptations will not be trivial and cannot be accomplished overnight. Prior planning is necessary, as well as program initiatives to provide appropriate hedges. As an obvious example, the small smart bomb is not necessary today, but would be exceptionally useful in many of the troublesome cases we discussed above. It would also be useful for other reasons, such as giving an air-to-ground variant of the F-22 and Joint Strike Fighter (JSF) more lethality per sortie and thus making it more cost-effective. Other hedges are less obvious. One is to plan for the enhancement of regional bases out of range of projected missiles and to ensure that those bases could be made operational for U.S. purposes quickly. This might involve mundane matters such as fuel hydrants and storage of appropriate fuels as well as timely stocking with precision weapons.

Table 8.1

POTENTIAL ACTIONS AND COUNTER ACTIONS

Potential Red Actions	U.S. Counters	Counters by Gulf States
Use advanced mobile air defenses, plus metered use to extend SEAD time.	Use very large number of Joint Air-to-Surface Standoff Missiles (JASSMs) to permit anti-armor operations well before all SAMs have been destroyed. Use semi-stealthy UAVs and space systems for early C^4ISR. Protect early shooters with stealth, electronic countermeasures (ECM), and attacks focused on front. Reassess risk; accept some losses.	Assist U.S. targeting efforts with elite troops on ground, reinforced by U.S. early-entry forces.
Create ambiguity during attack preparations, reducing warning time.	Increase permanent presence. Routinely use strategic warning and punish Red politically and militarily for causing buildups. Insist on agreed red line. Hedge with increased long-loiter, large-weapon bomber capability.	Support U.S. presence, use of strategic warning, and red line. Participate in routinized punishing of Red for provocative actions and costly Blue responses.
Attack on multiple axes and columns, which would reduce effectiveness of leading-edge attacks (but perhaps slow movement).	Plan to deal with axes sequentially. Use weapons with larger, cross-column footprints.	Maneuver capabilities sufficient, in principle, to force concentration.
Increase movement rate of dash to first objective.	Exploit red line; preempt attack and delay initial movement by days.	Embrace red line concept; incorporate in exercises. Have rapid-action ground forces designed for delay and disruption operations, rather than stand-and-die operations. As part of this or separately, create temporary barriers to road-bound logistics.
Devise "hides" (e.g., using a combination of camouflage and other tactics) to permit episodic dashes that would frustrate continuous interdiction efforts (less plausible for the long-distance invasion through the desert; more plausible for ground-force maneuvers within Iraq).	Use CAP stations with long-endurance, high-lethality platforms (e.g., stealthy bombers, UCAVs, or even fighter aircraft with small smart bombs). Use strip-alert forces able to augment CAP stations on short notice.	Use elite ground forces (perhaps augmented by U.S. forces) able to penetrate deep into enemy territory to provide improved warning of when maneuvers will begin. Use ground-force ambush teams that could prolong the duration of marches.
Pose WMD threat to forward bases, prepositioning, and force; and to Gulf-state cities.	Deter with announced reprisal attacks. Enhance naval air's capabilities. Enhance capacity and stocking of secure but more distant regional bases. Prepare use of 1st week joint strike force with ground units from sea.	Support U.S. reprisal plan to enhance deterrence. Use gas masks for population; suits for critical workers at bases. Enhance capability and stocking of more distant regional bases. Enhance long-range bomber capability: more bombers, smaller weapons, regional bases, and prepositioning.
Increase size of army.	Increase number of best-effectiveness precision-guided munitions (PGMs) per platform (e.g., small smart bombs).	

Table 8.2

SYSTEM PROBLEMS AND FIXES

Problem	Solution
Slow buildup of command-control and C^4ISR competence (in a future crisis in a post-sanctions regime with reduced U.S. presence).	Standing groups (consistency of technical expertise, not top leadership) (AF and Joint). National doctrine of using strategic warning to spin up C^4ISR systems. Virtual rehearsal training of command and control groups as they are alerted and deploy.
Prolonged SEAD, making classic phased campaign ineffective for early halt.	Plan early anti-armor employment, with risks, but reduce risks by lavish use of anti-SAM missiles, escort jammers, and use of long-range missiles (Air Force and Joint).
Short tactical warning.	Sizable permanent presence.
Inability to deal with sheer speed of invasion.	Plans for early strikes inside Iraq, after red line crossing. Effects-based planning for strikes immediately after start of invasion, strikes designed to cause maximum disruption and delay, even if not massive attrition. Focus may be choke points, but also logistics train (trucks count). Leading-edge attacks may be quite valuable with real-world opponent forces.
Inconsistency of capabilities over time as presence rotates from Navy to Air Force, etc.	Increased jointness in planning.

Appendix A

REPRESENTING DIFFERENT SHOOTER TYPES

A.1 GENERAL DISCUSSION

The closed-form mathematics used in this monograph can be generalized to reflect explicitly many types of anti-armor shooters (e.g., bombers, Air Force fighters, Navy fighters, Army attack helicopters, Multiple Launch Rocket System (MLRS) missile batteries, and naval missiles). The problem treated is linear: The attrition to the attacking ground force attributed to "equivalent shooters" can be regarded instead as the sum of attritions from different types of shooter. To accommodate this generalization, one merely defines the key variables as mathematical arrays indexed (or "dimensioned") by type of shooter. The resulting arrays are one dimensional and are thus nothing more than simple vectors of the sort found in elementary calculus and analytical geometry. We shall use bold type, rather than italics, to indicate such vectors.

As an example, the number of shooters at time t is represented by a vector $\mathbf{A(t)} = \{A_1, A_2, \ldots\}$, where $A_i(t)$ is the number of the *ith* type of shooter at time t.

Recall that in the main text, the key to solving for the halt time was a simple integral equation

$$\xi = \int_0^{T_{halt}} N(s)\delta(s)ds, \qquad (A.1)$$

in which ξ is the number of armored fighting vehicles (AFVs) to be killed to bring about a halt through attrition, N(s) is the number of anti-armor shooters employed at time s, and $\delta(s)$ is the kills per shooter day as of time s. In the generalization, $\mathbf{N}(t)$ is a vector indexed by type of shooter. Ignoring for illustration the complications of theater capacity, the *ith* component of N(t) (i.e., the number of the *ith* shooter type at time t) is given by

$$N_i(t) = F_i(t)\{A_{0i} + R_i t\}. \qquad (A.2)$$

That is, a particular shooter type (e.g., a Joint Strike Fighter) might be present at some level A_{JSF} on D-Day, would deploy at some rate R_{JSF}, and would be allocated and used against armor over time according to $F_{JSF}(t)$.

Equation (A.2) involves a multiplication of vector components, but not the usual dot-product multiplication of standard analytical geometry. Let us adopt a notational convention that is quite useful here, although nonstandard. For any two vectors $\mathbf{X}$ and $\mathbf{Y}$ that are indexed in the same way (i.e., by shooter type in this case), let a bar denote a product vector as follows:

$$\overline{\mathbf{XY}} \equiv \{X_1Y_1, X_2Y_2, \ldots X_nY_n\}. \tag{A.3}$$

That is, the *ith* component of the product $\overline{\mathbf{XY}}$ is X_1Y_1.

With this convention, Eq. (A.2) can be replaced by the vector equation

$$\mathbf{N}(t) = \overline{\mathbf{F}(t)\mathbf{A}_0} + \overline{\mathbf{F}(t)\mathbf{R}}t. \tag{A.4}$$

We shall also need dot-product multiplication. For example, the product appearing in the integrand of Eq. (A.1) generalizes to

$$N(s)\delta(s) \rightarrow \mathbf{N}(s) \bullet \boldsymbol{\delta}(s) = \sum_i N_i(s)\delta_i(s). \tag{A.5}$$

where $\boldsymbol{\delta}$ (s) is a vector because the time dependence of the different shooters' effectiveness may be different. For example, less stealthy aircraft might—early in conflict before air defenses are suppressed—have fewer kills per day because of having fewer suitable target sets to attack.

Having defined notation for the two types of vector multiplication arising in the equations, we can straightforwardly rewrite all the expressions of the main text.

To illustrate this without too much complexity, ignore here the complications of finite theater capacity, weapon exhaustion, ground forces in close combat, and losses to air defense, but include the phasing effect distinguishing before and after SEAD operations are complete. Assume that the halt time exceeds the SEAD time and that the wait time is zero.

With notation analogous to that used in the main text, then, we now have:

$$\xi = \int_0^{T_{halt}} \left\{\overline{\mathbf{F}(s)\mathbf{A}_0} + \overline{\mathbf{RF}(s)}s\right\} \bullet \boldsymbol{\delta}(s)ds$$

$$\xi = \int_0^{T_{SEAD}} \left\{\overline{\mathbf{F}_{\mathbf{post}}\mathbf{A}_0} + \overline{\mathbf{RF}_{\mathbf{post}}}s\right\} \bullet \boldsymbol{\delta}\, ds + \int_{T_{SEAD}}^{T_{halt}} \left\{\overline{\mathbf{FA}_0} + \overline{\mathbf{RF}}s\right\} \bullet \boldsymbol{\delta}\, ds. \tag{A.6}$$

Since the elements of the integrand are now constants, except for s itself, this can be integrated to obtain

$$\xi = \mathbf{A}_0 \bullet [\overline{\mathbf{F}_{\mathbf{post}}\boldsymbol{\delta}} - \overline{\mathbf{F}\boldsymbol{\delta}}]T_{SEAD} + \frac{1}{2}[\overline{\mathbf{RF}_{post}} - \overline{\mathbf{RF}}] \bullet \boldsymbol{\delta}T_{SEAD}^2 + \overline{\mathbf{FA}_0} \bullet \boldsymbol{\delta}T_{halt} + \frac{1}{2}\overline{\mathbf{RF}} \bullet \boldsymbol{\delta}T_{halt}^2. \tag{A.7}$$

This can be rearranged to be in standard quadratic-equation form:

$$\frac{1}{2}T_{halt}^2 + \frac{\overline{FA_0} \bullet \delta}{\overline{RF} \bullet \delta} T_{halt} - \left\{ \frac{\xi + [A_0 \bullet \overline{\delta[F - F_{post}]}]T_{SEAD} + \frac{1}{2} R \bullet \overline{\delta[F - F_{post}]}]T_{SEAD}^2}{\overline{RF} \bullet \delta} \right\} = 0. \tag{A.8}$$

If ζ and ψ are defined as

$$\zeta = \frac{\overline{FA_0 \delta}}{\overline{RF} \bullet \delta} \tag{A.9}$$

and

$$\psi \equiv \left\{ \frac{\xi + [A_0 \bullet \overline{\delta[F - F_{post}]}]T_{SEAD} + \frac{1}{2} R \bullet \overline{\delta[F - F_{post}]}]T_{SEAD}^2}{\overline{RF} \bullet \delta} \right\}, \tag{A.10}$$

then as in the main text:

$$T_{halt} = \sqrt{\zeta^2 + 2\psi} - \zeta. \tag{A.11}$$

A.2 APPLICABILITY OF THE GENERALIZATION

It is rather elegant mathematically to represent a problem as complex as the one treated in this monograph with closed-form array equations. However, the practical applicability is limited. If one wishes to represent multiple types of shooters, but without all the complications of delays, weapon exhaustion, and so on, then the generalization here can be used straightforwardly (Davis and Carrillo, 1997), particularly in a system such as Analytica. However, when all the complications are added in, our own assessment is that workers should instead shift to a simulation model—such as our own EXHALT. With all the complications added, the closed-form expressions, however "elegant," are not as understandable or easy to work with as the simulation equations. Nor do they have the richness of the full simulation. Recall that EXHALT-CF (the model described in this monograph) was developed for some very special purposes—the most important of which were probably: (1) the desire to illustrate the analytical bare bones of the analytical problem and (2) the desire to be able to do extremely fast and interactive exploratory analysis with perhaps 8–12 parameters being varied simultaneously. For other purposes, however, simulation is often preferable.

A.3 SPECIAL ISSUE: CLUMPY ARRIVALS OF NAVAL AVIATION

A special problem arising in the use of equivalent shooters is that naval aviation would enter the real-world problem in clumps as aircraft carriers arrive, undercutting the concept of a constant average deployment rate used throughout this monograph. However, since the purpose is to find outcomes (halt distances and halt times) rather than dynamics along the way, it is not necessary to deal directly with the clumpiness issue. The question is merely what average deployment rate should be used to represent the arrival, at time T_{CVBG}, of a clump of naval aircraft? If a first carrier is accounted for in A_0, the number of D-Day shooters, then the issue would be the effects of a second, late-arriving carrier. In what follows, we limit ourselves to discussion of effects on an in-depth strategy.

As in Chapter 3, calculating a good estimator of the carrier's contribution to R requires estimating the halt time itself. If the SEAD time and other factors limiting early performance are small in comparison with the halt time, then the effective deployment time can be estimated by equating two calculations of the shooter days contributed by the carrier's aircraft over the halt time. The correct number is just the difference between the halt time and the time the carrier arrives. The effective deployment rate for aircraft actually deployed on an aircraft carrier (CVBG) can then be estimated by requiring

$$\frac{1}{2}\hat{R}_{CVBG}\hat{T}_{halt}^{2} = FA_{CVBG}(\hat{T}_{halt} - T_{CVBG})$$
$$\hat{R}_{CVBG} = \frac{2FA_{CVBG}(\hat{T}_{halt} - T_{CVBG})}{\hat{T}_{halt}^{2}}. \quad \text{(A.12)}$$

If the carrier's aircraft were ineffective—even if present—for a time T_x because of the various complications of SEAD and the like, then this formula could be amended to read

$$\hat{R}_{CVBG} = \frac{2FA_{CVBG}(\hat{T}_{halt} - T_{CVBG})}{(\hat{T}_{halt} - T_x)^2}. \quad \text{(A.13)}$$

The second carrier's contribution to R is only part of a much larger total and halt time is rather insensitive to R—varying more slowly than the inverse square root. Thus, this estimate is typically adequate. Since R is one of the highly uncertain variables anyway, and should routinely be varied by factors of two or three in exploratory analysis, the error is negligible.

Appendix B

SUMMARY OF VARIABLES USED IN MODELS

Table B.1

INDEPENDENT VARIABLES (INPUT PARAMETERS) OF THE MOST GENERAL CLOSED-FORM MODEL (from Chapter 6)

Variable	Definition	Comment
A(t)	Number of aircraft (and other equivalent shooters) at time t	
A_0	Number of D-Day shooters (for all missions, not just anti-armor missions)	Result of deployments based on strategic and tactical warning
A_{00}	Initial number of shooters (for all missions)	Number present before crisis (optional)
A_{max}	Maximum number of shooters	Constraint due to infrastructure
B	Initial kills (e.g., on D-day) from hitting assembly areas or major choke points	
b	Constant daily rate of AFV kills by ground forces	Vehicles/day
C	Time of full-scale deployment, subject to access and capacity limits. Treated as fully actionable warning time.	Assumed used for full-scale deployment. May be small because of surprise, initial access restrictions, etc.
D_{line}	Defense line (km) at which ground forces may attempt to halt residual attackers	
F_{pre}	Fraction of shooters allocated to and employed on anti-armor missions for times up to T_{wait}	
F_{post}	Fraction of shooters allocated to and employed on anti-armor missions for times between T_{wait} and T_{SEAD}	
F	Fraction of shooters allocated to and employed on anti-armor missions after T_{SEAD}	Other shooters may be used for strike missions, etc., and some shooters may be withheld temporarily because of vulnerability
$G_{capability}$	Ground-force capability as measured by the number of armored vehicles a ground force at a defense line can halt	
H	Break point fraction	Fractional attrition at which point attacking army is considered halted
K	Kills per sortie	The nominal kills per sortie, assuming that sorties need not be distracted by air defenses and have nominal command and control
L_0	Initial D-Day loss rate per sortie	Fraction of sorties lost, per sortie
$L_{dailyaverage}$	"Average" daily loss rate during the SEAD phase	Depends on sortie rate during SEAD phase
M	Multiplier of kills per shooter day for SEAD period (from reduced sortie rate or reduced kills per sortie)	

Table B.1 (continued)

Variable	Definition	Comment
$N(t)$	Number of anti-armor shooters employed at time t $N(t) = F(t)A(t)$	
N_0	Number of anti-armor shooters employed on D-Day	Referred to as λ in earlier work. N_0 is a tricky variable because it is nonphysical: It represents the product $F(0)A_0$.
N_{div}	Number of attacking divisions	
N_{vpd}	Number of AFVs per division	
Obj	Objective of attacker (km of penetration)	
R	Full-scale deployment rate of shooters	The unconstrained average rate
R_0	Deployment rate after C-Day, but before full access is granted	
R_{strat}	Deployment rate of shooters upon strategic warning only	
S	Sortie rate of shooters	The nominal average sortie rate. Actual rates may be lower due to command and control or logistical problems
S_{avg}	Average sortie rate, during the period T_{wait} to T_{SEAD} of vulnerable shooters	Used only in casualty estimates
T_{delay}	Delay (days) caused by "special" strikes	Can reflect the effects of striking assembly areas, critical bridges, etc., or of preemptively attacking before invader reaches border
T_{gain}	Gain-competence time	
T_{halt}	Halt time	
$T_{defense}$	Time (days) at which ground forces can fight effectively at defense line	
T_{SEAD}	SEAD time	Time required to suppress air defenses enough to permit full-scale operations with nominal sortie rates and effectiveness
T_{wait}	Time (days) for which the vulnerable fraction of the shooters is withheld to reduce losses	
$\hat{T}_{halt}$	An a priori estimate of T_{halt} for use in estimating losses within calculations	An upper bound might be 10–20 days
V	Movement speed (km/day)	Average movement speed except for special disruptions.
W_{strat}	"Strategic" warning time	Assumed used for precautionary naval deployments, preparation of command and control, etc.

Table B.1 (continued)

Variable	Definition	Comment
A_0	D-Day shooters	All shooters, not just anti-armor shooters being employed
ΔT_{access}	$T_{access} - C$	
ΔT_{strat}	$C - T_{strat}$	
Ω (omega)		
α (alpha)	$\alpha = \delta/\xi$	Shooter days nominally needed for halt (ignoring complications)
δ (delta)	Kills per shooter day for nominal high-quality weapons. For in-depth strategy.	May be calculated from product of kills per sortie and sorties per day, or equivalent
δ_B	Kills per shooter day for lesser-quality weapons (relevant when A weapons are exhausted). For in-depth strategy.	May be calculated from product of kills per sortie and sorties per day, or equivalent
δ_{edge}	Kills per shooter-day for nominal high-quality weapons. Leading-edge strategy.	May be calculated from product of kills per sortie and sorties per day, or equivalent
γ	Kilometers of invasion depth "killed" by each shooter in a day; reduction of effective speed	Reflects multiple axes and columns
ξ_{line}	Number of AFVs that must be destroyed before the enemy reaches the defense line if the ground forces are to be able to halt and defeat the residual forces at that defense line. $\xi_{line} = \xi - G_{capability}$	Applies only if ground forces can be at the defense line in time
ξ	Number of AFVs to be killed to bring about a halt	"Vehicles" means "armored fighting vehicles" unless otherwise stated

Table B.2

INTERMEDIATE VARIABLES

Variable	Definition	Comment
Approx $L_{dailyavg}$	$Min[L_{dailyavg}, R]$	Used only to calculate other variables; eliminates need to consider very unusual cases
Approx Losses	$Min[Losses, A_0]$	Used only to calculate other variables; eliminates need to consider very unusual cases
N_{avg}	Average number of anti-armor shooters during the period T_{wait} to T_{SEAD} $N_{avg} \approx Max[F_{post}A_{max}, F_{post}A_0 + RT_{wait} + \frac{1}{2}R(T_{SEAD} - T_{wait})]$	A better approximation is given in the text, but this is typically a good approximaton
$L_{dailyavg}$	Average *daily* loss rate of shooters during the period T_{wait} to T_{SEAD} $L_{dailyavg} \approx \frac{F_{post}S_{avg}}{T_{SEAD} - T_{wait}} \frac{T_{SEAD}}{2} \left[e^{-2\frac{T_{wait}}{T_{SEAD}}} - 0.135 \right] L_0$	
T_{max}	Time at which theater capacity is reached (not accounting for effects of losses to air defenses)	
T_{toline}	D_{line}/V + Delay	
Ω	Reduction in daily movement (km) per AFV killed $\Omega = A_{spacing}/(N_{div}N_{col}H)$	May be directly inputted
α	Shooter days needed to kill the specified number of AFVs $\alpha = \xi/\delta$	May be directly inputted
A_0	Number of D-Day Shooters See Table 3.2 for functional dependence on A_{00}, R_{strat}, R_0, ΔT_{strat}, ΔT_{access}	May be directly inputted
ξ	Number of AFVs that must be killed to cause a halt, if accomplished by interdiction alone $\xi = (N_{div}N_{vpd} - B)H$	May be directly inputted
Δ	$N(t)\gamma$	

Table B.3

DEPENDENT VARIABLES (OUTPUTS) OF THE CLOSED-FORM MODELS

T_{halt}	Time to Halt Invading Army (days)	
D	Maximum penetration of invading army (penetration at time of halt)	
Losses	Losses of shooters from air defenses	
Utility of outcome	A subjective utility balancing values of D and Losses	
G_{req}	Ground-force capability required to achieve halt at a specified defense line, given characteristics of the threat and interdiction force	Based on "inversion" of basic model
$T_{line, req}$	Time at which defense line must be effective to achieve halt, for a specified threat and interdiction capability	Based on "inversion" of basic model

Appendix C
SUMMARY DESCRIPTION OF EXHALT 1.5

This monograph describes the mathematical basis of EXHALT-CF (the implementation in Analytica of the model developed here). Some readers may need the greater richness of the EXHALT 1.5 simulation model, an expansion of the original EXHALT (McEver, Davis, and Bigelow, 2000a), which includes all of the factors treated in this monograph. EXHALT 1.5 can be used explicity with many different shooter types and weapon loadings (e.g., F-15E with six Skeets), whereas the "CF" (for closed form) version of EXHALT uses equivalent shooters. Also, CF is a closed-form analytic model, whereas EXHALT 1.5 is a simulation. That is, it undertakes a timestep-by-timestep modeling of the flow of forces into the theater and the employment of Blue's instantaneous force levels against Red's armored fighting vehicles. Likewise, the progression of Red's advance is tracked throughout the simulation. Thus, the in-progress dynamics of the halt campaign are explicitly played out in EXHALT 1.5 and can be explored and analyzed. This is in contrast with EXHALT-CF, in which these interim phenomena are taken into account in the calculation of the halt time and distance, but the details of the day-to-day activity are lost. Of course, this loss in detail comes with the benefit of faster calculation time and lower computational requirements for the implementation of EXHALT-CF, as well as the ability to examine closed-form solutions and gain insight into the important factors determining Blue's ability to halt Red in various circumstances.

EXHALT 1.5, as usually employed, tracks many different shooter types (e.g., F-15Es, MLRS/ATACMS, F/A-18 E/Fs) from aircraft carriers, etc. For example, a current application with EXHALT 1.5 includes 19 shooter types. The associated data may be classified. EXHALT tracks these shooters as they arrive, are used, and are possibly lost to air defenses. Although EXHALT 1.5 does not depend on the equivalent shooter formulation, as does EXHALT-CF, the multiresolution/multiple-perspective (MRMP) design of EXHALT 1.5 allows users to input shooter information at the level of equivalent shooters if they choose to do so.

During each timestep, EXHALT 1.5 determines the number of shooters of each type assigned to interdiction attacks against Red and calculates the AFV kills obtained by these aircraft (as well as any attrition suffered by Blue as a result of Red's air defenses). Although EXHALT 1.5 has the capability to adjust shooter effectiveness based on many considerations (C^4ISR capability, Red dash tactics, and terrain, among others), in this analysis these considerations are presumed to be included in the input values of the nominal effectiveness for the various munitions types, or in choices of T_{wait} and F_{pre} and F_{post}.

The enhancements represented in EXHALT 1.5 are primarily parallels to matters described in detail within this monograph. These modifications include:

Delay times, in which Red's movement is assumed to be delayed by Blue attacks on assembly areas and the like. This is modeled by holding Red's advance velocity at zero until the simulation time reaches D-day plus the delay time.

Red lines, which allow Blue to begin his attacks against Red some distance before Red crosses the border (which would normally trigger D-Day). This is implemented by having Red's starting point be negative, with magnitude of the distance from the red line to the border. Thus, Red must travel some time (while under attack) before he crosses into the territory defended by the United States and her allies.

Ground forces, which are represented as in the monograph. EXHALT 1.5 includes a defense line, a time the ground force is prepared to defend the defense line, and the strength of Red force that can be handled by the ground force. If the ground force is able to reach and defend the defense line before Red's force arrives at that defense line, and if Red's force level is at or below that which the Blue ground force can handle, the Red advance is stopped at the defense line. Otherwise, the Red advance continues unabated (it is assumed that Blue will not attempt to defend the defense line if Blue will be overrun).

Exhaustion times for good munitions are represented through the explicit modeling of munitions stocks and their consumption via use in Blue sorties. Four munitions types are assumed (in order of Blue's preference: premium standoff area munitions, premium direct area weapons, good direct area weapons, and direct 1-on-1 weapons). These weapons have some initial stock, which may be augmented during the campaign. As Blue sorties engage Red, they will draw down the Blue munitions stock, in accordance with the number of munitions that can be carried by each shooter type per sortie (which may be dependent on whether the SEAD campaign is ongoing) and the number of munitions remaining in stock. Note that Blue will draw down his preferred weapons first until they are exhausted, and then move on to the next-preferred type.

In addition to these enhancements to make the EXHALT simulation consistent with this monograph, other changes were made to enrich the EXHALT 1.0 model generally.

The wait time (during which Blue withholds a portion of his shooters out of concern for Red's air defenses, which are relatively robust early in the halt campaign) was made shooter type-specific.

In EXHALT 1.5, the simulation begins not at zero (as in v1.0), but at the strategic warning time, and counts up to D-Day (t = 0), where it becomes positive. This allows users to view the buildup of forces during the pre-D-Day period.

Other minor improvements have been made as well (cleaning up equations, etc.), which have no major substantive effect on the simulation's processes or conceptual model.

The purpose of this monograph was to develop a set of closed-form solutions with which to study the early-halt problem, and we have discussed some of the benefits provided by EXHALT-CF in terms of conceptualization, insight-gathering, and computer run-time and memory requirements. That said, and consistent with our general philosophy that, in analysis, there is inherent value in the construction and use of families of models at different resolutions and from many points of view, the strategic evolution of EXHALT 1.0 to EXHALT 1.5 to gain consistency with EXHALT-CF provides benefits of its own:

- *The intermediate dynamics of the processes that make up the halt campaign are directly modeled.* The simulation nature of EXHALT 1.5 is easier both to model and to troubleshoot, since each progressive node in the model represents a smaller cognitive portion of the overall simulation. This is not to suggest that EXHALT 1.5 is simple or even easy to understand, but rather to point out that corrections usually do not involve rederivation of the entire model. Of course, lost in this process are runtime performance and the ability to examine functional forms for insight.
- *The intermediate dynamics of the halt campaign can be directly observed.* Often, analysts are interested not only in the final result of a campaign, but in the dynamics of how that result was generated. Analytic insight can be gained from being able to observe the behavior of the processes that make up the halt campaign at different points in that campaign. As an extension, simulations also allow users to place decision rules within the simulation to allow Blue (or Red) to learn and strategically change his behavior based on past events.
- *EXHALT 1.5 is implemented in Analytica,* a visual modeling environment that is relatively easy to walk through and visualize data flows.
- *EXHALT 1.5 is much easier to adapt and customize to emerging analytic needs* than closed-form-solution models, which often require complete reformulation and rederivation from the ground up when changes are made. Analytica allows users to add to or change EXHALT 1.5 very easily as, again, each node represents only some small part of the whole.

EXHALT 1.5 and its closed-form-solution counterpart EXHALT-CF are two components of a family of models designed for the analysis of the early-halt problem. Each has its own strengths and weaknesses, but together are powerful tools in understanding these kinds of interdiction problems.

Appendix D

AN APPROXIMATION FOR CASES IN WHICH T_{exh} OCCURS BEFORE T_{wait}

The main text suggests constraining T_{exh} to be no less than T_{wait}[1] and accepting the error in the unusual cases in which that occurs. If such cases are of sufficient interest to warrant the trouble, one can either generalize the formulas or, at least, improve the approximation by adding a correction to the estimate of halt time generated by the basic formulas of Chapter 6.

The basic formulas generate a systematic error if the true exhaustion time is less than T_{wait}. The basic formulas assume that such exhaustion times are instead equal to T_{wait}. The error, then, is in underestimating the halt time by overestimating the number of AFVs killed before exhaustion. Suppose that it underestimates the preexhaustion kills by Q. Then the halt time will be overestimated by approximately the marginal additional time it takes to kill those Q vehicles at the end of the halt campaign. A simple expression for the error in days then would be

$$\text{Error} \approx \frac{F_{pre}}{F_{halt}} \frac{\text{Min}[A_0 + (1/2)RT_{wait}^B, A_{max}]}{A_{halt}} \frac{(\delta - \delta_B)(T_{wait} - T_{exh})}{\delta_B}, \tag{D.1}$$

where the numerator is the error in the estimated number of kills prior to T_{wait} and the denominator is the rate at which AFVs are being killed at the time of halt. Here A_{halt} and F_{halt} are the values of A and F that apply at the halt time. Table D.1 gives rough estimates for both. The Min operators in Eq. (D.1) and Table D.1 mitigate the errors that arise when T_{max} occurs in the intervals of importance.

The final expression, then, is

$$\begin{aligned} &\text{If} \quad T_{exh} \ge T_{wait}, \\ &\text{then } T_{halt} \approx T_{halt}^0 \\ &\text{else } \; T_{halt} \approx T_{halt}^0 + \text{Error}, \end{aligned} \tag{D.2}$$

where T_{halt}^0 is the estimate of the halt time obtained by using the basic equations of the text, which artificially constrain T_{exh} to be no smaller than T_{wait}. The error is evaluated by using Table D.1 to determine $\hat{F}_{halt}$ and $\hat{A}_{halt}$.

The correction—when it applies—will typically be on the order of a fractional day, or perhaps a day. That is a small fraction of the halt time in most cases, but not always. The unusual cases are those in which, for example, Blue has a large number of shooters present on D-Day, a significant fraction of those shooters can be operated imme-

---

[1]By this we mean using only input values of exhaust time greater than the wait time or, if T_{wait} is calculated, constraining the result to be no greater than T_{wait}.

diately, the A-weapons are many times more effective than the subsequent weapons, and the size of the threat is small. Again, then, this correction is usually unnecessary.

Table D.1

APPROXIMATE VALUES OF A_{halt} AND F_{halt} FOR USE IN ESTIMATING T_{halt}

Condition	$\hat{F}_{halt}$	$\hat{A}_{halt}$
$T^B_{halt} < T_{wait}$	F_{pre}	$Min[A_0 + (1/2)RT^B_{halt}, A_{max}]$
$T_{wait} \leq T^B_{halt} < T_{SEAD}$	F_{post}	$Min[A_0 + RT_{wait} + (1/2)(RT^B_{halt} - T_{wait}), A_{max}]$
$T^B_{halt} \geq T_{SEAD}$	F	$Min[A_0 + RT_{SEAD} + (1/2)R(T^B_{halt} - T_{SEAD}), A_{max}]$

Appendix E

GENERAL FORMULAS FOR LEADING-EDGE STRATEGY

E.1 INITIAL COMMENTS

This appendix develops solutions for the leading-edge strategy. There are a number of mathematical subtleties caused by the exhaustion of weapons and the need to treat different sequences of critical times.

In contrast to the case of the in-depth strategy, the relevant functions have sharp discontinuities. These can be confusing, and care must be taken to evaluate some of the variables at the proper side of a discontinuity. Furthermore, the ability of the interdiction force to slow the attacker is not a monotonic function of time. Instead, it can rise, drop, and then rise again, depending on the order of events. This is illustrated in Figure E.1, which shows the slowing effect $\Delta(t)$ versus time for the various cases.[1] The various thresholds are indicated in the figure; some of them occur at discontinuities (not mere kinks), so it becomes necessary to distinguish between values at the different ends of the discontinuous jumps.

The complexities indicated in Figure E.1 reflect annoying mathematical details, but unless they are accounted for adequately, charts of halt time versus the various parameters will be numerically inaccurate and also visibly ill-behaved. That ill behavior can be a serious distraction in exploratory analysis, even when the size of numerical errors is small.

In Section E.2, we solve for the halt time that would arise from the slowing effect alone. When the threat is quite large, this may be the limiting factor determining overall halt time. As shown in Section E.3, however, when "good weapons" are limited in number, the slowing-effect halt time may be quite large and the limiting factor determining halt time then turns out to be attrition to the overall force—as in the in-depth strategy. Even so, as shown in Section E.4, the slowing effect is important because it reduces halt distance.

E.2 THE HALT TIME THAT WOULD ARISE FROM THE SLOWING EFFECT ALONE

Tables E.1 and E.2 define the thresholds and slowing-effect-only halt-time solutions for the leading-edge strategy, using case conventions as earlier. Not all of the thresholds in Table E.1 are actually needed, but they are included for completeness and for use in possible model modifications.

---

[1]The abbreviations here are, respectively, D, W, S, E, and M for D-Day (0), wait time T_{wait}, SEAD time T_{SEAD}, exhaustion time T_{exh}, and the time the theater capacity is reached T_{max}.

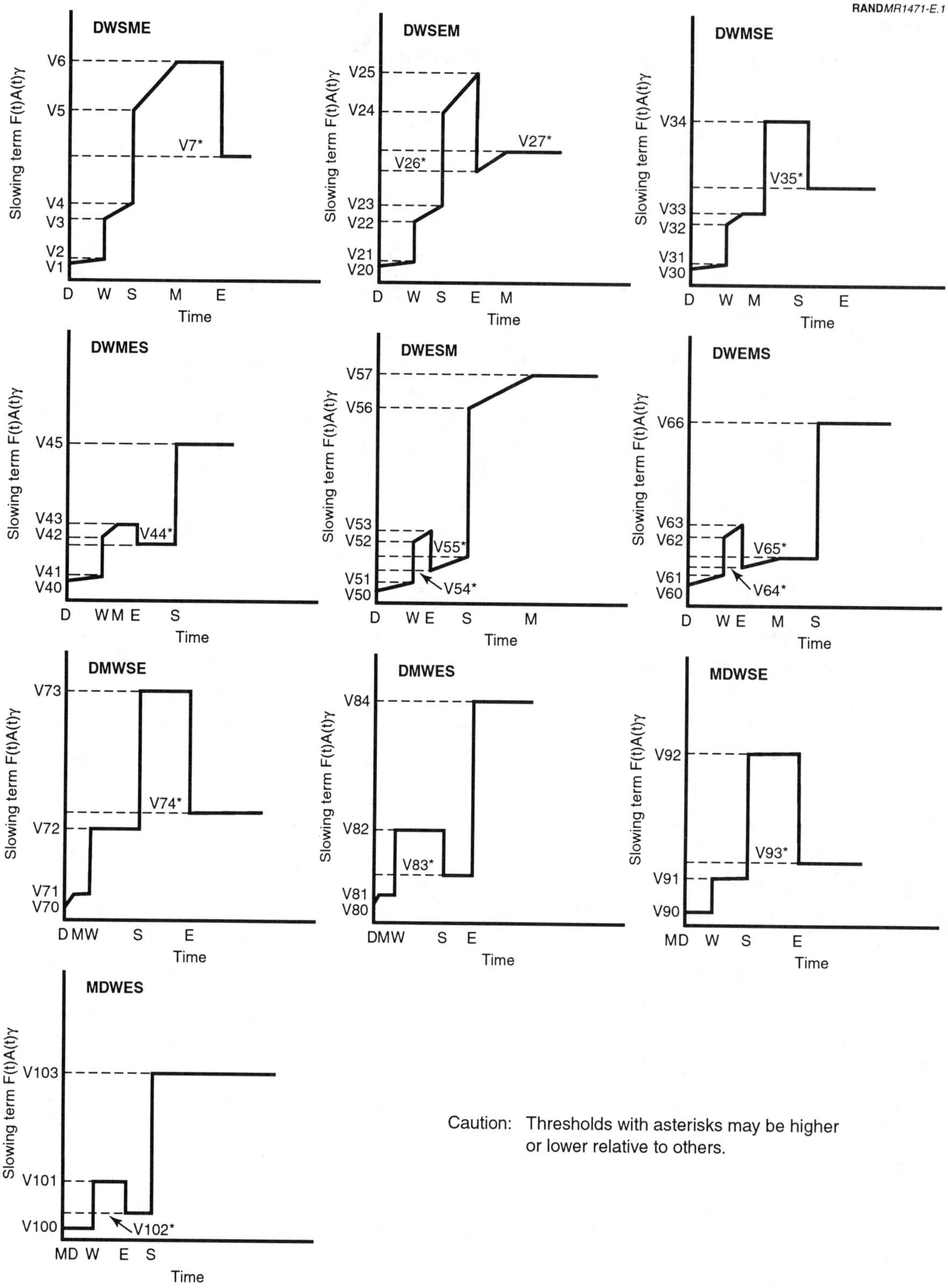

Figure E.1—Slowing Effect Versus Time

Table E.1

TRANSITION POINTS FOR LEADING-EDGE STRATEGY, INCLUDING WEAPON INVENTORY LIMITS

Ordering	Threshold	Value
DWSME	V1 (at 0)	$F_{pre}A_0\gamma$
	V2 (at W–)	$F_{pre}(A_0 + RT_{wait})\gamma$
	V3 (at W+)	$F_{post}(A_0 + RT_{wait})\gamma$
	V4 (at S–)	$F_{post}(A_0 + RT_{SEAD} - ALosses)\gamma$
	V5 (at S+)	$F(A_0 + RT_{SEAD} - ALosses)\gamma$
	V6 (at M)	$FA_{max}\gamma$
	V7 (at E+)	$(\delta_B/\delta_A)FA_{max}\gamma$
DWSEM	V20 (at 0)	$F_{pre}A_0\gamma$
	V21 (at W–)	$F_{pre}(A_0 + RT_{wait})\gamma$
	V22 (at W+)	$F_{post}(A_0 + RT_{wait})\gamma$
	V23 (at S–)	$F_{post}(A_0 + RT_{SEAD} - ALosses)\gamma$
	V24 (at S+)	$F(A_0 + RT_{SEAD} - ALosses)\gamma$
	V25 (at E–)	$F(A_0 + RT_{exh} - ALosses)\gamma$
	V26 (at E+)	$(\delta_B/\delta_A)F(A_0 + RT_{exh} - ALosses)\gamma$
	V27 (at M)	$(\delta_B/\delta_A)FA_{max}\gamma$
DWMSE	V30 (at 0)	$F_{pre}A_0\gamma$
	V31 (at W–)	$F_{pre}(A_0 + RT_{wait})\gamma$
	V32 (at W+)	$F_{post}(A_0 + RT_{wait})\gamma$
	V33 (at M)	$F_{post}A_{max}\gamma$
	V34 (at S+)	$FA_{max}\gamma$
	V35 (at E+)	$(\delta_B/\delta_A)FA_{max}\gamma$
DWMES	V40 (at 0)	$F_{pre}A_0\gamma$
	V41 (at W–)	$F_{pre}(A_0 + RT_{wait})\gamma$
	V42 (at W+)	$F_{post}(A_0 + RT_{wait})\gamma$
	V43 (at M)	$F_{post}A_{max}\gamma$
	V44 (at E–)	$(\delta_B/\delta_A)F_{post}A_{max}\gamma$
	V45 (at S+)	$(\delta_B/\delta_A)FA_{max}\gamma$
DWESM	V50 (at 0)	$F_{pre}A_0\gamma$
	V51(at W–)	$F_{pre}(A_0 + RT_{wait})\gamma$
	V52 (at W+)	$F_{post}(A_0 + RT_{wait})\gamma$
	V53 (at E–)	$F_{post}[A_0 + RT_{exh} - L_{dailylosses}(T_{exh} - T_{wait})]\gamma$
	V54 (at E+)	$(\delta B/\delta A)Fpost\,[A0 + RT_{exh} - \Delta R(T_{exh} - T_{wait})]\gamma$
	V55 (at S–)	$(\delta_B/\delta_A)F_{post}(A_0 + RT_{SEAD} - ALosses)\gamma$
	V56 (at S+)	$(\delta_B/\delta_A)F(A_0 + RT_{SEAD} - ALosses)\gamma$
	V57 (at M)	$(\delta_B/\delta_A)FA_{max}\gamma$
DWEMS	V60 (at 0)	$F_{pre}A_0\gamma$
	V61 (at W–)	$F_{pre}(A_0 + RT_{wait})\gamma$
	V62 (at W+)	$F_{post}(A_0 + RT_{wait})\gamma$
	V63 (at E–)	$F_{post}[A_0 + RT_{exh} - \Delta R(T_{exh} - T_{wait})]\gamma$
	V64 (at E+)	$(\delta B/\delta A)Fpost\,[A0 + RT_{exh} - \Delta R(T_{exh} - T_{wait})]\gamma$
	V65 (at M)	$(\delta_B/\delta_A)F_{post}A_{max}\gamma$
	V66 (at S+)	$(\delta_B/\delta_A)FA_{max}\gamma$

Table E.1 (continued)

Ordering	Threshold	Value
DMWSE	V70 (at 0)	$F_{pre}A_0\gamma$
	V71 (at M)	$F_{pre}A_{max}\gamma$
	V72 (at W+)	$F_{post}A_{max}\gamma$
	V73 (at S+)	$FA_{max}\gamma$
	V74 (at E–)	$(\delta_B/\delta_A)FA_{max}\gamma$
DMWES	V80 (at 0)	$F_{pre}A_0\gamma$
	V81 (at M)	$F_{pre}A_{max}\gamma$
	V82 (at W+)	$F_{post}A_{max}\gamma$
	V83 (at E+)	$(\delta_B/\delta_A)F_{post}A_{max}\gamma$
	V84 (at S+)	$(\delta_B/\delta_A)FA_{max}\gamma$

NOTE: Values used for the deltas should be those for the leading-edge strategy.

Given the diagrams of Figure E.1 and the thresholds of Table E.1, the solutions for slowing-effect halt time follow straightforwardly, albeit tediously, with if-then-else logic. To illustrate this, consider that the row in Table E.2 labeled DWSHME and all rows below it are irrelevant in a given model calculation unless the condition of the first row fails. Thus, if we are seeking the solution DWSHME, we know that $V \leq V_7$. This simplifies the logic required for implementation, which would otherwise be more torturous because the function involved is nonmonotonic.

The solutions in Table E.2 have Max functions because the analytical expressions for halt time, such as $(1/R)[(V/F_{pre}\gamma) - A_0]$, give the value of time at which the relevant straight line equals V. For large values of A_0, the line extends beyond the region for which it is valid (see Figure E.2). The correct solution, for a given interval, is then the maximum value of the expression and the lower bound of the interval (e.g., D-Day in DHWSME cases or T_{wait} in DWHSME cases). In Figure E.2, since $V \geq V_4$, the halt time falls in the interval $[T_{SEAD}, T_{max}]$ (see the dark straight line) and is either the value of time at which V intercepts the straight line for that interval (T_1) or—when V occurs at the discontinuity—T_2, which is T_{SEAD} itself. T_1 is outside the correct interval; T_2 is correct.

E.3 THE LIMITING FACTOR IN HALT TIME

Halt Time as the Shortest of Several Candidates

Tables E.1 and E.2 define the halt time that would obtain in a leading-edge strategy if the slowing effect of that strategy caused a halt before other factors. However, in cases in which the "good" weapons (Type A) are few, the lesser weapons (Type B) are poor or mediocre, and the threat substantial, the slowing effect will not in fact be the limiting factor, but will instead be large. Although the enemy's movement might be stopped temporarily by the good weapons, it could pick up again later when the good weapons are exhausted (see Figure E.2). This also leads to the apparently paradoxical result that the halt time of Table E.2 worsens as the number of good weapons increases.

The actual halt time, then, should be taken as the lowest of three quantities:

Table E.2

SOLUTIONS FOR LEADING-EDGE STRATEGY, INCLUDING WEAPON INVENTORY LIMITS (SLOWING EFFECT ONLY) (IF-THEN-ELSE LOGIC)

Case	Ordering	Halt Time
V > V7	DWSMEH	∞
V ≥ V4	DWSHME	$\text{Max}\left[\frac{1}{R}\left[\frac{V}{F\gamma}-(A_0-\text{ALosses})\right],T_{SEAD}\right]$
V ≥ V2	DWHSME	$\text{Max}\left[\frac{1}{R-\Delta R}\left[\frac{V}{F_{post}\gamma}-A_0\right],T_{wait}\right]$
V ≥ V1	DHWSME	$\text{Max}\left[\frac{1}{R}\left[\frac{V}{F_{pre}\gamma}-A_0\right],0\right]$
V ≥ 0		0
V > V27	DWSEMH	∞
V ≥ V26	DWSEHM	$\text{Max}\left[\frac{1}{R}\left[\frac{V}{(\delta_B/\delta)F\gamma}-(A_0-\text{ALosses})\right],T_{exh}\right]$
V ≥ V23	DWSHEM	$\text{Max}\left[\frac{1}{R}\left[\frac{V}{F\gamma}-(A_0-\text{ALosses})\right],T_{SEAD}\right]$
V ≥ V21	DWHSEM	$\text{Max}\left[\frac{1}{R-\Delta R}\left[\frac{V}{(\delta_B/\delta)F_{post}\gamma}-A_0\right],T_{wait}\right]$
V ≥ V20	DHWSEM	$\text{Max}\left[\frac{1}{R}\left[\frac{V}{F_{pre}\gamma}-A_0\right],0\right]$
V ≥ 0		0
V > 35	DWMSEH	∞
V ≥ 33	DWMSHE	T_{SEAD}
V ≥ V31	DWMHSE	$\text{Max}\left[\frac{1}{R-\Delta R}\left[\frac{V}{(\delta_B/\delta)F_{post}\gamma}-A_0\right],T_{wait}\right]$
V ≥ V30	DHWMSE	$\text{Max}\left[\frac{1}{R}\left[\frac{V}{F_{pre}\gamma}-A_0\right],0\right]$
V ≥ 0		0
V > V45	DWMESH	∞
V ≥ V44	DWMEHS	T_{SEAD}
V ≥ V41	DWHMES	$\text{Max}\left[\frac{1}{R-\Delta R}\left[\frac{V}{F_{post}\gamma}-A_0\right],T_{wait}\right]$
V ≥ V40	DHWMES	$\text{Max}\left[\frac{1}{R}\left[\frac{V}{F_{pre}\gamma}-A_0\right],0\right]$
V ≥ 0		0

Table E.2 (continued)

Case	Ordering	Halt Time
V > V57	DWESMH	∞
V ≥ V55	DWESHM	$\mathrm{Max}\left[\frac{1}{R}\left[\frac{V}{(\delta_B/\delta)F\gamma}-(A_0-\mathrm{ALosses})\right],T_{SEAD}\right]$
V ≥ V54	DWEHSM	$\mathrm{Max}\left[\frac{1}{R-\Delta R}\left[\frac{V}{(\delta_B/\delta)F_{post}\gamma}-A_0\right],T_{exh}\right]$
V ≥ V51	DWHESM	$\mathrm{Max}\left[\frac{1}{R-\Delta R}\left[\frac{V}{F_{post}\gamma}-A_0\right],T_{wait}\right]$
V ≥ 50	DHWESM	$\mathrm{Max}\left[\frac{1}{R}\left[\frac{V}{F_{pre}\gamma}-A_0\right],0\right]$
V ≥ 0		0
V ≥ V66	DWEMSH	∞
V ≥ V65	DWEMHS	T_{SEAD}
V ≥ V64	DWEHMS	$\mathrm{Max}\left[\frac{1}{R-\Delta R}\left[\frac{V}{(\delta_B/\delta)F_{post}\gamma}-A_0\right],T_{exh}\right]$
V ≥ 62	DWHEMS	$\mathrm{Max}\left[\frac{1}{R-\Delta R}\left[\frac{V}{F_{post}\gamma}-A_0\right],T_{wait}\right]$
V ≥ V60	DHWEMS	$\mathrm{Max}\left[\frac{1}{R}\left[\frac{V}{F_{pre}\gamma}-A_0\right],0\right]$
V ≥ 0		0
V > V74	DMWSEH	∞
V ≥ V72	DMWHSE	T_{SEAD}
V ≥ V71	DMHWSE	T_{wait}
V ≥ V70	DHMWSE	$\mathrm{Max}\left[\frac{1}{R}\left[\frac{V}{F_{pre}\gamma}-A_0\right],0\right]$
V ≥ 0		0
V > V84	DMWESH	∞
V ≥ V83	DMWEHS	T_{SEAD}
V ≥ V81	DMHWES	T_{wait}
V ≥ V80	DHMWES	$\mathrm{Max}\left[\frac{1}{R}\left[\frac{V}{F_{pre}\gamma}-A_0\right],0\right]$
V ≥ 0		0

NOTE: This is an if-then-else table and must be implemented that way or errors will be created.

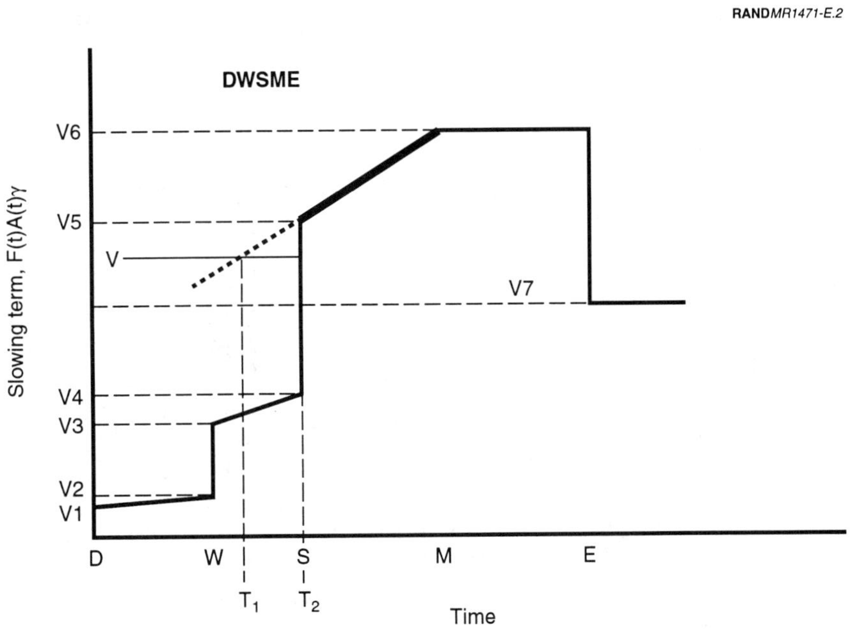

Figure E.2—Example of V Occurring at a Discontinuity

- When attrition to the overall force brings about a halt.
- When the attacking forces reach the defense line—*if* ground forces are in position before then and have enough strength to stop the portion of the attacking force remaining at that time.
- When the slowing effect brings about a permanent halt (not merely a temporary halt during the period of good weapons).

The halt, then, may occur before the attacker reaches the defense line, at the defense line, or subsequently. To implement this algorithm, it is necessary to calculate—even when assuming the leading-edge strategy—both the attrition halt time of the full enemy force and the attrition halt time for the hypothetical smaller force amounting to the full enemy force minus what ground forces could stop at the defense line. It is also necessary to calculate the time at which the attacker reaches the defense line.

Estimating Time to Defense Line

The rigorous solution for the attacker's time to defense line requires accounting for the increase of shooters during a given time period (lower curves in Figures E.3 and E.4). In these figures we begin using the notation Q for delay time T_{delay} and exploit the fact that all of the critical times can be considered to be larger than or equal to D-Day (0), which we then do not mention explicitly. The rigorous solution requires solving a quadratic equation in time, which is doable, but it is a good approximation to linearize (solid curves of Figure E.3). To see this, note that the slowing effect at time t is given by

$$S(t) = F(t)[A(t_x) + R(t - t_x)]\gamma, \qquad \text{(E.1)}$$

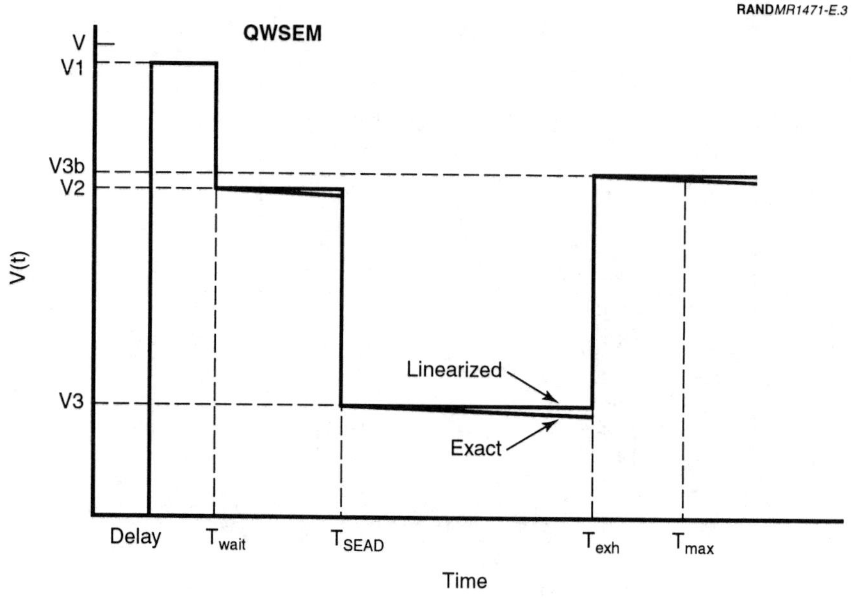

Figure E.3—Schematic of Attacker's Movement Rate Versus Time

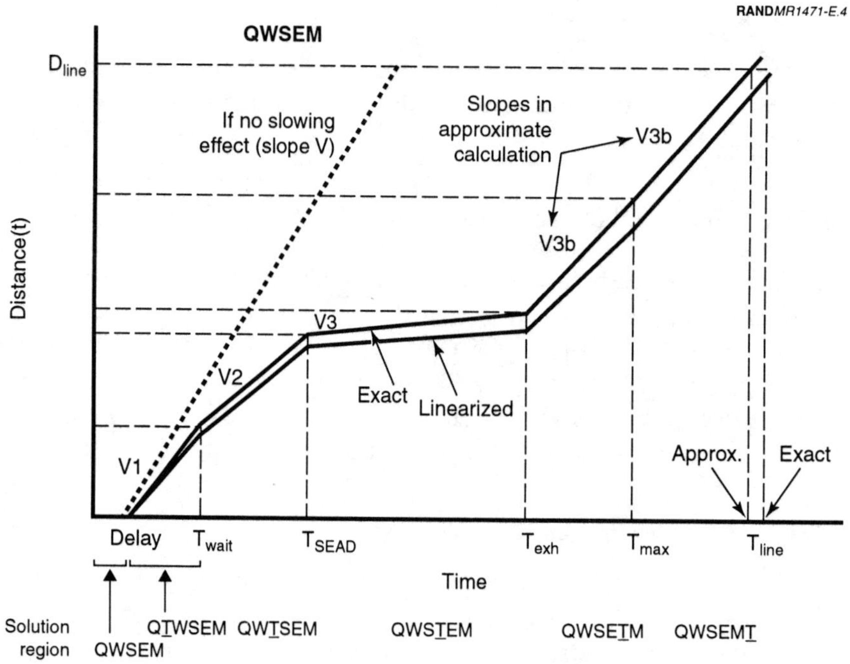

Figure E.4—Schematic of Attacker's Movement Versus Time When Subject to the Slowing Effect of a Leading-Edge Attack

where t_x is the critical time previous to t. For example, if t is between T_{SEAD} and T_{exh}, then t_x is T_{SEAD}. The approximation is to ignore the term $R(t - t_x)$, which is small compared with $A(t_x)$ for cases of interest in the larger problem.[2]

With the linearization, the time for the attacker to reach the defense line can be solved by merely writing, for each solution region (e.g., QWSEM):

$$D_{line} = \sum_{i}^{n} V_i \Delta t_i = \sum_{i}^{n-1} V_i \Delta t_i + V_n (T_{line} - t_n)$$

$$T_{line} = \frac{D_{line} - \sum_{i}^{n-1} V_i \Delta t_i + V_n t_n}{V_n}, \qquad \text{(E.2)}$$

where i indexes the time interval (e.g., 0 to T_{wait}), ΔV_i is the speed during the *ith* time interval, the sum is taken over the intervals needed to reach D_{line}, except for the last, and t_n is the last critical time before reaching the line. Which intervals apply depends on the "case"—i.e., on the ordering of the critical times.

Although formalistic, Eq. (E.2) is helpful in developing and checking formulas—i.e., in understanding the form the formulas should take.

As elsewhere in this monograph, we are plagued with a multiplicity of cases. A "case" can be considered to be an ordered sequence of critical times Q, W, S, M, and E denoting the delay time, wait time, SEAD time, time of maximum theater capacity, and exhaustion time, respectively. We can assume that all of these are greater than or equal to 0 (D-Day). Mathematically, there are 5! or 120 combinations, but we can reduce the number of cases in several ways. First, as discussed throughout the monograph, we require

$$T_{wait} \le T_{SEAD}. \qquad \text{(E.3)}$$

Second, as discussed in Chapter 6, we approximate calculations involving the exhaustion time by requiring that the value of T_{exh} (which is calculated elsewhere) be constrained to be no smaller than T_{wait}. Since smaller values of T_{exh} can therefore not arise in the calculation anyway, we can reduce the number of cases by requiring that

$$T_{wait} \le T_{exh}. \qquad \text{(E.4)}$$

These conditions reduce the number of combinations from 120 to 40.[3] For each such case, there may be a number of subcases distinguishing solutions. For example, for

[2]The effect of the approximation is a slight conservatism in that it slightly overestimates the size of the ground force needed to halt the attacker at the defense line.

[3]This may not be intuitive. Of the 120 original cases, half are eliminated by requiring that W < S. However, the requirement that E > W does not cut the cases by half again because the distribution of cases is already "lopsided." Consider the problem with three objects A, B, and C. This has 3! or six combinations. If A < B, then only three remain: ABC, ACB, and CAB. If we require that A < C, that eliminates only the last one.

the case QWESM, the potential subcases would be denoted TQWESM, QTWESM, QWTESM, QWETSM, QWESTM, and QWESMT, where T denotes T_{line}. Each requires a separate formula. Thus, we might have as many as 180 subcases to deal with. This is still far too many.

Fortunately, another major simplification is possible. Instead of treating T_{max} as a critical time in the same list as the others, let us approximate the number of shooters in a given time interval defined by Q, W, E, and S as being the lesser of the number at the beginning of the interval or A_{max}. The error introduced is typically small even if we don't linearize and, if we do, no further error is introduced by this treatment of A_{max}.

It follows that we have only 4! cases to deal with, of which half are eliminated by Eq. (E.3). Equation (E.4) eliminates one-third of those that remain, leaving a total of eight. Those are shown in Table E.3.

To better define this concept, it is convenient to define the speeds for the various time periods first, and then write the formulas for T_{line}. This is accomplished in Tables E.4 and E.5. It is necessary to understand the speeds in Table E.4 to proofread Table E.5 (or its equivalent in computer code).

Table E.3

VALID CASES USING THE LINEAR APPROXIMATION AND CONSTRAINTS

QWSE: Delay, wait, SEAD, exhaustion
QWES: Delay, wait, exhaustion, SEAD
WQSE: Wait, delay, SEAD, exhaustion
WQES: Wait, delay, exhaustion, SEAD
WEQS: Wait, exhaustion, delay, SEAD
WESQ: Wait, exhaustion, SEAD, delay
WSEQ: Wait, SEAD, exhaustion, delay
WSQE: Wait, SEAD, delay, exhaustion

Table E.4

ATTACKER SPEEDS, AFTER SLOWING, FOR DIFFERENT ORDERINGS OF CRITICAL TIMES (IN LINEAR APPROXIMATION)

Attacker Speed for Particular Region	Applicable Times
$V_1 = V - F_{pre}\mathrm{Min}[A_0, A_{max}]\gamma$	$t \le T_{wait}$
$V_2 = V - F_{post}\mathrm{Min}[(A_0 + RT_{wait}), A_{max}]\gamma$	$T_{wait} < t \le T_{SEAD}, T_{exh}$
$V_3 = V - F\ \mathrm{Min}[(A_0 + RT_{SEAD}), A_{max}]\gamma$	$T_{SEAD} < t \le T_{exh}$
$V_{1b} = V - F_{pre}\mathrm{Min}[A_0, A_{max}](\delta_B / \delta_A)\gamma$	$T_{exh} < t \le T_{wait}$
$V_{2b} = V - F_{post}\mathrm{Min}[(A_0 + RT_{wait}), A_{max}](\delta_B / \delta_A)\gamma$	$T_{exh}, T_{wait} < t \le T_{SEAD}$
$V_{3b} = V - F\ \mathrm{Min}[(A_0 + RT_{SEAD}), A_{max}](\delta_B / \delta_A)\gamma$	$T_{exh}, T_{SEAD} < t \le T_{SEAD}$

NOTE: When implemented, these should be defined as positive definite.

Table E.5

TIME FOR ATTACKER TO REACH DEFENSE LINE, FOR DIFFERENT ORDERINGS OF CRITICAL TIMES

Broad Case	Specific Case	Time for Attacker to Reach Defense Line
QWSE	qwset	$\frac{D_{line} - [V_1(T_{wait} - T_{delay}) + V_2(T_{SEAD} - T_{wait}) + V_3(T_{exh} - T_{SEAD})] + V_{3b}T_{exh}}{V_{3b}}$
	qwste	$\frac{D_{line} - [V_1(T_{wait} - T_{delay}) + V_2(T_{SEAD} - T_{wait})] + V_3T_{SEAD}}{V_3}$
	qwtse	$\frac{D_{line} - [V_1(T_{wait} - T_{delay})] + V_2T_{wait}}{V_2}$
	qtwse	$\frac{D_{line} + V_1T_{delay}}{V_1}$
QWES	qwest	$\frac{D_{line} - [V_1(T_{wait} - T_{delay}) + V_2(T_{exh} - T_{wait}) + V_{2b}(T_{SEAD} - T_{exh})] + V_{3b}T_{SEAD}}{V_{3b}}$
	qwets	$\frac{D_{line} - [V_1(T_{wait} - T_{delay}) + V_2(T_{exh} - T_{wait})] + V_{2b}T_{exh}}{V_{2b}}$
	qwtes	$\frac{D_{line} - [V_1(T_{wait} - T_{delay})] + V_2T_{wait}}{V_2}$
	qtwes	$\frac{D_{line} + V_1T_{delay}}{V_1}$
WQSE	wqset	$\frac{D_{line} - [V_2(T_{SEAD} - T_{delay}) + V_3(T_{exh} - T_{SEAD})] + V_{3b}T_{exh}}{V_{3b}}$
	wqste	$\frac{D_{line} - [V_2(T_{SEAD} - T_{delay})] + V_3T_{SEAD}}{V_3}$
	wqtse	$\frac{D_{line} + V_2T_{delay}}{V_2}$
WQES	wqest	$\frac{D_{line} - [V_1(T_{exh} - T_{delay}) + V_2(T_{SEAD} - T_{exh})] + V_{3b}T_{SEAD}}{V_{3b}}$
	wqets	$\frac{D_{line} - [V_1(T_{exh} - T_{delay})] + V_{2b}T_{exh}}{V_{2b}}$
	wqtes	$\frac{D_{line} + V_2T_{delay}}{V_2}$
WEQS	weqst	$\frac{D_{line} - V_{2b}(T_{SEAD} - T_{delay}) + V_{3b}T_{SEAD}}{V_{3b}}$
	weqts	$\frac{D_{line} + V_{2b}T_{delay}}{V_{2b}}$
WESQ	wesqt	$\frac{D_{line} + V_{3b}T_{delay}}{V_{3b}}$
WSEQ	wseqt	$\frac{D_{line} + V_{3b}T_{delay}}{V_{3b}}$
WSQE	wsqet	$\frac{D_{line} - [V_3(T_{exh} - T_{delay})] + V_{3b}T_{exh}}{V_{3b}}$
	wsqte	$\frac{D_{line} + V_3T_{delay}}{V_3}$

As before (e.g., Chapters 3 and 6), the logic for choosing a solution from Table E.5, given that one has already identified the case (first column), is easily implemented using thresholds. In this case, the thresholds pertain to distances that the attacker can move in the various cases. The appropriate thresholds are defined in Table E.6.

As an example, if the case is WQES, then the logic would be as shown in the following pseudo code.

[For Case WQES]
If Defense_line $\leq X_6$
Then T_{tl} = wqtes
Else (E.5)
If Defense_line $\leq X_7$
Then T_{tl} = wqets
Else wqest

Table E.6

THRESHOLDS FOR USE IN CALCULATING ATTACKER'S ARRIVAL TIME AT THE DEFENSE LINE

Case	Threshold	Definition
QWSE	X_1 (at W)	$V_1(T_{wait} - T_{delay})$
	X_2 (at S)	$X_1 + V_2(T_{SEAD} - T_{wait})$
	X_3 (at E)	$X_2 + V_3(T_{exh} - T_{SEAD})$
QWES	X_1(at W)	X_1, above
	X_{2b}(at E)	$X_1 + V_2(T_{exh} - T_{wait})$
	X_3 (at S)	$X_{2b} + V_{2b}(T_{SEAD} - T_{exh})$
WQSE	X_4(at S)	$V_2(T_{SEAD} - T_{delay})$
	X_5 (at E)	$X_4 + V_3(T_{exh} - T_{SEAD})$
WQES	X_6 (at E)	$V_2(T_{exh} - T_{delay})$
	X_7 (at S)	$X_6 + V_{2b}(T_{SEAD} - T_{exh})$
WEQS	X_8 (at S)	$V_{2b}(T_{SEAD} - T_{delay})$
WESQ	None	None
WSEQ	None	None
WSQE	X_9 (at E)	$V_3(T_{exh} - T_{delay})$

E.4 SOLVING FOR HALT DISTANCE UNDER THE LEADING-EDGE STRATEGY

Initial Comments

Solving for halt distance is similar in some respects to solving for the time at which the attacker reaches the defense line. That is, once again we must consider the complex movement possibilities and the many combinations of critical times. In this calculation, however, linearizing could introduce an excessive error. Thus, our approximation will be merely that the average number of shooters in a given interval is the minimum of the unconstrained number and A_{max}.

Curve Shapes. It follows that the distance moved by the attacker will also have a complex shape. Figure E.4 illustrates this for the same sequence of critical times QWSEM, but with somewhat different assumed values of the parameters. In particular, Figure E.4 assumes that the slowing effect is large enough between T_{SEAD} and T_{exh} so that there is little or no movement.[4] Movement picks up again abruptly at T_{exh}. Figure E.4 also shows—for an illustrative sequence only—when the attacker reaches the defense line, which might also be where halt occurs.

The halt distance is affected by when movement begins (perhaps after an initial delay caused by air and missile strikes) and the subsequent movement rate versus time until halt is achieved. As discussed above, the attacker's movement rate decreases with time as the number of shooters increases and decreases sharply as larger allocations are made at times T_{wait} and T_{SEAD}. The movement rate *increases*, however, when the exhaustion time T_{exh} is reached. Thus, as mentioned above, V(t) may not be a monotonic function of time, depending on the order of the critical times.

A Convention for Labeling Speeds. To simplify the equations it is helpful to define and abbreviate a number of speeds that occur in the various intervals. We adopt a convention in which V is labeled with three indicators. The number 1, 2, or 3 indicates whether the relevant time period is at or before T_{wait}, greater than T_{wait} but no more than T_{SEAD}, or greater than T_{SEAD}. The presence of a "b" indicates that the relevant time period follows T_{exh}. The presence of an "f" or "e" indicates that the upper end of the time period is T_{halt} or T_{exh}, respectively. If neither "e" nor "f" appears, the upper end of the time period is T_{wait} or T_{SEAD}, for V_1's, and V_2's, respectively. This notation works because not all of the mathematically possible 18 combinations are feasible. Recall that we require that T_{exh} be no less than both T_{wait} and T_{SEAD}.

As mentioned above, we approximate the implications of T_{max} by approximating the average number of shooters in the relevant time period as the minimum of the unconstrained number and A_{max}.

With this background, Table E.7 defines the various speeds and Table E.8 gives the halt distances for the eight cases that arise when the T_{max} effect is handled approximately. The cases are QWSE, QWES, ...

---

[4]Arguably, one may also have negative speeds if the interdiction "rolls back" the invader force (see Ochmanek, Harshberger, Thaler, and Kent [1998]). For the purposes of this monograph, we do not permit negative speeds.

Table E.7

SPEEDS

Abbreviation	Attacker Speed (if not within a delay period)
V_1	$V - F_{pre}\gamma Min\left[A_0 + \frac{1}{2}RT_{wait}, A_{max}\right]$
V_{1e}	$V - F_{pre}\gamma Min\left[A_0 + \frac{1}{2}R(T_{exh} + T_{wait}), A_{max}\right]$
V_{1f}	$V - F_{pre}\gamma Min\left[A_0 + \frac{1}{2}RT_{halt}, A_{max}\right]$
V_2	$V - F_{post}\gamma Min\left[A_0 + \frac{1}{2}R(T_{SEAD} + T_{wait}), A_{max}\right]$
V_{2e}	$V - F_{post}\gamma Min\left[A_0 + \frac{1}{2}R(T_{wait} + T_{exh}), A_{max}\right]$
V_{2f}	$V - F_{post}\gamma Min\left[A_0 + \frac{1}{2}R(T_{wait} + T_{halt}), A_{max}\right]$
V_{2b}	$V - F_{post}\gamma \frac{\delta_B}{\delta} Min\left[A_0 + \frac{1}{2}R(Max[T_{exh}, T_{wait}] + T_{SEAD}), A_{max}\right]$
V_{2bf}	$V - F_{post}\gamma \frac{\delta_B}{\delta} Min\left[A_0 + \frac{1}{2}R(Max[T_{wait}, T_{exh}] + T_{halt}), A_{max}\right]$
V_3	$V - F\gamma Min\left[A_0 + \frac{1}{2}R(T_{SEAD} + T_{exh}), A_{max}\right]$
V_{3e}	$V - F\gamma Min\left[A_0 + \frac{1}{2}R(T_{SEAD} + T_{exh}), A_{max}\right]$
V_{3f}	$V - F\gamma Min\left[A_0 + \frac{1}{2}R(T_{SEAD} + T_{halt}), A_{max}\right]$
V_{3b}	$V - F\frac{\delta_B}{\delta}\gamma Min\left[A_0 + \frac{1}{2}R(Max[T_{SEAD}, T_{exh}] + T_{halt}), A_{max}\right]$
V_{3bf}	$V - F\frac{\delta_B}{\delta}\gamma Min\left[A_0 + \frac{1}{2}R(Max[T_{SEAD}, T_{exh}] + T_{halt}), A_{max}\right]$

NOTES:

1. As written, the speeds may be negative, corresponding to a rollback effect in which the interdiction destroys more column length per day than the advance rate. If this effect is unwanted, then all of the speeds should be constrained to be nonnegative.

2. When implementing this material, care should be taken to use δ values (kills per shooter day) for the leading-edge strategy, rather than the in-depth strategy. That is, a better notation here would be to use δ_{le}.

3. The use of $Max[T_{wait}, T_{exh}]$, etc. is a trick allowing us to reduce the number of speeds needed. Knowing that the speed is V_{2b} tells us that it applies after the wait time and the exhaustion time, but does not tell us which order these occurred in. That has a small effect on the estimate of shooters.

Table E.8

LEADING-EDGE HALT DISTANCES BY CASE AND SUBCASE

HQWSE	0
QHWSE	$V_{1f}(T_{halt} - T_{delay})$
QWHSE	$V_1(T_{wait} - T_{delay}) + V_{2f}(T_{halt} - T_{wait})$
QWSHE	$V_1(T_{wait} - T_{delay}) + V_2(T_{SEAD} - T_{wait}) + V_{3f}(T_{halt} - T_{SEAD})$
QWSEH	$V_1(T_{wait} - T_{delay}) + V_2(T_{SEAD} - T_{wait}) + V_3(T_{exh} - T_{SEAD}) + V_{3bf}(T_{halt} - T_{exh})$
HQWES	0
QHWES	$V_{1f}(T_{halt} - T_{delay})$
QWHES	$V_1(T_{wait} - T_{delay}) + V_{2f}(T_{halt} - T_{wait})$
QWEHS	$V_1(T_{wait} - T_{delay}) + V_2(T_{exh} - T_{wait}) + V_{2bf}(T_{halt} - T_{exh})$
QWESH	$V_1(T_{wait} - T_{delay}) + V_2(T_{exh} - T_{wait}) + V_{2b}(T_{SEAD} - T_{exh}) + V_{3bf}(T_{halt} - T_{SEAD})$
HWQSE	0
WHQSE	0
WQHSE	$V_{2f}(T_{halt} - T_{delay})$
WQSHE	$V_2(T_{SEAD} - T_{delay}) + V_{3f}(T_{halt} - T_{SEAD})$
WQSEH	$V_2(T_{SEAD} - T_{delay}) + V_3(T_{exh} - T_{SEAD}) + V_{3bf}(T_{halt} - T_{exh})$
HWQES	0
WHQES	0
WQHES	$V_{2f}(T_{halt} - T_{delay})$
WQEHS	$V_2(T_{exh} - T_{delay}) + V_{2bf}(T_{halt} - T_{exh})$
WQESH	$V_2(T_{exh} - T_{delay}) + V_{2b}(T_{SEAD} - T_{exh}) + V_{3bf}(T_{halt} - T_{SEAD})$
HWEQS	0
WHEQS	0
WEHQS	0
WEQHS	$V_{2bf}(T_{halt} - T_{delay})$
WEQSH	$V_{2b}(T_{SEAD} - T_{delay}) + V_{3bf}(T_{halt} - T_{SEAD})$
HWESQ	0
WHESQ	0
WEHSQ	0
WESHQ	0
WESQH	$V_{3bf}(T_{halt} - T_{delay})$
HWSEQ	0
WHSEQ	0
WSHEQ	0
WSEHQ	0
WSEQH	$V_{3bf}(T_{halt} - T_{delay})$
HWSQE	0
WHSQE	0
WSHQE	0
WSQHE	$V_{3f}(T_{halt} - T_{delay})$
WSQEH	$V_3(T_{exh} - T_{delay}) + V_{3bf}(T_{halt} - T_{exh})$

NOTE: The overall halt distance should be constrained to be no less than zero. If one does not want to allow "rollback effects," the speeds used in Table E.5 should each be similarly constrained.

Appendix F

NOTES ON IMPLEMENTATION IN ANALYTICA

F.1 PROGRAM VERSUS MODEL

EXHALT-CF, in Analytica, is intended to be a faithful implementation of the models in this monograph. As analysts and modelers know well, however, stand-alone documentation seldom keeps up with actual programs. Further, programs inevitably have implementation-specific features such as name differences, computational tricks, and additional machinery to assist in testing and explanation of results. EXHALT-CF collects changes made in a Notes item on the top page of the program (Figure F.1). Also, each variable is described where it is defined and these descriptions—along with the diagrammatic nature of the model (Figure F.2)—should help sort out distinctions between this monograph and the active program. For example,

RANDMR1471-F.1

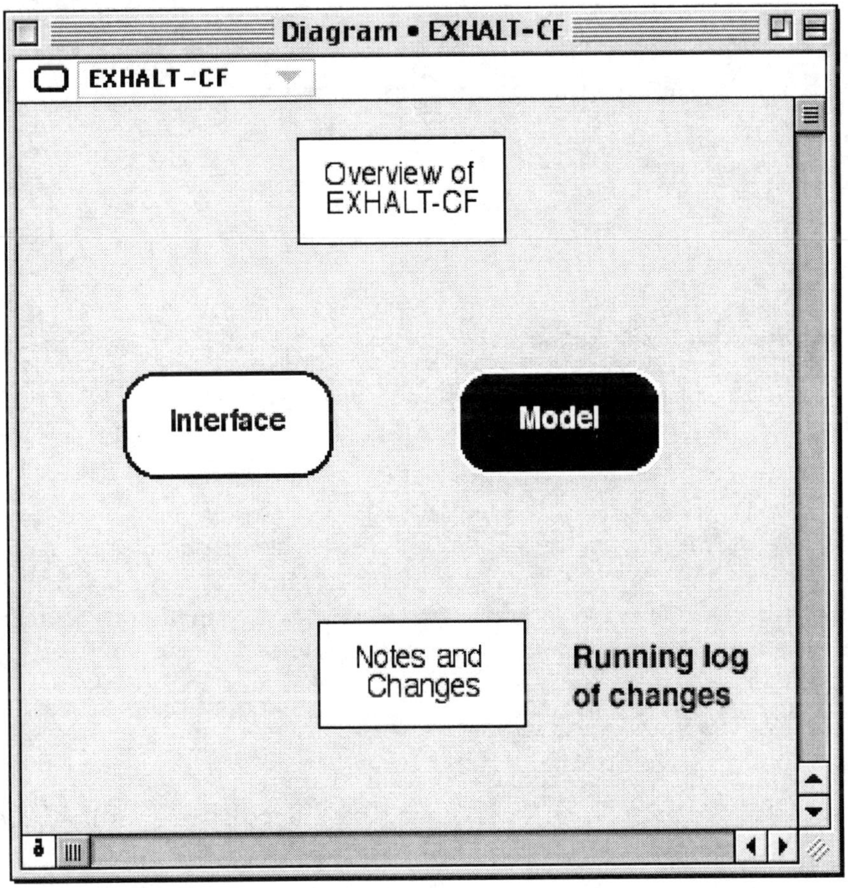

Figure F.1—Documenting Differences Between Program and Model Documentation

RANDMR1471-F.2

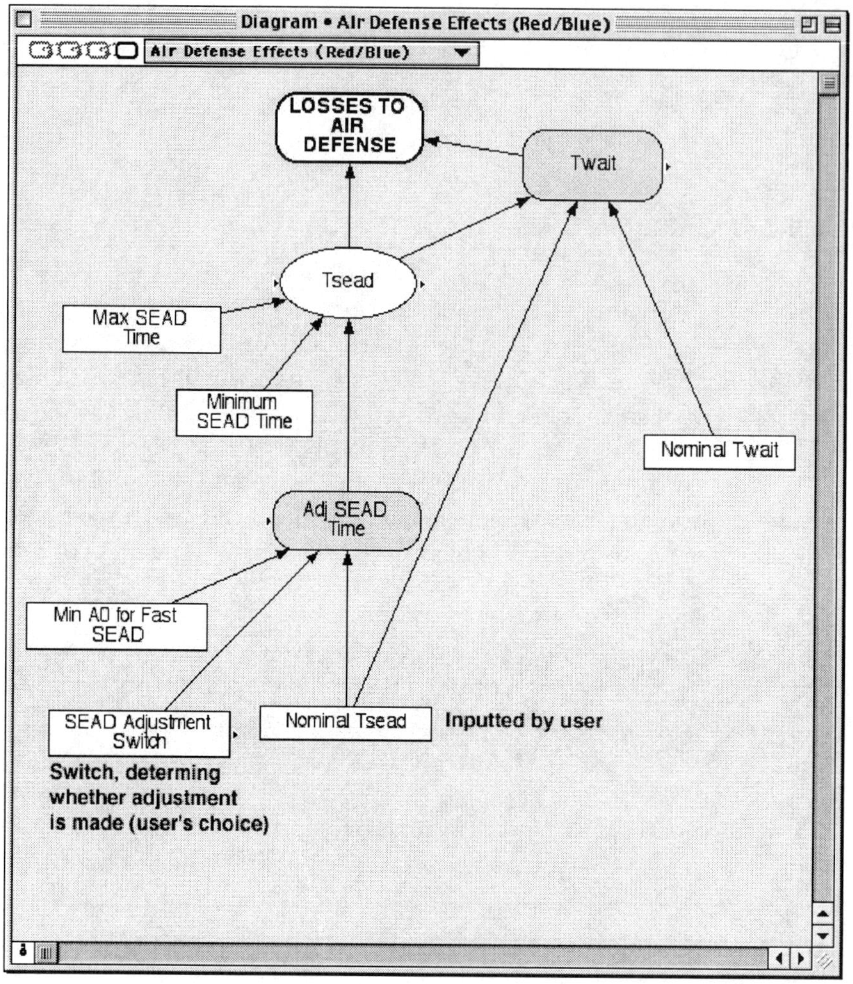

Figure F.2—Insertion of an Optional Adjustment

Figure F.2 introduces an optional adjustment for T_{SEAD}: If one wishes to use the adjustment (note the presence of a switch variable), then the nominal value of T_{SEAD} inputted by the user is replaced by an adjusted value when the input A_0 is very small (see Figure F.3). The adjustment accounts for the fact that shooters must deploy to a theater before the SEAD process can begin. That is, T_{SEAD} should not be treated as *entirely* exogenous, because a short T_{SEAD} makes no sense if A_0 is zero.

F.2 VERIFICATION AND VALIDATION

Verification and validation of models is notoriously difficult.[1] Fortunately, modern programming systems such as Analytica facilitate some of this. Although some

[1]A good survey of related issues is Pace (1998) in Cloud and Rainey (1998). Davis (1992) discusses validation from a pragmatic perspective and also identifies (Appendices A and B) important features

RANDMR1471-F.3

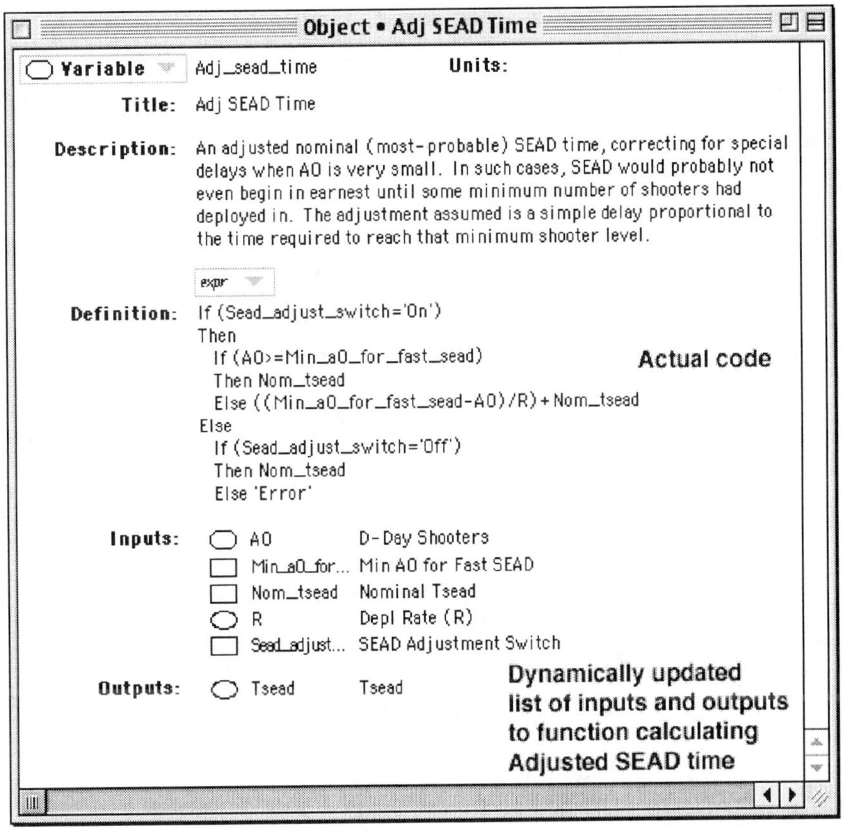

Figure F.3—Definition of an "Adjusted SEAD Time"

residual errors probably exist, as in nearly all nontrivial computer models, we have checked and refined EXHALT-CF extensively. We next describe our approach.

As a preface, we draw a contrast between classical and modern approaches. The classic idealized version of model building long called for distinct design and implementation stages, with verification testing a matter of ensuring correct implementation of a fully specified model. In contrast, a better modern approach involves a closed loop between design of the model and implementation. Although this monograph gives a language-independent specification of the model (which we have realized in C, EXCEL, and Analytica), much of the design was worked out by working within Analytica, rather than with paper and pencil. By working in this way we could design, test, and iterate rapidly: By testing as we went along, we could often clarify issues, discover logical errors (e.g., failure to recognize implications of a discontinuity), and improve the design. Further, by testing along the way, module by module, we made steady progress but always had "something"; that is, as time went on, we had increasingly complete versions of the model and an increasingly rich set

needed in future modeling environments to facilitate testing, many of which are now achieved in Analytica, EXCEL/Visual Basic, iThink, and other modern systems available commercially.

of optional tested modules.[2] Even early on, however, we had a properly running simple version. As so often happens with such an approach, we were still making minor refinements of design in individual modules until a few days before we began production runs for this monograph.[3]

With this background, let us touch briefly on the principal techniques used for testing, in both Analytica and C versions of the model. We used these techniques recursively at the various levels of the multiresolution design.

- *Graphical review of model structure.* Reviewing the model concepts critically by studying the diagrammatic relationships displayed by the Analytica implementation was very helpful in sharpening our understanding of the model and program while testing. It also laid bare some logical clumsiness that could be avoided with modest redesign.
- *Code reading.* Although proofreading the formulas in code to check against those in the monograph may seem tedious, doing this uncovered a number of errors that would likely have taken much more time to discover in other ways—if they would have been discovered at all. Further, by reducing errors in this way we were left with fewer errors overall, which meant that when we later observed a problem, it was almost always due to a single cause.
- *Graphical observation of model behavior.* Many of the more serious errors in programs are not subtle when viewed graphically: Curves that should be monotonically increasing show kinks, after which values decrease; curves go to infinity or drop to zero when they should not; curves cross each other, when that makes no sense physically. We found many errors in this way.[4]
- *Special diagnostics.* If a program were merely a perfect implementation of a perfect mathematical formula, one could dispense with intermediate calculations. In practice, however, it is useful to show intermediate calculations so that when errors are observed, they can be tracked back to their point of origin. In EXHALT-CF, a particularly important set of intermediate diagnostics involves identifying the "case" applicable to the calculations in a particular run. That is, for a given set of inputs, any of a great many different formulas might determine halt time. If an error is apparent in the results, then knowing which formula generated it is important.
- *Exploratory analysis using Monte Carlo methods.* By generating input variables with uniform distributions over the variables' plausible values, and by then using Monte Carlo methods to generate hundreds or thousands of cases, it is easy to identify cases where calculations go seriously awry (e.g., generating infinity, un-

---

[2]In many respects, our approach is consistent with that described in Bellman and Landauer (1998; see, e.g., admonitions on pp. 236–245).

[3]We have not used the term "rapid prototyping" here because that often suggests a version of the approach in which even key features of the eventual model "emerge" after numerous iterations, rather than being part of an initial conceptual design. In our work, there was a strong design from the outset, although many of the embellishments and subtleties evolved from the numerous iterations.

[4]Our testing of the C models used the CARs system developed by Stephen C. Bankes and Norman Shapiro. Analytica has built-in graphics.

defined results, or zeros where that makes no sense). The approach is to scan the values of intermediate and higher-level variables quickly on a run-by-run basis.[5] More extensive visual behavior checking can be done by downloading the various runs—along with their input data (outputs of the Monte Carlo sampler)—into a spreadsheet program and then generating graphs. We used Microsoft EXCEL for this purpose when working with the Analytica version of EXHALT-CF.[6]

- *Limiting cases.* We tested results by looking at numerous limiting cases for which paper-and-pencil calculations were possible.
- *Comparisons.* Since we and colleagues have implemented halt-problem formulas in a number of models and languages over the last few years, we could compare results in relatively simple cases.

As a final observation here, the program implementing EXHALT-CF is not ultimately simple and transparent. The basic principles underlying it are straightforward and the mathematics required involve nothing more than calculus and linear algebra. Nonetheless, the details are complex because of the proliferation of analytic cases dictated by the order of the various critical times, and because some of the mathematical terms do not have a readily apparent physical meaning. In some respects, verifying, validating, and understanding results in EXHALT-CF is *harder* than for a more complex simulation model (e.g., EXHALT), where one can follow the behavior of objects step by step in time. In other respects, however, it is much easier. In any case, details of testing are quite different for something like EXHALT-CF than a simulation model.

F.3 USER INTERFACE

The top level of EXHALT-CF, as implemented in Analytica, refers to a user interface (Figure F.1). By double clicking that, one obtains the interface itself (Figure F.4). By clicking on one of the gray buttons of independent variables, one finds a menu of permitted values. Those buttons that show "All" have been set so that Analytica will run cases for each value of the menu. At the bottom of the display is a button marked "More detailed inputs." Those inputs are provided, in the same format, in a subsequent interface sheet. However, they are relevant only if one chooses to use a higher-resolution module (e.g., as in calculating the number of D-Day shooters from inputs such as C-Day, strategic warning, and so on). Figure F.4 is the complete user interface if one is using the default version of the model intended for initial ex-

---

[5]For complex reasons having to do with our particular problem's mathematics and the way Analytica processes calculations with arrays, we sometimes turned off the error-warning feature because it gave false reports. The problem is that if one is interested in variable X, which is defined in terms of variable Y, and if variable Y has nonsense values for certain logically possible combinations of the input possibilities, then an error will be shown for the calculation of X even though the nonsense values of Y never arise in the actual calculations of X.

[6]A more direct approach was possible using the CARs system with the C version of EXHALT-CF. CARs can use Monte Carlo methods to generate the points that it plots.

ploratory analysis. There are no "hidden variables," so long as the switch buttons in Figure F.4 refer to the low-resolution version of the modules.

RANDMR1471-F.4

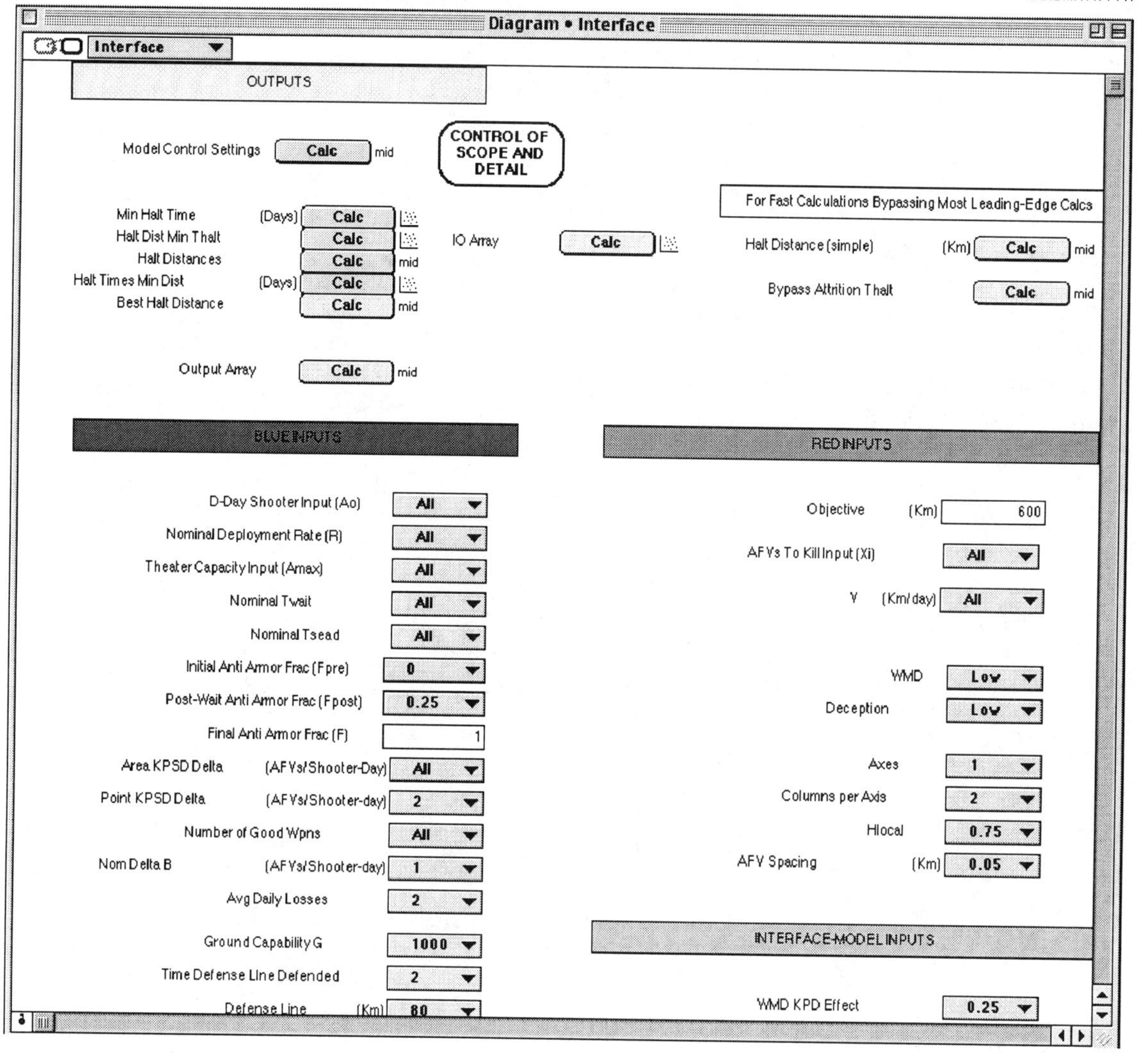

Figure F.4—User Interface

BIBLIOGRAPHY

Alberts, David, John Garstka, and Frederick Stein (1999), *Network Centric Warfare: Developing and Leveraging Information Technology*, CCRP Publication Series, Department of Defense, Washington, DC.

Albus, James, Alexander Meystel, and James Sacra (2001), *Intelligent Systems: Architecture, Design, and Control*, John Wiley and Sons, New York.

Bellman, Kirstie, and Christopher Landauer (1998), "Designing Models," in Cloud and Rainey (1998).

Biddle, Stephen (1996), "Victory Misunderstood: What the Gulf War Tells Us About the Future of Conflict," *International Security*, Vol. 21, No. 2, pp. 137–146.

Biddle, Stephen (1997), "The Gulf War Debate Redux: Why Skill and Technology Are the Right Answer," *International Security*, Vol. 22, No. 2, pp. 163–174.

Bigelow, James H., Paul K. Davis, and Jimmie McEver (2000), "Case History of Using Entity-Level Simulations as Imperfect Experimental Data for Informing and Calibrating Simpler Analytical Models for Interdiction," *Proceedings of the SPIE*, Vol. 4026. A later version is Davis, Bigelow, and McEver (2000b), reprinted in Davis et al. (2001).

Bowie, Christopher, Fred Frostic, et al. (1993), *The New Calculus: Analyzing Airpower's Changing Role in Joint Theater Campaigns*, RAND, MR-149-AF, Santa Monica, CA.

Brzezinski, Zbigniew (1986), *Game Plan: A Geostrategic Framework for the Conduct of the U.S.-Soviet Contest*, Atlantic Monthly Press, Boston, MA.

Bush, George, and Brent Scowcroft (1998), *A World Transformed*, Vintage Books, Alfred Knopf, New York.

Cloud, David, and Larry Rainey (eds.) (1998), *Applied Modeling and Simulation: An Integrated Approach to Development and Operations*, McGraw Hill, New York.

Cohen, Eliot, and John Gooch (1990), *Military Misfortunes: The Anatomy of Failure in War*, Free Press, New York.

Cohen, Secretary of Defense William S. (1999), *Annual Report to the President and the Congress*, Department of Defense, Washington, DC.

Davis, Paul K. (1988), *Toward a Conceptual Framework for Operational Arms Control in Europe's Central Region*, RAND, R-3704-USDP, Santa Monica, CA.

Davis, Paul K. (1992), *Generalizing Concepts and Methods of Verification, Validation, and Accreditation (VV&A) for Military Simulations*, RAND, R-4249-ACQ, Santa Monica, CA.

Davis, Paul K. (ed.) (1993), *New Challenges for Defense Planning: Rethinking How Much Is Enough*, RAND, MR-400-RC, Santa Monica, CA.

Davis, Paul K. (2000), "Exploratory Analysis Enabled by Multiresolution Modeling," *Proceedings of the 2000 Winter Simulation Conference,* Orlando, FL. Reprinted in Davis et al. (2001).

Davis, Paul K. (2001a), *Effects-Based Operations: A Grand Challenge for the Analytical Community,* RAND, MR-1477-USJFCOM/AF, Santa Monica, CA.

Davis, Paul K. (2001b), "Transforming U.S. Forces," in Frank Carlucci et al., *Taking Charge: A Bipartisan Report to the President-Elect on Foreign Policy and National Security,* RAND, MR-1306, Santa Monica, CA.

Davis, Paul K., and James H. Bigelow (1998), *Experiments in Multiresolution Modeling,* RAND, MR-1004-DARPA, Santa Monica, CA.

Davis, Paul K., James H. Bigelow, and Jimmie McEver (1999), *Analytic Methods for Studies and Experiments on Transforming the Force,* RAND, DB-278-OSD, Santa Monica, CA.

Davis, Paul K., James H. Bigelow, and Jimmie McEver (2000a), *Effects of Terrain, Maneuver Tactics, and C4ISR on the Effectiveness of Long-Range Precision Fires: A Stochastic Multiresolution Model (PEM) Calibrated to High-Resolution Simulation,* RAND, MR-1138-OSD, Santa Monica, CA.

Davis, Paul K., James H. Bigelow, and Jimmie McEver (2000b), "Informing and Calibrating a Multiresolution Exploratory Analysis Model with High Resolution Simulation: The Interdiction Problem as a Case History," *Proceedings of the December 2000 Winter Simulation Conference.* Reprinted in Davis et al. (2001).

Davis, Paul K., James H. Bigelow, and Jimmie McEver (2001), *Exploratory Analysis and a Case History of Multiresolution, Multiperspective Modeling,* RAND, RP-925, Santa Monica, CA (a reprint volume).

Davis, Paul K., David Gompert, and Richard Kugler (1996), *Adaptiveness in National Defense: The Basis for a New Framework,* RAND, IP-155, Santa Monica, CA.

Davis, Paul K., David Gompert, Richard Hillestad, and Stuart Johnson (1998), *Transforming the Force: Suggestions for DoD Strategy,* RAND, IP-179, Santa Monica, CA.

Davis, Paul K., and Manuel Carrillo (1997), *Exploratory Analysis of "the Halt Problem:" A Briefing on Methods and Initial Insights,* RAND, DB-232-OSD, Santa Monica, CA.

Davis, Paul K., and Richard Hillestad (forthcoming), "Exploratory Analysis of Strategy Problems with Massive Uncertainty," RAND (in draft).

Davis, Paul K., William Schwabe, Bruce Narduli, and Richard Nordin (1997), "Mitigating Access Problems in Persian Gulf Contingencies" (unpublished work).

Defense Science Board (1996), *Capabilities for 21st Century Operational Superiority,* Office of the Under Secretary of Defense for Acquisition and Technology, Department of Defense, Washington, DC.

Defense Science Board (1998), *Joint Operations Superiority in the 21st Century: Integrating Capabilities Underwriting Joint Vision 2010 and Beyond,* Volumes 1 and 2, Office of the Under Secretary of Defense for Acquisition and Technology, Department of Defense, Washington, DC.

Department of Defense (1992), *Conduct of the Gulf War: Final Report to Congress*, Department of Defense, Washington, DC.

Dupuy, Trevor N. (1979), *Numbers, Predictions, and War*, Bobbs-Merrill, Indianapolis, IN.

Flournoy, Michèle (ed.) (2001), *QDR 2001: Strategy-Driven Choices for America's Security*, Institute for National Strategic Studies, National Defense University, Washington, DC.

Fogleman, General Ronald (1997), *Confirmation Hearings for William S. Cohen for Secretary of Defense*, Senate Armed Forces Committee, January 22, 1997.

Gonzales, Dan, Louis Moore, Chris Pernin, David Matonick, and Paul Dreyer (2001), *Assessing the Value of Information Superiority for Ground Forces: Proof of Concept*, RAND, DB-339-OSD, Santa Monica, CA.

Gritton, Eugene C., Paul K. Davis, Randall Steeb, and John Matsumura (2000), *Ground Forces for a Rapidly Employable Joint Task Force: First-Week Capabilities for Short-Warning Conflicts*, RAND, Santa Monica, CA (government publication; not for public release).

Han, Yong-Sup, Paul K. Davis, and Richard Darilek (2000), "Time for Conventional Arms Control on the Korean Peninsula," *Arms Control Today*, Vol. 30, No. 10, pp. 16–22.

Hillestad, Richard, and Paul K. Davis (1998), *Resource Allocation for the New Defense Strategy: The DynaRank Decision Support System*, RAND, MR-996-OSD, Santa Monica, CA.

Hiro, Dilip (1992), *Desert Shield to Desert Storm: The Second Gulf War*, Routledge, NY.

Hosmer, Stephen (1987), *Constraints on U.S. Strategy in Third-World Conflicts*, Crane-Russak, New York.

Hosmer, Stephen (1996), *Psychological Effects of U.S. Air Operations in Four Wars, 1941–1991: Lessons for U.S. Commanders*, RAND, MR-576-AF, Santa Monica, CA.

Institute for National Strategic Studies (INSS) (2000), *Report of the National Defense University Quadrennial Defense Review 2001 Working Group*, a study led by Michèle Flournoy, National Defense University, Washington, DC.

Keaney, Thomas A., and Eliot A. Cohen (1993), *Gulf War Air Power Survey: Summary Report*, United States Air Force, United States Government Printing Office, Washington, DC.

Lucas, Thomas (2000), "The Stochastic Versus Deterministic Argument for Combat Operations: Tales of When the Average Won't Do," *Military Operations Research*, Vol. 5, No. 3.

Mahnken, Thomas, and Barry Watts (1997), "What the Gulf War Can (and Cannot) Tell Us," *International Security*, Vol. 22, No. 2, pp. 151–162.

Matsumura, John, Randall Steeb, John Gordon, Russell Glenn, Tom Herbert, and Paul Steinberg (2000), *Lighting over Water: Sharpening America's Light Forces for Rapid Reaction Missions*, RAND, MR-1196-A/OSD, Santa Monica, CA.

McCarthy, General Jim (USAF, ret. (2001), "Report of the Transformation Panel, a study reported to the Secretary of Defense." VuGraphs and a press conference can be found on the web at www.defenselink.mil.

McCrabb, Maris (2001), "Explaining Effects," unpublished draft for the Research Laboratory's program on effects-based operations.

McEver, Jimmie, Paul K. Davis, and James H. Bigelow (2000a), *EXHALT: An Interdiction Model for Assessing Halt Capabilities in a Larger Scenario Space,* RAND, MR-1137-OSD, Santa Monica, CA.

McEver, Jimmie, Paul K. Davis, and James H. Bigelow (2000b), "Implementing Multiresolution Models and Families of Models: From Entity-Level Simulation to Desktop Stochastic Models and a 'Repro Model,'" *Proceedings of the SPIE,* Vol. 4026, pp. 16–25. Reprinted in Davis et al., 2001.

McKenzie, Kenneth F. (2000), "Presentation: A Methodology for Assessing Risk," in *Quadrennial Defense Review 2001: Options and Issues for the Next Administration,* November 8–9, 2000, National Defense University, Fort McNair, Washington, DC.

McNamara, Robert (1968), *Essence of Security: Reflections in Office,* Harper and Row, New York.

McQuie, Robert (1988), *Historical Characteristics of Combat for Wargames,* U.S. Army Concepts Analysis Agency, Research Paper CAA-RP-87-2, Bethesda, MD.

Meystel, Alexander (1995), *Semiotic Modeling and Situation Analysis: An Introduction,* AdREM Inc., Bala Cynwyd, PA.

Morgan, M. Granger, and Max Henrion (1990; reprinted in 1998), *Uncertainty: A Guide to Dealing with Uncertainty in Quantitative Risk and Policy Analysis,* paperback reprint edition, Cambridge University Press, Cambridge, MA.

National Defense Panel (1997), *Transforming Defense: National Security in the 21st Century,* U.S. Government Printing Office, Washington, DC.

National Research Council (1996), *Understanding Risk: Informing Decisions in a Democratic Society,* National Academy Press, Washington, DC.

National Research Council (1997), *Post Cold War Conflict Deterrence,* National Academy Press, Washington, DC.

Ochmanek, David, Edward Harshberger, David Thaler, and Glenn Kent (1998), *To Find and Not to Yield: How Advances in Information and Firepower Can Transform Theater Warfare,* RAND, MR-958-AF, Santa Monica, CA.

Ochmanek, David, et al. (2000), unpublished work on an interdiction study for the Joint Staff and Office of the Secretary of Defense.

O'Malley, William D. (2001), *Evaluating Possible Airfield Deployment Options: Middle East Contingencies,* RAND, MR-1353-AF, Santa Monica, CA.

Pace, Dale (1998), "Verification, Validation, and Accreditation," in *Applied Modeling and Simulation: An Integrated Approach to Development and Operation,* McGraw Hill, New York.

Press, Daryl (1997), "Lessons from Ground Combat on the Gulf War and the Revolution in Military Affairs," *International Security,* Vol. 22, No. 2, pp. 137–146.

Riggins, Jack, and John Snodgrass (1999), "Halt Phase Plus Strategic Preclusion: Joint Solution for a Joint Problem," *Parameters*, Autumn 1999, pp. 70–85.

Savkin, V. Ye (1972), *The Basic Principles of Operational Art and Tactics: A Soviet View*, translated and published in the Soviet Military Thought series by the U.S. Air Force, U.S. Government Printing Office, 1975.

Shlapak, David, et al. (forthcoming), "A Global Access Strategy for the United States Air Force," RAND (in draft).

Stewart, Richard A. (1988), *Sunrise at Abadan: The British and Soviet Invasion of Iran, 1941*, Praeger, New York.

Stillion, John, and David Orletsky (1999), *Airbase Vulnerability to Conventional Cruise-Missile and Ballistic-Missile Attacks*, RAND, MR-1028-AF, Santa Monica, CA.

Watman, Kenneth, Dean Wilkening, John Arquilla, and Brian Nichiporuk (1995), *U.S. Regional Deterrence Strategies*, RAND, MR-490-A/AF, Santa Monica, CA.